FIR

Fire in Our Hearts

The story of the Jesus Fellowship/Jesus Army

SIMON COOPER
and
MIKE FARRANT

MULTIPLY PUBLICATIONS

Northampton

Copyright © Jesus Fellowship Church 1991, 1997

First published in 1991 by Kingsway Publications Ltd

Second, expanded, edition 1997

All rights reserved.
No part of this publication may be reproduced or
transmitted in any form or by any means, electronic
or mechanical, including photocopy, recording, or any
information storage or retrieval system, without
permission in writing from the publisher.

Unless otherwise noted, biblical quotations are from the
New International Version © 1973, 1978, 1984 by
The International Bible Society.

British Library Cataloguing in Publication Data
A catalogue record for this book is available from
the British Library.

ISBN 1–900878–05–4

Published by
MULTIPLY PUBLICATIONS
An imprint of Jesus Fellowship Resources
Nether Heyford, Northampton NN 3LB, UK

Produced for the publishers by
Bookprint Creative Services
P.O. Box 827, BN21 3YJ, England
Printed in Great Britain

Contents

Foreword by Gerald Coates — 9
Introduction by Noel Stanton — 11
Authors' Preface — 17

The Lord Took Hold of Bugbrooke
(1805–1973)

1 Forward Through the Desert — 21
2 Free! I'm Free! — 31
3 Gathering For Power — 38
4 Winds of Change — 44
5 Angels and Freaks — 52
6 Birth of a Culture — 63

Awake O Zion!
(1973–1978)

7 Community — 77
8 Mud, Sweat and Tears — 88
9 New Creation Chaos — 98
10 Zion, City of God — 107
11 Take That Land — 116
12 The World Strikes Back — 129
13 My Friend, My Brother — 141

City on a Hill
(1979–1983)

14	The Cloud Moves on	155
15	Into the Eighties	166
16	A Crown of Thorns	177
17	Dambusters!	186
18	Visions	195

On the March
(1984–1988)

19	Jesus 84	207
20	Fire! Fire! Fire!	215
21	When They Exclude You	226
22	A Sound of Marching	237
23	The Anointing	249

Communicate!
(1989–1993)

24	Flowing with the Mainstream	261
25	Refiner's Fire	272
26	Jesus Revolution	284
27	New Horizons	296
28	Spiritual Searchers	308

New Generation
(1994 onwards)

29	Passing the Torch	323
30	UK, We Love You!	334
31	Wild Spirit	346
Roger Forster Interviews Noel Stanton		357
Afterword		367

Keep up to Date — 369

Notes — 371

Index — 375

To the people of God everywhere
who long for the Fire of the Holy Spirit
to spread through the nations.

To the homeless, the exploited and the poor,
whom Jesus loves.

And to all spiritual searchers
in our post-modern culture.

Our Thanks

To Christian friends who have believed in us, loved us, forgiven us, stood with us and encouraged us through the good times and the bad.

To Roger Forster of Ichthus Christian Fellowship, for representing us on many occasions.

And to all the other Christian leaders who have supported us through the pain and pleasure of our pioneering journey.

Foreword
by
Gerald Coates

'There is only one thing worse than being talked about,' quipped one raconteur, 'and that is *not* being talked about.'

The Jesus Fellowship and the Jesus Army are among the most talked about groups in the U.K. Why?

Firstly they are *different*! Their predecessors, the Salvation Army, did not only start with uniforms, ranks, an alcohol ban and an aggressive approach to evangelism and social action. They also marched for Jesus (before either my colleagues or I ever thought about it!) They were visited by the 'Toronto Blessing' before any of them had been to Toronto! Shaking, falling, crying, laughing and trance-like positions marked many of their early meetings. They were ostracised by the respectable church, and attracted many of the broken, poor and dysfunctional individuals and families that rarely darkened church doors. Familiar!

Secondly they have made mistakes. Being different invites controversy. Being controversial, for whatever reason, invites comment, attack and abuse. People under attack can appear to be – and indeed often are – highly defensive. Shutters go up, doors are closed and an apparent elitism can result. Controversial people have to pray for the wisdom of Solomon if they are going to be influential.

New movements are usually a prophetic reaction to the

dull, dry and boring church that surrounds them. But the time for action can unintentionally become a reason for reaction – which is quite different.

Demonising the opposition and lack of humility (with even a whiff of superiority) can mark the early years of such a movement. I was around in the early days of the New Church Movement (house churches) so I know. It is an almost inescapable situation for such pioneer groups.

Thirdly they reach the untouchable. Part of the 'difference' and 'controversy' is that the Jesus Fellowship and Jesus Army is filled with people found on the streets or in a broken state. They not only get the emotional, spiritual and relational help they need, but the Jesus Army provides jobs for them in their many businesses. This is a holistic approach to the gospel and discipleship.

Small wonder occasional problems among such a group hit the press. If most churches had such a high percentage of untouchables, I suggest they would do no better than the Jesus Army. The likelihood is that they would fare much worse. This field of ministry is costly, intensive and a legal and moral minefield.

My own position is one of amusement when I hear of the Jesus Army being criticised and berated. It often comes from those whose churches remain much the same as they were ten years ago, have rarely done anything controversial and have little or no ministry to the untouchables.

We should let such institutional Christianity, unwilling to change, die in peace. In its place we need fresh, vibrant and spiritual movements, in line with the word of God. The Jesus Army is such a movement.

Such networks are the main hope for Europe. The future of the church will consist of groups that are small enough to care but are large enough to celebrate and influence our culture.

The Jesus Army has an important part in that future.

Gerald Coates
Speaker, author, broadcaster, Team Leader of Pioneer

Introduction
by
Noel Stanton

At the start of the 90s, the London *Daily Mirror* published a feature article with colour photographs of a Jesus Fellowship meeting and a descriptive write-up with testimonies. It carried the banner headline 'Rock Onward Christian Soldiers'. A subheading read 'Born-again youngsters find happiness belting out their love for Jesus'. It said, 'While more traditional forms of religion are in decline, the new churches – noisy, informal, passionate – go from strength to strength.' I am quoted as saying, 'We are part of a revolution that is taking place in this land. A revolution of love, of joy, of justice.' The article ends: 'The new Christians are indeed on the march.'

That article was a sign of the times. The media had realised that a new Jesus movement was spreading through the UK. Now, in the late nineties, the so-called 'Toronto' blessing, with its manifestations of laughter, shaking and falling, has been with us. Other strands of revival have been emerging. New fires are beginning to burn. Churches are stirring! The saving of souls, signs and wonders, and church-building revival mark these days. A Jesus movement, at grassroots level, is gathering momentum.

Fire in Our Hearts is the record of a growing community church which has seen the reviving activity of the Holy Spirit through the years. It is intended to be honest and open. Christian biography and history is often triumphalistic. Our two authors determined to 'tell it as it is' including struggles and disappointments. I believe it is a balanced record.

So you will read here of traumas and triumphs. Laughter and tears mingle together. The baptism of power brings also the baptism of suffering. The call has ever been to sacrifice, to tread the way of the cross. The church cannot be built without pain, pressure and persecution. The Jesus Fellowship/Jesus Army has been shaped by the free grace of God and by the unwavering commitment, whatever the cost, of a large body of pioneers. It has been a learning experience and sadly some have got hurt as we pressed forward to capture the vision.

In 1968 Michael Harper, then of the Fountain Trust, wrote a booklet called *The Baptism of Fire*. The charismatic movement was gathering momentum. The Fire was spreading. In that year, with a mixture of eagerness and trepidation, I read and heard of numerous people in non-Pentecostal churches receiving the baptism of the Spirit, speaking in tongues and bubbling with holy joy. I learned that the laying on of hands brought power and healing to people. I heard of demons being cast out. And churches and small groups were catching fire!

As a proud, evangelical Baptist pastor, the very thought that I needed the baptism of fire sent shock waves through my nervous system. The New Testament experience available now? Becoming Pentecostal? Actually speaking in tongues? Feeling drunk? Being taken over by God? But early in 1969 it happened. It was devastating, powerful, releasing and full of worship. It was, and has continued to be, a baptism of love, faith, vision and courage.

Way back in 1951 I had bought, in my search for an effective walk with God, a second-hand book by Samuel Chadwick (the Methodist leader who died in 1932) called *The Way to Pentecost* (Hodder & Stoughton, 1935). When I at last reached my personal Pentecost eighteen somewhat unfruitful years later, I was able to testify with Chadwick, as he describes the result of his baptism in the Spirit:

> There was a new sense of spring and vitality, a new power of endurance, and a strong man's exhilaration in big things. Things began to happen. What we had failed to do by strenuous endeavour came to pass without labour. The experience gave me the key to all my thinking, all my service, and all my life.

'Things began to happen.' For the Jesus Fellowship, this book records some of those things. The Holy Spirit led us into them. We did not always walk with him. His directives were perfect, our obedience was not. But with caring love and many chastisings, he caused a people to arise, pledged together to be a kingdom brotherhood and a force for mission to the underprivileged, an expression of the lively body of Christ on earth today.

In 1989, twenty years after my initial baptism of fire, MARC Europe conducted a census of church attenders in England. The results were published just before the first edition of this book. They stirred the media into action, for they showed the growth of the charismatic movement especially in the new churches. Churches which have the baptism of fire had expanded fast. Many other churches showed a significant loss.

Nearly ten years later, in what is called a post-modern culture with spiritual hunger apparent everywhere, there is great interest in the Christian faith, especially where it can be embraced with informality and emotion. Two-thirds of the population claim belief in God, with the majority believing in Jesus Christ, Son of God. Little wonder, as the barriers between church and people are broken down, that the response is big, and getting bigger! A culture-shift has taken place.

These are years of gospel-harvest in the UK. It's time to get into harvest mode! We've been too used to merely sowing! At Wembley Praise-Day 1996 we called on Christian leaders 'to recognise how God is moving in the nation, to embrace the closing years of the millennium and the opening years of the 21st Century as a time of Christian awakening, claiming the landmark year 2000 (2000 years from Christ's birth) as "The Jesus Year".'

As I write, young men in this large community house are singing the modern Jesus songs. They, and the friends they've made in the streets, pubs, and clubs, wear red crosses, one of the signs of this Jesus movement. They sing songs about Generation J replacing Generation X. The magazine *Net User* (Christmas issue 1996) giving a five-star award to the Jesus Army for their Internet Web site, quotes one of the songs: 'We're wild and we're Christian, Christ Jesus is our scene, we've met him and we love him, we're all part of his team.' There is excitement in the air! Hundreds of thousands of young people in the UK are part of this new advance. Accept them – they are unorthodox, their music can be loud, but they love Jesus, have networks of friends, spread the gospel easily, and can be willing disciples.

Says Samuel Chadwick:

> Wesley, Whitefield and General Booth wrought wonders by the Fire, kindled of the Holy Ghost. Men ablaze are invincible. Hell trembles when men kindle. Sin, worldliness, unbelief, hell are proof against everything but Fire. The church is powerless without the Fire of the Holy Ghost. Destitute of Fire, nothing else counts; possessing Fire nothing else really matters. The one vital need is Fire... How we may receive it, where we may find it, by what means we may retain it are the most vital and urgent questions of our time. Fire comes only with the presence of the Spirit of God. He Himself is the Spirit of Fire.

The character of the Jesus Army is summarised in the slogan which appears on our jackets: 'Love, Power and Sacrifice'. But the message of the Jesus Army must ever be: 'Blood, Fire and Covenant'. This speaks of the saving, cleansing blood of Jesus, the coming of the Spirit of fire and the building of Christ's church through covenant relationships.

Read this book with kindness! It is not perfect! Read it with a heart that cries to be used of God, whatever the cost. And the God who answers by fire will come to you. The Holy Spirit will fall on you and you will find, as we have found, that 'things will happen'!

To the God of all wisdom and might, the Father, the Son and the Holy Spirit, be all praise and honour!

Noel Stanton
Senior Pastor, Jesus Fellowship
November 1997

Authors' Preface

It was in early 1988 that we finally decided to write this book. The Jesus Fellowship had always been controversial since its beginnings at Bugbrooke Baptist Chapel. But after the dramatic launch of the Jesus Army in 1987 people were keener than ever to hear our story.

Our first experience of charismatic renewal was back in 1969. Since then we'd established an 'Acts 2' community lifestyle, spread across much of England, and taken the gospel to the streets. At times it was a lonely road. But now, after almost twenty years of pioneering, we felt God urging us to stand with others and share our heart and vision.

And so, with some added encouragement from Kingsway Publications, we sat down to write. One of our main leaders, Mike Farrant, had a lot of ideas for the book, but, when it came to it, he was hopelessly busy in administration. So Mike and I worked together.

I left my job as a school technician in Northampton and began to grapple, weep and laugh my way through a story that was both epic and passionately dear to my heart. As I dug through the archives, listened to old tapes, and talked with the many characters, memories flooded back. Then I poured out my soul into the word-processor and tried to capture the spirit and vision of those years. Mike got me to tidy it all up! As it's seen somewhat through my eyes, you'll have to bear with me when 'I' (Simon Cooper) wander in and out of the story.

Though this isn't exactly an official history of the Jesus Fellowship, there has been a good deal of hard research, discussion, polishing and editing. We've also tried to provide some biblical framework for what God has led us into and to set our own story in the context of the wider Christian scene.

You'll find that there are a lot of names in this book. We've tried to keep them distinct without resorting to the formality of surnames too often. (Within the Fellowship we often give people unofficial 'virtue' names, and these are mostly used to describe people.)

Neither of us could have produced this book on his own, but then that's really the theme of the whole book. This isn't a story by or about any one person. It's too big for that. As we've worked through this text, we've often been unashamedly moved and humbled. For this is a story of a bunch of widely different individuals whom God blessed, though they didn't often deserve it; changed, when they didn't always want it; and joined together – as a people with fire in our hearts.

Preface to Second Edition

And now, six years on, *Fire in our Hearts* has travelled the globe. It's been read in prisons and stately homes. But, like any good story, people keep asking, 'What happens next?' So the time has come to update and expand the story. I've enjoyed writing about the last few years. I'm sure you'll enjoy reading about them!

Simon Cooper

The Lord Took Hold of Bugbrooke
1805–1973

1

Forward Through the Desert

1805–1968

It all began in a village with a funny name. Bugbrooke, just south of Northampton, was a very English village with small sandstone cottages, a spired church and a large old rectory that dominated the southern edge. Its parkland of meadow, oak and copper beech added a touch of grandeur to a scene that nestled peacefully beneath the rolling hills of the Northamptonshire uplands.

Mind you, it hadn't always been peaceful. The East Midlands had a long history of religious rebels and, in the seventeenth century, had gaoled men like George Fox and John Bunyan. At that time, Bugbrooke had the highest proportion of nonconformists of all the villages in Northamptonshire. The Bugbrooke Quakers, Presbyterians and Independents were none too popular and some of them had to worship out in the fields at a spot called 'Hallelujah Corner'.

Baptists continued this tradition over a century later when a young farmer and a plumber from Bugbrooke were baptised in Northampton. The two men 'excited violent persecution' and 'some very base means were resorted to in order to prevent the entrance of the gospel of Christ'.[1]

But as they persevered in prayer, two young women joined them and they determined to plant a church in the village (it was a five mile walk into town!). God eventually blessed them with a young preacher, John Wheeler, and his wife, and in August, 1805, Bugbrooke Baptist Church was born.

That day the six pioneers made a 'solemn covenant' and promised, 'in the presence of God and our Lord Jesus, the crowned head of Zion...to promote his glory and walk together in the gospel...and, with the aid of the Holy Spirit, to deny ourselves and suffer for Christ's sake, to live above all undue influence from the present world, and to exhort, reprove, and comfort one another in the love of God...'[2]

Three years later they built a chapel, but John couldn't resist baptising in the river. Crowds came to see 'the Dipper' in action. By the end of his ministry, over a hundred people had joined them and congregations had been planted in the nearby villages. Bugbrooke became known as the 'cathedral of the chapels'. One of her noted converts, John Brown, was kicked out of Bristol College for 'quivering with laughter' while trying to say grace. He later became the President of the Baptist Union!

Bugbrooke had fire in its blood, and a memorial to the pioneers was fixed on the chapel wall:

> Your fathers, where are they?

'Well might they ask!' thought Verna, the chapel organist, as she gazed at the ancient plaque Sunday after Sunday. They gospel was in her blood, too. Verna's grandfather had been a Primitive Methodist preacher, and her parents were godly people. Her warm-hearted father was a shepherd and would come home from the fields and say grace before dinner. Her mother taught her to play hymns on an old harmonium. Verna grew up to love Jesus, and it was no surprise when she was baptised as a teenager and made a Sunday school teacher.

Then, at twenty-three, soon after the Second World War, she went away for a fortnight to Hildenborough Hall, a new Christian Conference centre down south. There two war heroes from the RAF told how they'd been converted to Christ. The talk that followed was simple and direct, and Verna saw that for all her religious upbringing she was still a sinner. For three days she barely ate or slept. 'Aren't I a Christian, then?' she thought. As God dealt with her, her pride was shattered. It was like waking from a dream. Then, as she took hold of her Saviour, she felt a deep sense of forgiveness and cleansing. God's love became real and peace flooded her heart.

When she came home her parents were delighted. But she had a big disappointment when she bounded up to her minister the next day. 'Oh dear, Verna!' he sighed, 'You've got in with one of those emotional groups. It will pass.' But it didn't, and the new life she'd found was infectious. That night, as sixteen girls from her Bible class crammed into her cottage, Verna just opened her heart. Some began to weep and soon eight of them had come to the Lord.

Verna was encouraged and began to pray for the gospel to make a real impact on the village. She threw herself into evangelistic work in Northampton. When she went off for a year's teacher-training in London, she thrilled to hear some of the best preachers of the day. Her horizons were widened and her faith stirred.

Then she came home to Bugbrooke to find her dear old chapel rather disappointing. Everyone was sincere, but the little group of evangelicals among them was discouraged. They tried to keep up their spirits and hope in God. But it was hard work.

By 1951, things had reached a low ebb. The third minister in ten years had moved on and the little flock was shepherdless yet again. The grass looked greener at the Free Evangelical Church in Northampton, where Pastor Barnes was a well-known champion of the gospel. In desperation, Verna and her friends went to see him. He listened thoughtfully as they unburdened their frustrations and he promised to seek God's wisdom for them.

When they returned a week later, he said: 'Well, I'd love to have you, but the Lord has given me a definite word for you: "Stay where you are. Be much in prayer and fellowship. Be faithful and obedient. The time will come when you will see the hand of the Lord stretched out in blessing on this church at Bugbrooke."'

So they took heart. One dauntless soul had never dreamed of giving up. Miss Campion simply prayed harder. This retired Rugby School matron had grown up in the days of Queen Victoria, and was a force to be reckoned with! As Chapel Secretary, she soon found a new minister. He and his wife were a pleasant couple, but, 'Where's the power of the gospel?' thought Verna.

Three years later news of a revival in the Hebrides began to filter through. Faith was rising in Britain and Billy Graham was making an impact with huge crusades in London. When, in 1954, Verna took some of the village youngsters down to hear him, they were stirred. Even the minister began to change and started a friendly after-meeting on Sunday nights. Things began to look promising. But within two years he'd moved on.

Tyres screeched as the motorbike swerved off the Bedfordshire lane and crashed through a hedge. A young man appeared, unhurt except for a few bruises. He was Noel Stanton.

Noel, born in 1926, had grown up on his parents' farm in Bedfordshire. On leaving school he worked for a bank, but at eighteen was conscripted into the Royal Navy. One day, when serving in Sydney, Australia, a man approached him on the street. 'My young friend,' he said, 'where do you expect to spend eternity?' The word struck home and, not long after, Noel gave his life to Christ.

After leaving the Navy, he was baptised by a pentecostal pastor, and in the laying-on of hands there was a call to ministry. Noel was soon out preaching with his friends from the National Young Life Campaign. Together they organised village crusades and gospel events. Then he went to All Nations Bible College and for a while acted as deputation secretary for what was then the West Amazon Mission.

Returning to Bedford, Noel worked as an accounts clerk and later in a business partnership. He lodged with a pentecostal family (with whose theology he disagreed!). He continued to evangelise and set his heart on pastoral ministry. The Ministerial Committee of the Baptist Union vetted him and he began to look for an opening.

At Bugbrooke they were having little success finding a pastor, and a local minister recommended Noel. Bristling with evangelical zeal, he stepped into the pulpit. The congregation warmed to this smart, fervent young man, and Miss Campion invited him for lunch. She found him polite, though a little reserved, and a man with strong vision. Miss Campion called a church meeting which invited him to become their full-time pastor. Noel accepted but offered to continue his secular work in order to help with the finances of the church.

So in March 1957 local Baptist leaders and the Principal of All Nations gathered for Noel's induction ceremony. It was a new day for the chapel as they all sang together:

> Forward through the desert,
>   Through the toil and fight!
> Jordan flows before us,
>   Zion beams with light!

Noel got to work immediately and urged them on into vigorous outreach and warmer, deeper fellowship. He was steeped in missionary zeal and fed his soul on Wesley,

Spurgeon and C. T. Studd. A recent book on revival – *In The Day Of Thy Power*[3] – had inspired him, and he invited the author, Arthur Wallis, to lead a week's retreat.

Bible weeks, evangelistic drives and missionary weekends followed, and in 1960 Noel and Ken Thomason, a neighbouring Baptist minister, invited the evangelist Don Summers to conduct a tent crusade to the surrounding villages. Fifty people came forward and a handful were baptised. Monthly rallies were started and Roger Forster led a Bible week that winter. The evangelicals were happy at last, and as that busy year came to an end, Noel was thanking God for their loyalty and for the many new friends.

However, after nearly four years of intense activity only a handful had actually joined the eighty or so members. Noel expressed his growing concern to the deacons: 'The crying need is for God to do his reviving work amongst us. Some show interest, but who is really won for Christ?' Other crusades followed, but the results were equally disappointing.

In the spring of 1963, the *Pilgrims* came for a weekend. This young music group talked about a Jesus you could know personally. That came as a thunderclap to Dave Lantsbery, the headmaster's son and an Anglican choirboy. Seventeen, fresh-faced and athletic, Dave would have been an 'all American boy' had he not been so English! Often he turned up at the chapel youth club, played table-tennis and chatted to the girls. As far as Dave was concerned, he was a Christian, a churchgoer, and all right, thank you very much!

At the next meeting with the *Pilgrims*, Dave sat at the back of the chapel, on the defensive, and trying to justify himself. On Sunday evening there was a call to make a commitment to Christ, and Dave stood up. Somebody came to counsel him, but still he held back.

'What about the Muslims?' he argued on – and on.

'The problem with you,' said the counsellor, 'is you won't admit you're a sinner. It's between you and God!'

Dave crumbled. As they prayed together, he saw a vision

of Christ on the cross, and he realised that it was for his own sin that Jesus died. He broke down and wept, and came out that night a changed young man.

But such signs of God's work were few and far between. Though the chapel was highly regarded in the area as an evangelistic centre, its members were often discouraged. Two more years of activity followed and still they waited. 'Here is a stack of decision cards,' thought Verna, 'but no real fruit.' Clearly energy alone wasn't enough.

'If we loved God, we would love one another,' Noel told the deacons, 'but where is the spirit of love and power amongst us?'

By 1967 he seriously wondered about the way forward. Ten years had flown by. Could he rely on the devotion of his flock? Should the next crusade go ahead? He felt desperate, and called a special church meeting. 'We are reaching a crossroads,' he said, 'and need to reassess things in the light of scriptural truth. Is the old style mission really the way? Should not growth spring from the vitality of the local church? We do a lot, but our heart is weak.'

Noel wondered whether he ought to stay on at Bugbrooke. Was he able to take the church any further? And were they willing for a deeper commitment to the Lord? The deacons stood by him and determined to go on with God.

Soon after that some of the village teenagers came to the Lord, and two were baptised. A new manse was built, and when £400 was needed to finish the work, Miss Campion organised a Gift Day. The exact amount came in. For a while, things seemed to be looking up and the Sunday after-meeting was attracting new people.

Dave was due to go to Africa on voluntary service, but before he left he helped form a Youth Council. The youngsters planned their own crusade, bought an old minibus, converted the chapel lounge into a coffee bar, and formed a Commando Team to go round the villages. It seemed the best thing yet. But over in Malawi, Dave soon heard how it was all petering out and the converts were going back to their old ways.

Verna visited friends in Ireland, who reminded her of the promise that Pastor Barnes had given them back in 1951. A pentecostal lady took her to one side. 'Verna,' she said, 'you're a lovely sister, but you need to receive the blessing.' Verna longed for this 'blessing' – whatever it was!

By now, they had a great hunger for spiritual power. There had to be a breakthrough. So in the summer of 1968, Noel started a Saturday night prayer meeting in the manse. About a dozen sought God and studied the Acts of the Apostles to see if they could find the secret of the early church.

All through that summer and autumn they searched the Scriptures. In Luke 24:49 they read how Jesus had told his disciples to wait in Jerusalem until they were 'clothed with power from on high'. They saw how transformed those disciples were after Pentecost when they were 'baptised with the Holy Spirit' (Acts 1:5) and spoke 'in other tongues' (Acts 2:4). They saw the radiance, the impact and the power of those early Christians. This was what they needed.

Noel began to cry to God and search his heart:

> I saw my own hypocrisy and got tired of saying the way of revival is to get filled with the Spirit. I wasn't living in the fullness and felt quite incapable of leading my people into it. A determination grew within me to get into the reality of God at all costs. His kingdom was hardly established in power amongst us at Bugbrooke and I felt a poor shepherd.[4]

Noel knew of revivalists like Moody and Finney who had experienced a 'baptism of power'. He had also heard something of the recent 'charismatic movement' and its emphasis on baptism in the Holy Spirit. In fact, old friends from Bedford were now 'speaking in tongues' and praying for him to get the blessing. Noel wasn't so keen!

But as the manse group continued to study the New Testament they kept coming across tongues. Even Paul did it – more than all of them (1 Cor. 14:18)! As Noel got more and more desperate, his theological reservations crumbled. At last he picked up *The Cross And The Switchblade* by Dave Wilkerson and read again how God gave this young pentecostal minister such amazing breakthroughs with the gang fighters of New York. Noel was impressed by their sudden deliverance from drug addictions.

'When did it happen?' Dave Wilkerson had asked them. And one after another they gave him the same answer: 'When I was baptised in the Holy Spirit!'[5]

One Saturday, the chapel teenagers visited a charismatic fellowship in Rugby. They sat waiting for someone to start the meeting. No one did! Everyone just started singing, dancing and speaking in tongues. It was all a bit overwhelming! However the youngsters realised they'd found something important and hurried back to tell Noel.

By now Noel was almost ready for God to baptise him in the Spirit. 'Any idea of a second experience,' he wrote, 'had been taught out of me. I now saw the early church had a baptism of power and I needed to ask for and receive the Spirit.'[6]

Out in Africa, Dave had met some Americans who spoke to him of a second blessing, and the Lord challenged him about his barrenness. After reading in a book by Catherine Marshall about surrendering the will to the Lord, he had a real experience of meeting with God. His prayer life came alive. He just asked for things and ticked them off when the answers came. By the end of 1968 he was praying for revival in Bugbrooke.

At the close of the annual church meeting in mid-December, Noel encouraged everyone to ask definitely for the Holy Spirit according to Luke 11:13: 'If you...know how to give good gifts to your children, how much more will your Father in heaven give the Holy Spirit to those who ask him!'

'I have a text for 1969,' he added. '"With God, all things are possible." Also this scripture from Ezekiel 34:26: "I will make them and the places round about my hill a blessing; and...there shall be showers of blessing"' (RSV).

Within days it came. Noel was praying in the manse when a tide of love broke over him and the Spirit came in power. Later he wrote of that moment:

> The experience was very much as Finney describes. Certainly it was so intoxicating, so exhilarating, and so intense that I felt I was just not going to live anymore! I became filled with the intensity of God. This went on for hours and hours and I moved into speaking in tongues and praising the Lord. It was a tremendous experience of life and fulness from which I didn't come down for a long time – and this was the changing point in my life.[7]

Around this time some of the chapel youngsters were baptised in the Spirit. Noel spoke in chapel of his own experience, and others began to enter in. Verna wrote to tell Dave. He was walking down a street in Malawi when he opened the letter. He leapt for joy. Quickly he wrote back to Verna: 'I was praying for an outpouring of the Spirit, and then you told me what happened. It was amazing! – I mean, it was the happiest day of my life!'

It looked as if the promise given in 1951 was reaching fulfilment. Verna herself received 'the blessing' in her own cottage a month later. The church had found a new path. Little did they know it would lead to them being called 'one of the most controversial Christian groups in the country'.[8]

2
Free! I'm Free!
1969

'Have you heard what's going on at Bugbrooke, John?'

Rev Ken Thomason stuck his head round the kitchen door.

'Oh dear!' thought John. 'What now!' He mumbled something negative.

'They're really different over there.'

'Oh?'

'Yes, you ought to go over. There's a fellowship supper at the chapel tomorrow. Go and see them, John...Go and see them.'

It was obvious his dad wasn't going to give him any peace.

'All right,' sighed John. 'I'll go! I'll go!'

So he went. His dad was right. Noel looked as though someone had polished his face! John had been to lots of things that Noel and his dad had organised, but the atmosphere here was different from anything he'd encountered before. He had 'made a decision' for Christ at eighteen, but now, at college, he'd grown cynical and holy huddles annoyed him. Communism was more appealing. Changing the world – that was where it was at.

He looked around.

'Good Lord!' he thought. 'Even Miss Campion is glowing!'

'Notice anything about Noel?' his dad asked when he got home. 'Well, yes,' said John. 'He looked like a 100 watt bulb! I had a good argument with them all about this "talking in tongues". Noel gave me this withering look. "Who are you to say a gift of God is no good?" he said. That really threw me. I thought, "You know what – he could be right!"'

The Holy Spirit had begun to invade the life of the chapel. The teenagers were very excited and encouraged one another along. Stories flew around of talking in tongues and seeing visions. The youngsters prayed together almost every night for revival to hit the chapel. Sometimes they ended up on the floor laughing in the Spirit. One of the lads felt something like a warm electric current come upon his head and travel down to his toes. The joy was immense and he shook for an hour.

One of their friends, Geoff, was a fiery redhead with a character to match. Extrovert and likeable, he thought the Youth Club was all a bit of a laugh. Then one evening when he walked in, Geoff looked really different. He'd given his life to Christ and was already baptised in the Spirit. It soon spread around the village. Geoff had 'got religion'!

Some of the youngsters joined the 'core' group. Around twenty, including Noel, Miss Campion, and Verna, now came together in the manse to seek God. Saturday nights were times of discovery as the delighted pastor stepped back, and allowed the Spirit to move. They didn't know what would happen next. One lad jumped up, took his glasses off, and peered out of the window. 'Hey! I can see the Baker's Arms sign really clearly now!' he shouted. Another youngster would laugh uncontrollably and then burst out crying. He couldn't help himself – it was like holding back the Niagara! But many in the group needed to struggle to express their feelings freely in worship and in the process they learned to open up and pray with one another.

Gradually they became aware of books and tapes going round which described how the Spirit was renewing churches all over the world. Thousands in Britain were speaking in tongues as on the day of Pentecost. Michael Harper, an Anglican curate, had organised the Fountain Trust to foster this growing renewal movement and one of the team, David Mills, visited Bugbrooke to encourage them.

'Free, I'm free! Praise the Lord, I'm free!' they sang in their Saturday evening meetings. At first they felt self-conscious as they raised their arms in the air and clapped their hands. But the barriers were coming down – a little. For traditional Baptists it was pretty good!

In the Sunday evening meetings the old hymn books were replaced by shiny, red pentecostal song books that spoke of blood, fire and the blessing. But clapping on Sundays was still regarded as rather offensive (and undignified) and the morning services were sacrosanct in the eyes of the more traditional members. So the new-found freedom was generally kept for Saturdays and after-meetings. At times it was like restraining a herd of well-mannered buffalo!

The Saturday evening group in the Manse began to explore the supernatural gifts of the Spirit – tongues, prophecy, wisdom, knowledge, healing, and so forth. One evening David Mills laid hands on them, and brought them all a word from the Lord. He also prophesied that one day the whole chapel would be full of people – arms raised and praising God. That was hard to believe!

The Fountain Trust was a great encouragement, and there was also input from leaders of the emerging 'house churches'. Peter Lyne came from Bristol and led them into singing in the Spirit. Other young leaders like Graham Perrins, Gerald Coates and John MacLaughlin visited the group. Hugh Thompson was the first to demonstrate the word of knowledge. 'Someone has a toothache,' Hugh announced. The someone refused prayer, however.

In July most of the group went off for a fortnight in Devon. The holiday helped them to get to know one another better. It brought a sense of family, and they began to refer to each other as 'brothers' and 'sisters'. Three others from Northampton turned up at this Devon retreat. John was a gentle young man seeking to lead a small group forward in the Spirit, Malcolm was a quiet sixth-former, studying music, and Phil had recently been converted. They quickly became part of the 'family', and Phil cremated a pile of his cigarettes in the garden.

John would often visit the manse group. When he spoke, he trembled with fear, but his words carried power. His Northampton group often brought people along to the meetings and gradually news spread around that 'something interesting is going on at Bugbrooke'.

Then Dave returned from abroad and took up Rural Science teaching at the local school. Even in Africa he had felt involved with the 'revival' in Bugbrooke, and now he'd come home. He knew he would spend the rest of his days with these people. With awe he sensed the presence of the Spirit in his old friends. Miss Campion showed a deep gladness at what God was doing, whilst in Verna there was a transparent joy. Noel too seemed warm and relaxed amongst the 'family'.

Dave went to his first meeting at the manse with fear and trembling. Some were quietly speaking in tongues and delighting in God. Heaven seemed very near. Then once again he had a vision of the Lord dying for him. The power and love of God came upon him and he could only worship God and weep for joy.

A week later he sought the gift of tongues and began praying by his bed in the dark. His parents came back and shouted upstairs, but Dave was lost in God and didn't hear. Later, when he called downstairs, they got the shock of their lives, and the young teacher had a good ticking off from his headmaster father!

Soon they heard that Don Basham, the author of *Face Up With A Miracle*[9], was speaking in Rugby. The group there was influenced by the highly-pentecostal South Chard fellowship who went for 'glory meetings' and the miraculous. Such groups were springing up all over. People said that this one was 'pretty wild' and Noel went along reluctantly.

The teenagers stepped boldly into the buzzing room. It sounded like a party. The rest followed cautiously and were hit by a hot wave of enthusiasm, as the blast of hugging, clapping, dancing, shouting, holy kissing, arm-waving and tambourine-bashing assaulted their ears. One lady went white as a sheet, John disappeared out of the back door, Noel looked aghast, and the rest were, to greater or lesser degrees, in a state of shock. Miss Campion had stayed at home, thank God!

Back at Bugbrooke, they vowed never to go again. However, when they heard that the evangelist Harry Greenwood was coming from Chard, they went over again. As they listened to his descriptions of the miraculous ways in which God can move in someone's life, their faith grew by leaps and bounds. Later, one young man was baptised down at Chard, but most felt that in this freewheeling scene there were theological and emotional excesses that needed to be guarded against.

As the year progressed, more Christians came around wanting to explore this new life in the Spirit. Peter Mattacola was a young man from the next village, who'd heard that they were 'laughing in the Spirit' at Bugbrooke. Pete was at university but went along in the spring vacation to investigate. Sure enough, he caught one of the teenagers rolling under the chairs in a state of spiritual intoxication. Pete went back to Newcastle, joined a house church and returned in the summer with a tambourine, and an enthusiasm for Wesley hymns and for hugging. Wesley was okay, and the tambourine was tolerable, but the hugging was a shock to the system!

In October a Christian couple arrived from London. Brian and Jill were aware of God's leading as they drove round searching for a house and a lively church. One look at the Chapel noticeboard convinced them that Bugbrooke was the place for them. Soon Brian and John were appointed deacons. Brian was an extrovert and a good balance to the cautious group. Evidently God was gathering them for a purpose. What that was, no one was quite sure.

There was some expectation of revival. They had listened with awe to accounts of the Awakening in the Hebrides, where people had been stopped in their tracks by the presence of God. Dave believed that within a few months the Spirit would sweep over Bugbrooke, the Baker's Arms would empty, the streets would be filled with repenting sinners, and God would do all the work. He wanted it the easy way!

Then tragedy struck. Geoff was enticed away by his old mates and backslid. A long-standing stomach ulcer got worse, and in hospital his condition became critical. Noel and other would often visit Geoff in hospital and would take his parents there after a service. Two weeks after being admitted, he found the Lord again and praised God so loudly he had to be quietened down! He amazed the nurses. How could someone that ill be so full of joy?

Geoff had five operations and was often near death. Everyone believed he would recover and prayed for him, but towards the end of the year he fell into a coma. The doctors were on the point of giving up when Noel and others gathered round and proclaimed the victory of Jesus. To the amazement of the doctors, Geoff recovered consciousness.

Geoff's illness was knitting the group together more closely and was a challenge to prove the power of faith. As for doubting John Thomason – well, the Lord cornered him on top of a London bus. The love of God welled up within him as he rushed back to his room and shut the door. Tongues burst forth, and flowed and flowed until, at two in the morning, his lips were sore! The next day he stood in the breakfast queue at Imperial College with his hand over his mouth. He couldn't stop speaking in tongues, and his boiled egg went cold before he could negotiate the difficulties of eating it!

The chapel was now a talking point for the whole village. 'Lily,' said an Anglican lady to Geoff's mum, 'I don't know what's going on there, but whatever they've got, we haven't!'

Some in the chapel weren't too keen on what they had got! Changes occurred in the weekday meetings. Some in the Young Wives were praising the Lord in new languages, and choir practice changed from 95% choir and 5% prayer to 0% choir and 100% prayer, praise and Bible Fellowship. Miss Campion's Friday afternoon prayer time was livening up as well. Homestead Cottage would never be the same again.

Miss Campion handed on the torch of Church Secretary to Verna. Deacons' meetings were now interspersed with praise and prayer, as they sought to know 'the guidance and witness of the Spirit'. That in itself was a miracle! Some expressed the gift of wisdom in picture form. One such 'wisdom picture' was of a beautiful lake obscured by trees. The lake represented the life of Christ in the church and the trees were its members. The wisdom was an encouragement not to block out the light of God's Spirit. They had to be humble before God and let him have his way if renewal was to continue.

Noel's ministry became more inspirational. The Spirit had opened up whole new horizons and he was learning as fast as he could. He was glad to listen to Brian, John, the youngsters, the Fountain Trust, anybody who could help. Slowly he was finding his feet and developing a distinctive ministry. The approach from man's side was 'softly, softly'. Prayer, patience and second-mile love was the way. After all, it was a traditional village Baptist chapel. But not for long. God was doing a new thing.

3

Gathering for Power

1970

Geoff died on the last day of January. He was just twenty. God's power was real, but there was no miraculous cure. The Thanksgiving service was full of victory, praise and tears. At his graveside they sang 'Blessed Assurance', while some wept and cried to the Lord. Geoff's parents, Arthur and Lily, were deeply moved by the love that had been shown them. Lily was a churchgoer, and Arthur was chapel. Both had felt reserved towards this move of the Spirit, but Lily began to go to the meetings, found the Lord, and was drawn into the centre of things. Arthur followed later.

The travail over Geoff proved to be the birthpangs of a new fruitfulness. The sense of God's presence increased, and Noel circulated a newsletter around the villages. The mid-week chapel meeting now moved around and met in homes. They were packed out. Expectation was still for revival and Noel, inspired by the example of Evan Roberts in the Welsh revival, got them all to pray in turn:

'Lord, fill me more powerfully with your Spirit.'

A wave of baptisms began in the spring, Malcolm being the first. He felt a new power as he came out of the water and soon the shy schoolboy musician was going around praying with people and ministering in the gifts of the Spirit.

John's sister, Carol, had become a Christian at thirteen, but later rebelled against her evangelical upbringing. The world had messed her up and now, at twenty-one, she'd hit rock bottom. People from Bugbrooke were often at her mum's house in Northampton, and she noticed the way they talked and prayed about this lad Geoff. Here was genuine love. And that was what she longed to find – real love.

Plucking up courage, Carol went along and sat at the back of the manse one Saturday evening. She tried desperately not to be noticed but felt increasingly awkward as the meeting progressed. They sang some songs, lifted their hands in the air and prayed. 'Let's pray for our sister Carol,' said Noel. She lifted her head unbelievingly. 'What, pray for me?' she thought, and burst into sobs. The tears streamed down and mingled with her mascara. Soon Carol was surrounded by caring arms as the sisters prayed with her. The awareness of her sin was overwhelming and she cried out to God. Then peace came. How amazed she was that night to be loved by God! It was a fresh start. Her worldly friends dropped her, but Carol didn't mind – she'd found a new family.

Carol had known the gospel well enough. She had heard it a thousand times over. But here was a real sense of belonging. It was amazing to see how all these people were on the same wavelength. They actually loved one another. This wasn't formal religion or even the type of evangelical Christianity she had known. 'For we were all baptised by one Spirit into one body...and we were all given the one Spirit to drink,' she read (1 Cor 12:13). She looked at the 'intoxicated' teenagers and smiled. That was what she was seeing before her very eyes.

A few weeks later she was in the manse again. 'Some of you will be baptised in the Spirit tonight,' Noel announced.

Carol wept again as God's love bubbled within her and she spoke in tongues. Immediately her barriers went down. She wanted to go around the room and hug everyone.

They often spoke of the 'body of Christ'. The church was not an organisation – it was a living organism. All over the world, believers were discovering this, and were meeting in their homes as a 'family'. In Scripture the manse group read of the body 'building itself up in love' (Eph 4:16), of the members having 'different gifts' (Rom 12:6) and of rejoicing and weeping together (Rom 12:15). All who experienced the Spirit felt this sense of unity, of being part of one another. But others in the chapel weren't finding God in such a way and some felt a little excluded. Not everyone wanted such an experience. Quite a few clung to the old ways. Some were confused or a little fearful. Others could be proud and quite rude!

It seemed that belonging to the 'body of Christ' and chapel membership were not exactly the same. The Spirit was a blessing and a trouble-maker. Jesus had warned against sewing a new patch on an old garment, and the chapel was feeling the strain. It was a heartache for those who sought to bridge the widening gulf. Some had already left.

Sunday evenings now began to change and baptismal services, especially, brought new freedom. Handclapping and raised arms began to appear. Up in the organ, Verna's fingers moved nimbly over the keyboard as the songs livened up.

In the summer vacation Peter 'Matt' came round again with his tambourine and found the chapel a strange mixture. Charismatic choruses were accompanied by a huge pipe organ and sung from old wooden pews with doors on the end, while the mixed bag of believers was led from the pulpit by an increasingly liberated Baptist minister. At one Sunday evening baptismal service they didn't wait for the preacher or the organist! The singing started spontaneously; someone spoke in tongues and it was followed by an interpretation of exuberant praise. As if that wasn't enough, the service was followed by a discreet exorcism! And that was the end of traditional formality on a Sunday evening.

Minister and deacons now began to review the Constitution, which had its limitations when looked at in the light of a renewed understanding of Scripture. One deficiency concerned 'body ministry'. In the early Church everyone was a disciple, all had spiritual gifts, and all were involved in worship and ministry. They saw this, and were keen to encourage ministry from within the church. Moreover Noel wanted to recognise fellow elders and the Constitution didn't allow for that. The matter was taken to a Special Church Meeting and they agreed to 'revoke the rules temporarily – to allow the Lord to guide us in the formulating of new ones'.

A gracious little bombshell! It meant they were breaking free from tradition and the battle was shifting from personal blessing to church renewal.

Meanwhile, Carol was feeling the need for water baptism. Jesus had been baptised, and the formula in Acts 2 was clear enough: 'Repent! Be baptised! Receive the Spirit!' Baptism spelt goodbye to the old life. It was the burial of a sinful nature already slain upon the cross. The old Carol with the sin-stained life, and the broken heart, had come to an end. She could bury it all, and rise with no shadow to follow her.

One July evening she stood in the warm water. All around the baptistry were friendly faces and cross-legged kids peering excitedly down. Carol was plunged into the water and up she came again spluttering and radiant. A ripple of laughter went through the chapel, and the organ groaned into action. A word of prophecy was given that she would be a 'fruitful vine'. A brief pause, then a tambourine swung into a song. 'Lifted! I've been lifted, I've been lifted by his love, out of sin and sorrow into boundless realms above!' The congregation burst into praise.

Within days a minibus and two cars were speeding through the night to Scotland. Another chapel holiday had begun. Carol had brought a friend, Mim, with her. Mim was excited but Carol slept peacefully on her shoulder. 'Thirty-two Spirit-filled Christians in a castle for two weeks!' thought Mim. 'Well, thirty-one plus me!'

Mim was from the Elim Pentecostal Church and there was a kinship between the two fellowships. The chapel admired their well-established pentecostalism, and the Elim youngsters who came round enjoyed the vitality and family atmosphere at Bugbrooke. Mim, though, hadn't been baptised in the Spirit yet.

No sooner had the first evening meeting begun, than Carol got up and delivered one of the 'words of knowledge' that God often gave her. 'Mim is going to get baptised in the Spirit – tonight!' she declared, and by the end of the evening Mim was speaking in tongues.

That night the sisters' dormitory was invaded by flying beetles, so Carol had an idea. She got out of bed, mustered up her spiritual authority and shouted: 'I rebuke you beetles in the name of Jesus!' The poor beetles were never seen again!

The theme for the fortnight at Kilravock Castle was 'Rejoice always'. Friendship, worship and fresh air combined to make, in Mim's words, 'a terrific holiday'. For Noel it was a chance to spend more time with leaders as they sought the way forward. One thing was clear – the change in Carol was amazing. It was a power conversion and a power baptism. They read in Acts of how Paul met some disciples who knew only 'John's baptism' (Acts 19:3). Something was wrong. They trusted in Jesus, but lacked life and power. Paul baptised them again and, as he laid hands on them, they 'spoke with tongues and prophesied'. The Holy Spirit had come upon them! Now Noel saw baptism in a new light. It was a gateway into further blessing, and Carol and Malcolm had passed through.

GATHERING FOR POWER

A few weeks on, and up to forty people crowded into the manse. It was hot and the windows were flung open. The room buzzed with life and there was hugging and praising. Kelly and Norma were two pentecostals who were so impressed with the change in Mim that they had come fifteen miles from Kettering to investigate. Kelly was a converted biker and hungry for God.

'How did you get on?' asked Norma, on the way home.

'Man! The liberty's worrying,' said Kelly, and smiled. 'It was great!'

They were very drawn by the love and were an immediate hit with the youngsters. Kelly had a leather jacket, dirty jeans and sideburns! What's more he played the guitar and was down to earth. Everybody liked them and before long they slipped into the heart of the fellowship.

Kelly felt they were laying a foundation for the future with their emphasis on the body of Christ. The spiritual gifts were fine, but it was the love that spoke volumes. Often a minibus-load would cram into their little house at Kettering. It was better brotherhood than among the bikers and there was no hangover!

Towards the end of the year they moved in next door to Verna, and soon took in one of the young men. The two cottages attracted people over the weekends and formed a little spiritual oasis. Kelly was invited to the leaders' meeting, and given responsibility for two minibuses and the cleaning of the outside toilets. Such was the price of fame!

Slowly people were gathering. Two years had now passed since the original group had first felt the shock waves of the Spirit. They'd discovered much, but perhaps the most important thing of all was the reality of bring knitted together in the love of God. Revival hadn't swept over Bugbrooke, but the winds of change were definitely blowing.

4

Winds of Change

1971

It was a normal Sunday morning in February. Miss Campion hovered around the front of the chapel and kept a maternal eye on the deacons who greeted people at the door with a handshake. She was pleased to see that a few of the new Saturday-nighters were now turning up for the morning service.

All was well. The flowers had been arranged, the communion table set out, and inside Verna was playing gentle hymn tunes on the organ. The congregation sat patiently in their pews until 10.30am, when the side door opened, the whispering of the children stopped, and in stepped a well-groomed Noel. The choir followed and as they positioned themselves on the platform, Noel stood casually next to the pulpit. (To the annoyance of some – he should have been in it!) Then he quietly prayed and announced the first hymn.

It was hardly the day of Pentecost! Yet that Sunday morning was different. The deacons had already agreed to introduce 'free ministry' during the communion service, but no one had dared break the ice. Then John Thom, the charismatic graduate, spoke out in tongues – loudly. Traditional hearts froze. The tongue was interpreted and another brother prophesied. For some, that was it. 'If we'd wanted a pentecostal church,' said one man, 'we would have gone to one.'

But the Holy Spirit could not be stopped. Now was the time to lose the 'wood, hay or straw' (1 Cor 3:12) of traditionalism and build according to the New Testament. The chapel doors must be flung open to allow the wind of the Spirit to blow right through!

The spring of 1971 saw an influx of young people. Lunch and tea were provided on Sundays, and Kelly and Dave led an afternoon gathering called TTMTT. In this Teens and Twenties Music and Testimony Time there were real breakthroughs in sharing, testifying and experimenting with gifts and ministries. Many more were around on Easter Monday when five people were baptised amid loud rejoicing and tears. On Sunday evenings the sound of tambourines carried into the night air. Sometimes there would be singing in the Spirit, the melodies weaving together in harmony. 'When they sing in these tongues, it's so beautiful,' one lady told her friends, 'you think you're in heaven.'

Some of the older members of the chapel were now catching up and entering into blessing. One elderly lady saw a vision of Jesus, with a beautiful glow around his face. She found a deep peace and entered into the worship. But not all the villagers were so keen. 'All that clapping and singing!' said one irate neighbour. 'You wouldn't think it was a place of worship.'

A facelift was now overdue for the chapel. The organ was riddled with woodworm, and the pews were large, hard and immoveable. The place needed heating, lighting and space. The evening congregation was growing and the mums and babies were taking over the vestry. A new building programme was needed.

The plan was to replace the old pews with lightweight, padded ones, and to redecorate the chapel in bright, cheerful colours. As for the organ, the cost of restoring it would be astronomical. The space could be better used for a new vestry. So they agreed to purchase an electronic one, versatile enough for a newer style of worship. The organist could then sit with the rest of the 'family'.

But, again, not everyone was happy. 'When that organ went, it was like someone had died,' lamented one old lady. Opposition was building up, not only from within the congregation, but from others who were suspicious of the charismatic movement.

Noel stood firm and reassured the deacons. 'As we allow the Lord to have his way, we shall know victory,' he said and quoted from 1 Peter 3: 'Love as brothers, be compassionate and humble...But even if you should suffer for what is right, you are blessed.'

Many, like Kelly, ached for a full release of worship and brotherly love, and had often grieved over those who were getting left behind. But in the end it was their choice whether or not they would yield to the Lord.

In May Gerald Coates came for a week. He was a dynamic young man, one of many charismatic leaders in the UK whom Arthur Wallis sought to draw together in a vision for restored, biblical Christianity. Two streams were emerging in the charismatic movement. One sought for 'renewal' within the denominations, the other for a 'restoration' of New Testament church life. Gerald had left his Brethren assembly to form a house group in Cobham. Like Bugbrooke they were finding real relationships and even greater liberty. The problems of dealing with people of widely different views didn't exist in their type of house church, and Noel envied their biblical simplicity.

Gerald ministered with great freedom, weeping as he spoke of the grace of Jesus. One of the ladies was healed of a deformed hand and news of this rippled through the village. As a reward, Gerald was given the task of visiting some of the traditional chapel folk. But he didn't get very far. The flamboyant young fellow was hardly their idea of 'the minister'!

Gerald taught from the book of Haggai, a prophet endeared to the house churches.

'"You expected much, but it turned out to be little,"' he read, referring to the hope of revival.

'"Why? Because of my house, which remains a ruin, while each of you is busy with his own house."' Gerald pressed for radical commitment.

'"Go...and build the house,"' he read with excitement, '"so that I may take pleasure in it and be honoured, says the Lord."'

'An enthusiastic remnant rebuilt the temple in their day,' Gerald explained, as he paced around. 'So must we in ours! We must restore the purity of the church. God is looking for pioneers – for worshippers – those who are going to get out of compromise and get into reality.'

The last ceremony in the unaltered chapel was Mim's wedding. Then, while work went ahead, sixty went down to an old rented Bible College in the New Forest for the summer retreat. Some major subjects were tackled in Noel's teaching sessions, including authority, spiritual ministries, church meetings and the nature of the church.

The function of the church was a vital topic. They began to see that it wasn't enough simply for chapel practices to be renewed. Throughout the world, the Spirit was bringing a fresh understanding of the nature of the church. Churches in the first days were planted by apostles and prophets and functioned more or less independently. Denominations and priestly systems were unknown, as were consecrated buildings, vestments and altars. Theological colleges were unheard of. Instead, on-the-spot training was given in the local churches.

With a full range of spiritual gifts and ministries, each local church should be a place of simple brotherhood and a real expression of the body of Christ. In Britain, many people who felt this were joining the house churches, and those who pioneered these 'new churches' were helping other fellowships and taking them under their wing – or 'covering' them.

Bugbrooke Chapel had received input from 'restoration' and from 'renewal' streams. Where did she stand? Basically, as an independent church. Bugbrooke had a remarkable heritage of independence, and the chapel, like others affiliated to the Baptist Union, was entirely self-governing.

The chapel fellowship was wary both of being restrained by denominational tradition and of being 'covered' by one of the new churches. The house church fellowships, being new, were inevitably immature and some were very middle-class. Noel had a good streak of the Puritan evangelical in him, and was wary of an overbalance on liberty. Members of house churches had discovered the joy of being 'not under law' in their front rooms, but there was plenty of evidence for ruling authority in New Testament churches. There was also the need for holiness and costly discipleship.

The chapel quietly asserted its independence as radical Baptists. The Lord was launching them out in a new direction, and it was a joy to have the Scriptures for a compass, and the Spirit blowing into their sails.

Towards the end of the retreat they began to plan a new offensive: the Jesus Lives Crusade. Kelly, in particular, got excited. It seemed that this little 'body' was being mobilised. There was talk of a music festival and a convoy through the villages. What's more, they'd ordered a load of Jesus tee-shirts in turquoise, orange and violet! JESUS IS LORD would soon be proclaimed in block capitals from their chests and HAPPY NEW LIFE IN JESUS from their backs.

The times were certainly changing. To cap all that, they had decided to drape a red and white banner across the old stones of the chapel. JESUS LIVES! it would proclaim — right over the chapel entrance!

Kelly winced as he thought of the reactions. He leaned back in his canary yellow shirt and red leather waistcoat and let out a low whistle. He wasn't your average Christian. But he didn't need to be — not for what was coming.

Back in the freshly-painted chapel, Kelly's eyes scanned the balcony. 'Perhaps violet was going a bit far,' he thought, and smiled as he watched Noel waiting for the choruses to end. Noel still looked the smart Baptist minister, but under the dark suit a charismatic rebel was burning.

Thirty youngsters had turned up in two minibuses that summer evening, and the chapel was packed and buzzing.

'Man!' whispered one lad, tugging at his friend. 'The love kinda hits you!'

'Yeh! They're all tripped out on something,' said the other. They sniggered and hid behind their song books.

Verna beamed behind the new electronic organ. A couple of guitars joined in as she played 'Sweep over my soul' for the umpteenth time. A murmur of praise then rose up and flowed into a new chorus: 'He has given me the wine to make my heart rejoice, and the oil to make my face to shine!'

Miss Campion sat towards the back with a twinkle in her eyes. Her Baptist severity had given way to a glow of glory. Some of the leather-jacketed youths didn't know what to make of it. They eyed each other and Miss Campion, and nervously edged towards the door. A few of their mates had already lit up outside. Soon Noel was throwing out the challenge of a radical following of Christ. His theme was the 'Jesus Revolution'.

News of a movement among the American hippies was leaking into Britain. Flower power had been invaded by the gospel and there were amazing stories of deliverance from drugs and the occult. The revival itself was turning into a counter-culture as transformed young 'Jesus People' followed the teachings of Jesus and lived a life of sharing. For them, Jesus was the revolutionary of revolutionaries.

In July the local Northampton paper had carried an article about the Jesus Revolution, and this coincided with the chapel's publicity for the Jesus Lives Crusade. In the minds of the locals the two were associated. Violet tee-shirts, bell-bottom jeans, and long hair, confirmed it. Bugbrooke Chapel was full of Jesus Freaks. They were, without a doubt, the Jesus People.

The Crusade began in August with a convoy around the villages. Cars and minibuses displayed stickers and posters, while, in the middle, a lorry chugged along full of tee-shirted youngsters on straw bales, sporting guitars and Jesus grins. Noel, in his posh Audi, led the convoy down the A5. When they got to the outskirts of Towcester, they turned round, and the whole procession did a U turn through a petrol station! The attendant stared unbelievingly as the lorry came through. 'Smile! Jesus loves you!' they shouted – and handed him a gospel tract.

The culmination of forty days of activity was a music festival on a village green near Bugbrooke. Gerald Coates came with a team, along with some music groups whose styles varied from gentle gospel to heavy rock. Carol and others told their stories from the back of the lorry as hamburgers and onions sizzled nearby.

Old friends from Bedford who had been praying for sober Noel to get the blessing turned up, and got a shock to see his bright red shirt, glowing face and long hair! They liked the new version and the group became Saturday night regulars.

Following the music festival, eight people were baptised. Johnny, a local fighter, wept his way to the Lord. The village was stirred and he was asked to speak at Dave's school. Some of the youngsters responded, and more came along to see what was going on down at the chapel.

In September, the American evangelist, Arthur Blessitt, hit town, leaving a trail of Jesus stickers and enthusiasm. Then a huge bonfire lit the skies over Northampton – the Nationwide Festival of Light had begun. In London the shouts of 'Praise the Lord!', the One Way signals, the music, the stickers and the joy all indicated the spiritual groundswell abroad.

At Bugbrooke that swell was rising fast. Some who had started coming to the chapel meetings were thinking of moving into the village, but not all could afford to. Noel suggested a Sharing Fund to meet particular needs and the formation of a housing association to provide homes at a low cost. This, he explained, put into practice the communal spirit of the New Testament. He admired the example of the early Christians and, to the amazement of some, started to lend out his Audi.

Christmas was approaching and many were uneasy about the worldliness and hypocrisy it involved. The festival, which was of pagan origin, and never recognised in the early church, brought so many temptations to drunkenness and greed. Sadly, Johnny, the local fighter, had already gone back to some of his old ways.

Nonetheless, a carol service went ahead and Noel hoped to reach the hearts of some of the traditional folk. Testimonies to the power of Christ were given, but Noel came away grieved. So many seemed to sing the carols with no real desire to follow Christ. The way of compromise seemed ineffective and he yearned for a clean break. Jesus revolutionaries needed the courage to stand against the tide and be true to God.

Christmas day was a Sunday. Normal services were held, but few came. The church was on holiday and the work of God took a back seat. Noel resolved that next year it would be different.

Two days later Johnny turned up late at night weeping outside the chapel. Kelly and Noel led him back to the Lord. Soon he got a burden to reach his drop-out friends in Northampton. Others sensed the leading of God in this and a vision for these people developed. As God urged them on to the streets, they launched out into deeper waters.

5

Angel and Freaks

1972

They knew where to find them. The Black Lion was known as a centre for the drug scene in Northampton. When the weather was warmer thy sat on the steps of All Saints Church, or chatted to each other in the coffee bar inside – an interesting mixture of hairies, acid heads, and bikers, ranging from flower power hippies to full blown Hell's Angels. Most were drop-outs, spending their money on dope. There was an openness amongst them, something of a brotherhood.

One Saturday morning in January the unlikely team from Bugbrooke dived in: Noel, the evangelical crusader; Kelly the pentecostal ex-biker; Johnny, the newly-converted fighter; Val, a teacher; and Malcolm, the refined schoolboy-musician.

John Cornish and Paddy were sitting up against the wall chatting when they spotted the middle-aged straight and his friends coming up the steps. Paddy was taken aback but liked their 'vibe'. Kelly and Johnny had some interesting stories.

Paddy and John Cornish were intrigued by this Jesus trip, and paid a visit to Bugbrooke. As a result, Kelly and Norma's cottage and the manse soon came to be known as places where you could get a lot of friendship and a good conversation about religion! Bugbrooke might be a bit 'far out' (five miles), but it was worth the ride.

The following week Noel met Rufus, a vegetarian and a religious freak. He was into the drug scene in London and frequently took the hippy trail to Glastonbury and Cornwall. At nineteen, he had done two years with the Royal Shakespeare Company, worked for television and appeared in the film of *War and Peace*. Rufus was on the road to stardom.

His wife, Jessie, lived with his mum in Northampton, and Rufus travelled to and fro, dealing acid on the quiet. He disdained the junk pushers (John Cornish and Paddy were already fixing heroin) but was happy to sell his 'sweet dreams'. LSD, in his eyes, was a mind-opening path to religious experience: enlightenment was his goal.

Noel sailed in. 'This guy's quite interesting,' Paddy whispered to Rufus as Noel approached. Rufus broke off his mantra and gave him a quick suss. Noel's face looked alive.

'Hello. Bless you!' Noel said warmly. 'I'm Noel from the Jesus People. Have you got a faith in God?'

'Yeh,' said Rufus, 'I've just been praying to the angels — you know — conversing with the powers of light.'

Noel smiled. 'I think we've got something that might interest you. Why don't you come along?'

So he did — that night. John Thom was leading a Bible study in the manse on Acts 2 — how the first believers 'had everything in common' (Acts 2:44). Rufus interrupted a few times and when the meeting finished, wandered into the kitchen where someone was frying sausages.

'Wow — carnage!' said Rufus. 'I thought you people were spiritual.' The brother smiled.

'Oh well, obviously it's a place for needy people who haven't got much savvy,' thought Rufus, '...certainly not for the philosophical.'

Noel walked in.

'Why, O why,' Rufus asked, 'do you feel salvation lies in your little structure? It's all so narrow. What about all the other spiritual masters?'

Noel laid his hand on his shoulder. 'Good to see you, Rufus.'

'Yeh...well, praise the Lord anyway!' grinned John Thom annoyingly and tucked into his sausages. Rufus sighed and asked for a lift home.

'That guy,' said Noel, after he'd gone, 'is going to be really good when he comes to the Lord.'

Six or seven weeks passed. Bonds with the drug scene increased. A 'Life Squad' went out to the Black Lion on Friday nights. Other hippies and bikers came along and enjoyed the atmosphere at Bugbrooke. They also appreciated the help — sometimes of a bed or a meal. One biker from the 'Apache Outlaws' was bailed out for theft. Slowly hearts were gained, a trust developed, and the Christians were welcomed on to hippy turf.

Chapel meetings grew in power, and increased to six evenings a week, with Friday night 'free in the Spirit' gatherings for the unconverted. Printed cards invited folk back to the Jesus Vibro! ('for under 30s life-seekers').

More teenagers were converted through Johnny's testimony and in March there were over a hundred people around. Among the seven baptised was Val, the teacher, who shook under the power of God as she entered the water. Spiritual gifts were much in evidence: one man's gums were healed; words of prophecy and wisdom flowed forth and many sang in tongues.

Clearly God was honouring this move on to the streets. Some of the new friends began to open up and come to meetings. 'I'm searching for the truth,' said an Apache Outlaw to

Malcolm one lunchtime. 'Last night I kicked in a Keep Left sign so I could read the Scriptures better.' More and more of these guys were identifying with the Jesus People and responding to their love.

Rufus came that Easter with Jess and some other freaks. Most of them were high on pot, and Rufus let his guard down. They were all encouraged to shut their eyes, hold hands, and feel God's love. Jess thought it an improvement on the Krishna mob, but was offended by a straight who offered to replace her best patched jeans. John Cornish was 'mainlining' heroin and Paddy was stoned, but they stayed around and watched the baptisms the next day.

'Let it flow! Let it flow!' they all sang. Someone shook their hands. '...Let the love of Jesus flow through you and let it flow through me!'

They peered hazily out of their long hair.

'Man,' said Paddy, '...this is better than any acid trip!' They decided to finish with dope and were prayed with. Paddy came off with no withdrawal symptoms.

A few days later, Paddy was praying in his house, asking God to make himself real. It was late morning and his friends had already gone to All Saints. A moment came that he never forgot. He felt a fire on his head that seemed to pass right down through him and out of his hands.

'It was like I was being flushed right through,' he was soon telling John Cornish excitedly. 'I felt clean – all white inside, and full of love.' Immediately he rushed down the street, bounded up All Saints steps and bought them all a cup of tea. 'That really freaked them out,' he chuckled. 'I'd never done that before!'

The fire spread. John came to the Lord and, in May, Paddy was baptised along with a friend, Mick. Mick had been mainlining heavily and his arms were full of ulcerations and scars. When he came up from the water the marks had all gone!

Trouble brewed up with the Outlaws. Some of them were

into witchcraft and violence and didn't take too kindly to these Christian creeps. Kelly and Johnny were in the Black Lion one Friday night when a fight broke out. They left quickly with a girl who needed help, but were pursued by two Hell's Angels with sticks. One took a swing at Kelly, but before the blow could land, the biker sank to the floor – Johnny was an experienced fighter! He turned to Kelly sheepishly. 'I thought it was right in the Spirit,' he said. Kelly grinned, took a look over his shoulder and ran to the car. They hopped in – just in time. The gang surrounded them and started to turn the car over.

'Kelly,' said Johnny, 'I think we ought to go home.'

'Yes, Johnny,' said Kelly, '...certainly!' Kelly hit the ignition and they lurched into the night.

Rumours went round that Johnny and Kelly were in for some 'treatment'. The following night the Apaches planned to bust the chapel open but, by a stroke of providence, a more important 'rumble' cropped up somewhere else.

A few days later the President, Nicky, came with a few mates and sat on the front row with knives and sticks. Nicky was huge and vicious. Kelly eyed him from the platform and swallowed hard; Norma gripped his arm; and Noel preached as normal. The rest was up to prayer, worship, and God. The presence of the Lord was real and, by the end of the meeting, Nicky's heart was softened. Kelly came down and embraced him. They struck hands and Nicky threw off his Angels' gear. When a reporter from Northampton came to investigate, Nicky told his story:

> We used to carry 12-bore shotguns in the Chapter and I really enjoyed violence. We came over to create a disturbance but by the end of the evening I really felt I had found some sort of truth. People were happy. I took off my colours, broke my stick in two, and gave it to Noel. It was notched for every time I used it.[10]

When John Thom and Nicky visited All Saints, Nicky told his mates what God had done for him. At first they couldn't believe it. Then John watched one of them go white and start to tremble. Hoss was into black magic and the occult.

That following Sunday, the chapel heard that Hoss was on his way to the service. The pre-meeting prayer time became very animated and God gave one brother an impression of Hoss lying prostrate on the floor. Hoss arrived with three of his coven, and settled down at the back. They sat with hands joined, chanting the Lord's Prayer backwards and trying to put a curse on people.

The worship grew in power and they began to panic at the sound of the name of Jesus. The chorus, 'Oh there's power, power, wonder working power in the blood of the Lamb!' was terrifying and the tambourines were deafening! Eventually the satanists clambered desperately out of the pew and rushed to the door. But before Hoss could reach the exit he turned sickly pale, clung to the pillar and keeled over. He hit the floor like a dead man and was carried down the aisle into the back room for deliverance ministry. After a while, he came to and found peace with God.

'It was love that cracked me!' he said, as he lay weeping on the floor. 'It was love that cracked me!'

Hoss and Nicky were changed men, but hardly instant saints, as Malcolm's diary reveals. 'Hoss renamed himself Isaiah. Nicky reacted and punched him in the eye. Theme tonight – love.'

Dave had to confess to Kelly that he'd broken the suspension by cramming eight people into his car! They also ferried people to the meetings in two minibuses. It seemed the village was being invaded by these colourful, hairy drop-outs and unwashed bikers. (Pete Matt and Carol had some interesting guests at their wedding!) Some hung around outside or even nipped over the wall into the neighbour's back garden to enjoy a quiet 'joint'. She wasn't very amused!

The police became aware of the chapel link with the drug scene and the amazing changes in some of their clients. Paddy appeared in court for supplying methadone. He would normally have been sent down, but in view of his conversion, the magistrate took a lenient course. 'The Jesus Movement,' said the defence, 'has done something for this young man when he was heading in one direction only — borstal.'[11]

There was a danger that the chapel would become a place of drug dealing. It wasn't easy to keep order. Noel spoke of 'upholding the holy name of God', and maintaining discipline in the camp. The chapel was to be treated with respect and smoking and drugs were strictly banned. However, a fight broke out in the manse car park between the bikers. The front door was kicked in and the police were called out.

Village teenagers would swarm around, too, fascinated by the goings on. They would sit on the wall of the Baker's Arms and cheer the Jesus freaks as they went in and out of chapel. Chapel members were losing their aura of respectability as they learned to share 'not only the gospel of God but [their] lives as well' (1 Thess. 2:8). Time, money, prayer and patience, burdens, disappointments and tears were all thrown into this work. John Thom was always on duty. He seemed never to sleep!

Homes were opened up and sometimes Kelly and Norma would be up all night nursing someone through 'cold turkey' and the traumas of withdrawal. Often there was heartbreak as, around the summer months, many came — only to vanish again. There were few to care for them, and a lot of those who received help and prayer went back to their old scene — some, to an early grave.

Verna, Dave, Kelly, and the rest, considered it an honour to serve these drop-out friends. How much they needed the love of God! Verna would weep with joy to see them come through to Jesus. It was the answer to so many prayers over the years.

'Let's have a feast and celebrate,' the father of the Prodigal Son had said. 'For this son of mine was dead and is alive again' (Luke 15:24). The fellowship was greatly enriched by these new young believers who brimmed over with gratitude and enthusiasm. But there was still the 'elder brother' tendency to reject them. Self-righteous Christianity has so frequently turned away those whom Christ loves. Those who identify with them are likewise scorned. At Bugbrooke, being pentecostal was bad enough, but now they had turned into a bunch of offbeat hippies! In the eyes of some village folk, and of some of the other churches, Bugbrooke Chapel had already gone too far.

Rufus bumped into a transformed Paddy in town, now into Jesus and looking really healthy. Paddy was off heroin and had a regular job. Rufus was impressed; both were miracles! 'This Jesus trip must be good – for a junkie – but, so shallow!' he thought, and continued on his way, chanting.

Noel started to visit Rufus and Jess at his mum's. One day Noel and John Thom came in when they were meditating. Noel chatted with Rufus but Gilly, his adopted brother, sat in the lotus position, oblivious.

"Ere! – Gilly, bro,' said John, 'don't you think you're being rather rude?'

'I reckon he's achieving more through meditation, John, than you are through talking,' Rufus objected angrily.

'You really ought to respect our friends here,' said Noel quietly. 'You ought to apologise, bro.'

John humbled himself and apologised. This amazed Rufus and Gilly: these guys were crashing through the barriers. They could relate.

Rufus was in the back garden one sunny day pruning his 'grass' plants when Noel appeared. A stab of guilt hit him and he dropped all the leaves.

'Why should this Christian guy make me feel unclean?' he thought as he ran around in a temper, picking them up.

'Praise the Lord!' said Noel.

'Yeh, but why don't you just praise Krishna as well?' answered Rufus.

But Noel would never argue. He listened as Rufus enthused about his books on astral projection and his times of fasting and meditation. Rufus felt someone appreciated him. He began to think that these were the most solid guys he'd met. He'd seen Gurus, talked to Zen masters and heard the pioneers of the LSD movement, but these Christians had something extra. Rufus and his friends spent ages trying to work out what it was. In the end they put it down to faith. These other guys had powers and abilities, but they hadn't got faith.

Most religious types managed to put Jessie's back up. Noel and John didn't. They treated her with respect, and she liked them.

'Jess would make a good New Testament woman!' Noel once said laughingly.

'What do you mean by that?'

'Well, the Bible says that wives find fulfilment in loving and serving their husbands. They have lovely, gentle spirits.'

That appealed to Rufus.

Meanwhile, the new Jesus hippies were heavily involved in church life and evangelism. John Cornish took over from Malcolm, supplying books, badges, Bibles and stickers, while Paddy helped edit a Jesus People-style paper, *Jesus Reality*. Headings appeared like 'High On Jesus!' and 'Satanist Finds The Only Way Out'. By June the press caught the scent. The Northampton *Chronicle and Echo* sent a young reporter around and she wrote this:

> Dumbo the elephant decorates the blackboard, second hand furniture fills the room and a middle aged Sunday School teacher is positioned at the piano, when suddenly a guitar starts up, tambourines join in and the Jesus Movement of Bugbrooke takes voice. And from that point, any connection with the Established Church ends. Their meetings are revivalist, Jesus is the focus and their religion is community based...Already £600 was raised in one collection, but a lot more is required for their Housing Association. Mr Stanton is unperturbed by the problem. 'Jesus will provide,' he says. And it's very easy to believe him![12]

ANGELS AND FREAKS

Noel commented in the chapel bulletin:

> When God moves everything happens! What a story! Large congregations, generous giving, a wonderful sense of love, and many turning to Jesus. There are many pressures, some disappointments, occasional abuse and false gossip. But Jesus is Lord and by the Spirit we have continuing victory. There is a great revival of faith arising in Britain. The Jesus Movement is hot news. We ourselves are receiving many letters and phone calls. People come from long distances. BBC Radio has contacted us. But in the midst of all this we must maintain a close walk with God.

At this time God gave them a prophetic 'wisdom-picture' of a wheel with hub and spokes, the hub representing the committed core of the church. Revivals have often failed as numbers increased. The hub at Bugbrooke must grow stronger to hold the growing church together.

The summer retreat in Matlock was a timely regathering of strength. Noel took the theme of deepening. Though their liberty was growing, they saw that the backdrop must be holiness and full surrender to Christ. The hymn, 'Burn fire of God, my ransomed soul possessing' moved many to tears. Jesus was to be all in all. They were choosing a path of fierce, loving abandonment to Christ and his kingdom.

Noel spoke from Timothy and Titus on God's order within the church. He also introduced them to the writings of Watchman Nee who had just died after twenty years' imprisonment in China. Nee had pioneered churches in China and many regarded him as a prophetic voice to the West. In his book, *The Normal Christian Life*[13], Nee emphasised baptism, separation from the world and the distinctiveness of the church. At Matlock the theme of commitment was foremost. Fulfilment of ministry in the church was a priority, and jobs in the world came second.

The leaders called six of those recently baptised into the centre of the room. Hands were laid on them, and words of wisdom and prophecy given concerning their ministries within the church. This became a regular practice after the example of Paul and the elders laying hands on Timothy (2 Tim 1:6), and the fellowship called it 'ministry for ministries'.

Matlock was a time of dancing and fun and sharing. Community whetted their appetite for closer fellowship, and the hub was restored. When they got back to chapel you could tell who had been to Matlock: they danced!

At this point, I (Simon*) turned up from Oxford with the latest Watchman Nee books under my arm. My home was nearby and I had just finished my zoology degree. I'd gone as a confirmed atheist but a sudden encounter with God's love had brought me to Jesus and gave me a longing for the reality of New Testament Christianity.

Entering Bugbrooke Chapel was like walking into a sea of life. It was very colourful, very diverse and very turbulent. I was met by warm unpretentious villagers, a host of Jesus tee-shirts, and a bunch of freshly converted hippies. Coming straight out of the Christian Union it was all a bit overpowering, but was just what I needed.

It was a good time to arrive. People were being converted and filled with the Spirit all over the place. The church had vision. Noel's preaching was biblical and full of passion. I liked him and figured that any friend of Watchman Nee was a friend of mine! I agreed with Val, the teacher, who had recently settled there. 'These people,' she said, 'have more potential for discovering what we see in the Acts of the Apostles than any church I know.'

---

* See preface

6

Birth of a Culture

1972–73

The afternoon was hot – even for August. Most of us had marched in a 'Jesus Demonstration' through Northampton. From Midsummer Meadow to All Saints Church we brandished our placards and shouted our Jesus shouts. Paddy rushed around with a broad grin accosting the general public. I felt highly embarrassed. But it was fun.

'Hi, man! Smile! Jesus loves you!'

Paddy thrust copies of *Jesus Reality* at some passers-by.

'Don't miss the Music Festival on Monday. It's far out!'

On All Saints' steps we knelt and prayed for the town. A few told their stories and we walked to a youth centre for the tea and Celebration Rally. As we worshipped, Val was laughing for joy. Yvonne, a schoolgirl, looked across at the liberated schoolteacher and smiled. The Spirit came upon her, too, and she sank to the floor and worshipped God.

'Oh no!' she thought. The Lord was urging her to speak. She got up, made her way to the front and began nervously.

'I was hearing things I hadn't even thought about – God working miracles today! People having a relationship with Jesus! I came the next night, and – wow! I felt warm inside. Then laughter started to flood from my mouth. I was so happy with Jesus – I felt my inside was bursting out!'

The congregation fell about laughing. Paddy waved a tambourine and shouted 'Glory!'

Yvonne blushed and giggled. 'My mum thought I'd gone off my rocker! But now she's really keen. She's here tonight and she's coming to my baptism tomorrow!' The hall burst into applause and her mum hid her face in her hands.

Yvonne was baptised with seven others the next evening. What a mix it was, too. It included a large housewife, a nurse, a black lady, Malcolm's physics teacher, and an eccentric old chap plastered in Jesus badges. It was beautiful to see them at the same level in Christ.

Kelly's and Verna's cottages were filling up and it was getting difficult to accommodate our many visitors. We began to think in terms of a large community house, and John Thom was keen to pioneer.

The seeds of community living had already been well sown. The last three holidays proved the worth of being together. What's more, Noel was impressed by Rufus. Something in Noel, the smart minister and business man, responded to his hippy lifestyle that scorned the world's values, lived simply, and sought some kind of spiritual brotherhood. It was out of this culture that the Jesus People had arisen, and Noel, already challenged by the early Christians, found them an inspiration.

It seemed to many that God had raised up this Jesus Movement in the States as a demonstration of real brotherly love. One author looked on in admiration:

> These young people who formed communes...are the pace-setters and innovators...They radiate a quiet joy such as the early Franciscans knew. Their music reflects a holy hilarity. They have offered the first inducement in years to make me want to

be young again...They do not discriminate because of age, sex, race or status. They have broken down the barriers.[14]

We watched a film on the Jesus Revolution and a music group visited us from the Jesus People in the States. We felt God's leading in all this and continued to pray for Rufus.

'Read Hamlet, Rufus. Read Hamlet!' Rufus' dad poked his head out of the window as his train pulled out of Northampton Station.

Rufus knew that his dad was deeply depressed and was obsessed with thoughts of suicide. As he waved goodbye Rufus' heart was heavy. He knew Hamlet all right – 'To be or not to be...' The words drummed in Rufus's mind.

Within hours his dad was dead. Rufus felt desperate and helpless. What comfort could he offer his mum? Chanting and meditation were great, but it didn't help anyone else. As soon as he left the lotus posture the world closed in on him.

He'd grown sick of his life as an actor – of the unreality of it all. Jess had a baby – his mum kicked them out and he rented an empty house. He felt the responsibilty of the baby. He worked a long hard day for an Irish ganger and broke with dope. After a police raid, friends in London had gone down for two years on drug charges, and Rufus felt he'd had a narrow escape.

Purity was his goal now. He shaved his hair, leaving a pony tail – which Jess cut off! She detested the Hare Krishna scene that seemed to dehumanise her friends. There were blow-ups between them and Rufus would sometimes lash out and hit her. Dope no longer soothed his conscience and guilts came crashing in. He meditated three hours a day and fasted, but out on the building site he wept with cold and exhaustion. Enlightenment seemed a million miles away.

In desperation, he read the New Testament and saw the idolatry in Krishna. The Gurus were also turning him off and stories of their affluence disgusted him. He plunged into macrobiotics and spent his money on special foods. Even the dogs were vegetarian! He dreamed of a houseboat on the river, and laid out £500, but the boat turned out to be rotten. It felt kind of symbolic.

Then in the new year he met John Cornish. John seemed everything that Rufus wasn't – contented, relaxed, a picture of sanity.

'Wow! You're looking great!' said Rufus. 'What's that under your arm?'

John flushed and unwrapped a Bible.

'Man, you're really into it!'

Rufus longed for what John had. A friend gave him a tract about a cartoon hippy who gets ripped off, burned out, and ends up in a mess. Then the guy meets some Jesus People, gets saved, and goes round spreading the good news. Somehow it really touched Rufus.

He was glad when Noel and John Thom appeared. They would sit on orange boxes and sip herbal teas with Rufus and Jess. On one occasion they prayed and God's presence filled the room.

The crunch came three weeks later when Rufus devoured a swiss roll at his mum's place. That was macrobiotic sin. He came away despairing and, in a burst of anger, slammed the dog against the wall. The dog followed meekly after. Rufus turned and asked Jess whether she still loved him. 'Yeah!' she said. Rufus felt like he was falling apart.

Back home, he ran upstairs and shut himself in an empty room. There in the darkness he saw it all so vividly. The Tibetan Book of the Dead, the I Ching, the mantras he had chanted, the mandalas he had looked at, the numerous yogic postures he had learned, the kohans he had read, the mescalin and acid he had taken – they all seemed to be laughing at him. Rufus broke down and out of the darkness, he cried out to God: 'I can never get to you, Lord. You've got to reach down and pick me up.'

In a moment he knew: it was Jesus. He went downstairs to Jessie. 'Jess, what if we left everything and went round just telling people about Jesus. Would you come, Jess?'

She paused. 'What – with the baby – just telling people?'
'Yeah, with the baby,' said Rufus.
'Yes – I'd come,' said Jess.

Rufus went out to the phone kiosk. 'Look, Noel,' he said, 'I know I'm a sinner. I just want to find Jesus.'

Rufus and Jess came to the next meeting. Rufus wore a greatcoat tied with string, and turned-down wellies. With two dogs and a baby they came in as tramps and were welcomed like kings. He looked around. These people were worshipping a powerful, invisible presence, and they looked radiant and fulfilled. Afterwards, Noel left him with a copy of *Run Baby Run*[15]. He found the book disgusting – all blood and guts, but when he reached the place where the gang leader finds Jesus, Rufus entered into a great sense of forgiveness.

At the next meeting Rufus joined in the praise. Suddenly the finger of God touched him and in a moment he knew the Father's love. It was neat, undiluted love – powerful, but superbly personal. As he felt the dirt drain away, his knees went weak and he fell to the floor, weeping for joy.

Soon he was in London seeing his old mates. One of them, Ralph, was like a brother to Rufus. Ralph was so Communist that he had painted his door red, and on his bedroom wall had fixed a huge poster of Che Guevara.

'Rufus, mate,' he used to say, 'you're too airy fairy.' He enjoyed bringing Rufus down to earth but would still let Rufus badger him into going to something way out. He loved Rufus but couldn't keep up with his fads.

Rufus blew in and hugged Ralph.

'Praise the Lord, Ralph!'

'You what?' said Ralph.

'Praise the Lord! Glory! I've found Jesus – the constant high!'

'Oh no!' said Ralph. 'Not Jesus! You'd praise a matchbox if it could save you.'

'That's right,' said Rufus. 'But I've found Jesus. Glory! You've got to come up and meet the Jesus People, Ralph.'

'Meet them! I'll come up and meet them!' said Ralph looking agitated. 'And I'll find out who's raking in the money!'

Ralph turned up in order to sort Rufus out. Rufus had really flipped this time. Christianity! Krishna had turned Ralph off – but Christianity! It reeked of all that was middle-class, imperialist and oppressive. Jesus was all right. He was for the people. But the church! The church! It was the religious facade of capitalist materialism.

Ralph sat next to Rufus in the upstairs lounge and sussed them all out. Most of them were right straights, he thought, but they looked pretty happy and liberated. Even Jess was getting into it. It must be the first scene they'd ever agreed on! Ralph smiled cynically. Then he felt uneasy. He was always going on about being free, breaking out, being yourself. But he wasn't. He was bound up like everyone else – and he knew it. Oh, but not God. That was old hat.

Out of the blue, a lady stood up. 'The Lord tells me there is a young man here who is very cynical. But he wants you to know that he really loves you and wants to set you free.'

Ralph was stunned. He felt totally exposed – as if God was looking inside him – and he started to crumble. After that he didn't say a word for two days. If he became a Christian, then what about his ideals – equality, freedom, the brotherhood of man?

In the end he turned it over to God and, as he surrendered, a great peace came into his soul. The following evening he listened in amazement as Noel quoted a political idealist

> We communists are the ones who get shot and jailed and slandered. We live in virtual poverty. We turn back to the party every penny we make above what is absolutely necessary. We don't have time for movies and concerts or T-bone steaks, or decent homes, or new cars. We are called fanatics. Our lives are dominated by one great vision. We have a philosophy no money can buy, and a purpose to fight for. It is my life, my business, my religion, my hobby, my sweetheart, my lover, my bread and my meat. I work at it in the daytime and dream of it

at night. Its hold on me grows, not lessens – therefore I cannot carry on a friendship or even a conversation without relating it to this force that drives my life. I have already been in jail, and if necessary, I am ready to go before the firing squad.[16]

'How much more,' said Noel, looking in Ralph's direction, 'should we be devoted to the cause of our Lord Jesus Christ!' With tears in his eyes, Ralph worshipped his new-found Saviour.

A week passed and another of Rufus' friends came to see what was going on. Mary was French – and the philosophical arty type. She was an 'acid head', her boyfriend was astrologer to the Beatles, and she was into Timothy Leary and the psychedelics.

When Rufus appeared in Chelsea, she watched him going round praising the Lord and hugging his old friends. It was bizarre, but unusually solid for Rufus, she thought. He was becoming human again!

Mary came up, and was lighting a fire when Ralph walked in, beaming. 'Mary,' he said, 'I've been converted.' She couldn't believe it: Ralph, the militant atheist!

'These Jesus People must be miracle workers!' she thought, and decided to go along to a meeting. Bugbrooke, she imagined, was a barn in the country full of turned-on Jesus Freaks.

But not so. One guy was over forty, sporting a big red tie, braces and long balding hair. 'A typical eccentric Englishman!' she thought, as he approached her down the aisle just before the meeting. It was Noel. He said a few friendly words but in this atmosphere of holiness she felt exposed, and was lost for words.

The meeting began and soon they were singing in strange languages. Suddenly she was aware of the presence of God and in a flash she saw the meaning of the gospel. Jesus had died for her! The Bible was true! She could receive the Holy Spirit!

Mary talked with Rufus into the early hours, and he told her she must give God her heart and love Jesus supremely. It was a simple choice of surrender, and Mary decided to give it a go. In the morning she hitched a lift to London and Jesus was the sole topic of conversation all the way! She packed up some essential things and gave the rest to her flat mate. Paintings, tapestries and writings were left unfinished. She said goodbye to London and returned that day to a new lifestyle – a sleeping bag on Rufus' floor!

Others friends got converted and moved in, and the little house was bursting at the seams. What with mattresses and sleeping bags, the baby, the dogs, and the frequent visitors, the new community hummed with life. Jesus People, bikers and freaks – converted, unconverted, or semi-converted – all sat where they could. Ralph and Mary cooked sausages in the kitchen, to Rufus' continued horror. But when he checked the Scriptures he failed to see a vegetarian Jesus, so he gave it up – much to the relief of the dogs!

Rufus also burned his mystical books. But the house quickly filled with black smoke and they all rushed into the garden! The police soon got interested in all these hippy comings and goings, and at two in the morning the innocent freaks were busted! In came the law with a search warrant but all they found was a pile of Jesus leaflets and One Way tee-shirts. Perplexed, they sniffed out a jar of herbal tea and took it away triumphantly for testing. As soon as the door closed, the hippies all rolled around laughing. Rufus had only just disposed of his last 'grass' plants.

By now John Thom was established in a house at Almond Close on the Bugbrooke estate. There he gathered some unlikely characters: a biker, an ex-monk, the eccentric chap with the badges, and a fairly normal Christian lad, who had turned up late one night on the back of his dad's Honda 50. It was a crash course in relationships; for John it was a crash course in leadership.

He also manned the 'Jesus Lifeline' telephone and recorded a new message late every night. 'Phone every day. Drive gloom away!' was the motto and up to sixty people a day left a recorded response to the message – some none too savoury!

Amidst all the excitement we needed to steer a firm course and see what God was doing. One thing was clear to us – a new society was emerging whose roots were not in an old tradition but in a new work of God.

There was a great mix. Students from Oxford began to visit us, three or four lay preachers had joined us, and God was sending professional people into our midst. The dropouts woke up to find themselves disciples of Jesus (and got jobs!). The straights were suddenly surrounded by converted freaks. We just wanted to be together and see the work of God go forward. Church life was of overwhelming interest and there was little time for the world and its pursuits.

We didn't think much of the 'goggle box' and quoted this piece of ironic verse in *Jesus Reality*: 'The TV is my shepherd. My spiritual growth shall definitely want. It maketh me to sit down and do nothing for his name's sake.'[17]

We began to see how unconventional the first disciples of Jesus were. They kicked the system. They broke the mould. They trusted God. They left all else and shared in great simplicity. Around Jesus arose an upheaval of such dramatic proportions that the establishment put him down.

Where did we stand? For revolution? Yes! A revolution of love. A revolution that would turn the world's values upside down. But that required commitment, and some among us didn't want the hassle. There were many new converts but too few of us poured out our lives for them. Revival was blessing at a cost. We had enjoyed the charismatic blessings, but would we get on the charismatic cross?

Some of the young Christians were overtaking us in their radical devotion to Jesus; others were rapidly backsliding. They could not be absorbed into our middle-class lives. God was forcing us to see that we had to make a choice between the world's culture and Christ's church. We knew that the spirit of British culture had to go. A marvellous thing then emerged. Relationships formed that were spiritually based, and as we worshipped together a sense of brotherhood was born.

God gave us wisdom urging commitment to each other. One of us saw a huge golden crown shining in the darkness, and many joined in a circle to lift it into the air. Its glory attracted many more, who helped to lift the crown. Others hung around, fascinated, but refused to shoulder the burden, and slowly shrank away into the darkness. We saw that coming under Christ's authority meant unity.

The path of discipleship seemed to blaze out before us from the Scriptures. Jesus compared the kingdom of God to a banquet which, sadly, most were too busy to attend. He also likened it to a tower, and told his disciples to count the cost of building it (Luke 14). The church would never be built on 'cheap grace'.

'Grace is costly,' Noel quoted from Dietrich Bonhoeffer, 'because it compels a man to submit to the yoke of Christ and follow him.'[18] For us, this would mean a new lifestyle. 'Any of you who does not give up everything he has cannot be my disciple,' Jesus had said (Luke 14:33). Some speak fearfully of these 'hard sayings', but obedience to them was the key that unlocked God's life amongst us.

We also found baptism in water to be increasingly significant. Alan was a busker and a registered heroin addict. With long blond hair and purple kaftan, he was a familiar sight in London. When he heard about Rufus, Alan came along to see us. In the first meeting he was born again and healed of addiction. In the second he was baptised in the Spirit. In the third he got baptised.

These young prodigals demonstrated that new birth, baptism in water and in the Spirit were power encounters with salvation. Alan had a lot of old life to bury. His eyes had grown so weak from drugs that he wore shades. When he came out of the water his eyes were healed. Baptism was no mere confession of faith: it was power.

BIRTH OF A CULTURE

It was also an exit from the world's value system. 'Repent and be baptised,' Peter had cried. 'Save yourselves from this corrupt generation!' (Acts 2:38, 40). It was going to be tough, but Alan was identifying with the people of God.

Around this time we discovered *Love Not The World* by Watchman Nee. Nee wrote: 'Salvation is essentially a present exit from a doomed order...[In baptism] a whole world goes down with you. When you come up, you come up in Christ – in the ark that rides the waves. You have entered a new order of things.'[19]

Clearly the hippy culture was not the Jesus culture, but neither was the status quo. Everything in the New Testament cried revolution, transformation and a new society. 'If anyone is in Christ,' declared Paul, 'he is a new creation; the old has gone, the new has come!' (2 Cor 5:17).

New creation became our theme song as we broke new ground. New creation called for a reassessment of values that had been drummed into us from birth. It meant hacking out a hallowed spot from the tangle of worldliness. It put a question mark on everything we did simply because everybody else did it. Television, theatre, sport, vacations abroad, religious festivals – they all came under the searchlight.

Many questions arose as we glimpsed the magnitude of God's will. 'Do not conform any longer to the pattern of this world,' he was saying, 'but be transformed by the renewing of your mind' (Rom 12:2). If it was a choice of moving with God or running with the crowd, then the matter was already settled.

The writings of A. W. Tozer encouraged us a great deal. He insisted that the church was 'a despised minority group standing in bold moral contradiction to the world...a division of soldiers on foreign soil, a brotherhood of like minded men.'[20] We agreed.

By the summer of 1973 we were getting known. Our stance towards traditionalism and worldliness upset a few people.

Some felt threatened. We appeared a provocative bunch and we no doubt lacked the depth and humility of a Tozer.

But here we were, a church of renewed village chapel-goers, converted freaks, pentecostals, professionals and the odd academic. Add to that the relentless energy of the Holy Spirit, and the melting power of God's love, and you had the ingredients of a new society.

Awake O Zion!
1973–1978

7

Community

1973

'Lord,' Victor had once said, 'if you want me to marry Sheila, then make this wart on my finger go down!' He opened his eyes. The wart had gone! Victor had these kind of dealings with God.

Back in 1961, as a young Anglican at Art College, he'd experienced God's forgiveness. Then one day he read in Acts 10: 'For they heard them speaking in tongues and praising God' (Acts 10:46). 'If this is for now, Lord,' Victor prayed, 'let me have it.' He got it, and immediately felt a strong urge to live and share with other Christians. But nothing came of it. Victor plunged into his career and got married.

Now in his early thirties, he dreamed of a yacht and a luxury home by the sea. He was already a qualified architect, a deacon in the Baptist Church, Superintendent of the Sunday school, and President of the Lay Preachers Association in Taunton. Things seemed good. However, his sensitive nature was stifled by ambition. Christian duties, a young family, and the strain of work were taking their toll and the doctor put him on tranquillisers.

Victor sought God afresh and decided to make a clean break. Northampton was a growing town and the Development Corporation was advertising for landscape architects. God gave him a positive nudge and a well-known charismatic leader suggested he check out a lively little church called Bugbrooke.

It was a cold February night when he turned out in a suit for the mid-week meeting. He just reached the top of the chapel lounge stairs when Noel greeted him warmly. Their eyes met. 'Whoops!' thought Victor, 'He can see right through me.' Somewhat unnerved, he looked around. Before him was a group of hairy hippies. Victor groaned inside as a heavy-looking biker caught his eye and walked over. Victor froze. 'Well, this is it!' he thought.

'Bless you, bro! It's great to see you!' Kelly gave him a warm hug and Victor relaxed. They talked a while and then the meeting took off. A brother prophesied powerfully and Victor was a bit awe-struck. Then Noel spoke on eldership and how it was a lifelong commitment to the church.

'Just as well I'm not an elder,' Victor thought.

He stayed with a couple in the fellowship for a few months and travelled home at weekends.

Noel chatted to him one evening. 'I'll look forward to seeing you at the elders' and deacons' meeting next Monday.'

'Help!' thought Victor.

He often went home to Sheila with interesting stories.

'This long-haired communist, Ralph, turned up the same night as me,' he related. 'He came to the Lord. Oh, and one ex-junkie called Paddy plays this weird instrument. It's a long pole with bottle tops on, and a boot at the end! He's getting married in July and the fellowship have bought a 'Jesus house' for them in Northampton.'

'They've started this meeting on Mondays called PLAN – Power and Love in Action Now. It's for all the dynamic young people – including me! Some of them reckon it's more real than the leaders' meeting. They're so committed! Last week God was so real some people were prostrate on the floor.'

'By the way,' said Victor, tucking into his breakfast, one Saturday morning, 'Noel's invited me to the leaders' meeting. We'd better pray, you know. If I accept this I think we're in it for life!'

Sheila came up and was taken aback by the love in the fellowship. They took the plunge and bought a house in Northampton. In June there was a house warming 'holy love-feast' at their new home. It was a timber-framed house with the lounge on the first floor and Victor's architectural mind did overtime as he watched sixty sweaty charismatics move into a time of worship! Sheila was a solid evangelical schoolteacher, but was delighted with all she saw. They had married on the understanding that Jesus would come first. He was taking them up on it. It looked as if they were in for an interesting future!

In July a hundred of us packed our suitcases and headed for the Yorkshire Dales. When we arrived at the hostel in Malhamdale we got a shock. So did the owner – it was a holiday centre for youngsters! We knew the Scripture, 'Unless you become as little children...' but this was ridiculous. They let us stay, but it was iron bunkbeds and small portions for the rest of the fortnight!

Every morning we were woken up by a loud bell and, after breakfast, the keen ones stayed for the morning Bible study. In the afternoon we went hiking, hill walking, cave exploring or swimming.

On the first day Noel went with Pete and Carol to visit the Brontë house on the moors. Carol went in with the baby while Noel read to Pete from a new book, *A New Way of Living* by Michael Harper. It described the Church of the Redeemer in Houston, Texas.

'Listen to this, Pete,' said Noel.

> During Lent 1965 the group began to study the Acts of the Apostles, and were struck by the account in the second chapter of the way the Spirit-filled Church shared so completely. The Lord impressed upon them all that he wanted them to live this life together.[21]

Pete smiled. 'Hey, we're eight years behind them!'

'Oh, bro! We're getting there. We just need to grasp the vision. Rufus' lot virtually share everything already.'

'Yes, but what about the middle-class?' said Pete, 'Do you think they'll swallow it?'

'We'll see – won't we?' smiled Noel.

Pete was silent and Noel buried himself in the book.

'Hey, bro,' said Pete, after a while, 'are you thinking about all of us moving into community?'

Noel looked up. 'Why not?'

'Yeh,' said Pete. He looked out of the window – it was a beautiful afternoon. 'Man!' he said – under his breath.

Practical sharing began in earnest that week. Apart from midnight distributions of apple pies and Mars bars, there were more serious needs. Some folk were only there because others had paid for them. Then there were all the requirements of the two new Jesus Homes in Northampton – the house for Paddy, and also a house for Rufus and his friends. Rufus' house was fairly run down and needed a lot of work, and they were still far short of the initial mortgage price. A hat was left out in the meetings. On one day alone they got £200. One brother pledged his life insurance and another threw in the £100 he was saving towards his dream minibus.

As the fortnight progressed we sat more lightly on our possessions. God wanted to own us completely: our affections, our time and our goods. The example of the Redeemer Church was a massive inspiration and Noel frequently read from the book. 'Each of them,' he read 'began to live a life of simplicity. They stopped buying new cars and televisions. Possessions were of value only for their usefulness to the community.'[22]

Our wallets continued to open along with our hearts. Somehow this material sharing released the floodgates of brotherly love. Laughter and tears flowed into the meetings as the bond of love increased.

One brother had been a sergeant major and wore a moustache to prove it! Long haired hippies weren't quite his scene, but the Lord burst his heart open. For him Malhamdale was unforgettable:

> The atmosphere was terrific. It was family. At Malhamdale we really saw the vision of community. It's hard to describe such deep ministry. We were crying with joy – I mean everybody, including Noel. You never wanted the meetings to end. You just wanted to sit there and know the love. It brought everyone through – I mean, if you weren't real for the Lord, you'd never have stood a fortnight of it!

'It was fun too!' said his wife. 'We played tricks on each other, like tying all the bedroom door knobs together. One night I jumped into bed and someone had put a load of dried peas in it!'

Many of us remembered worshipping down in the caverns and tunnels of White Scar cave. 'Jesus, Jesus, let me tell you what I know,' rang out in echoing harmonies and rounds as the Jesus People made their way singing through the underworld, accompanied by some skilful playing on the stalactites.

At Malhamdale the Spirit was bringing a new sense of unity and power which confronted the forces of darkness. Noel taught on the spiritual warfare and there were quite a few demonic manifestations. Some from the nicest people you could know.

At this point I made an exit. I felt as though I had a hard shell around me that wouldn't break and I couldn't get into the flow. So I went home to lick my wounds and try to pray. I passed Victor and his family arriving for the second week and saw his acute embarrassment as an older sister flung her arms around him! I wished him luck! But he fared better than I, being a humbler man. Victor was determined to lose his reserves and relate to people. Already he was wearing jeans and letting his hair grow longer. From the hippy side, Ralph also made a concession. His waist-long hair was cut back to his shoulders!

Victor sat comfortably in the evening meeting surrounded by his new 'family', and enjoyed the wealth of ministry.

'I saw coloured drops of water,' said Verna. 'They were falling into a pool and being absorbed; it produced a thing of great beauty.'

'That's us losing our independence and getting "lost" in the body of Christ,' Victor thought.

'Yeah! I saw this really long piano. I mean reeeaally long,' said a new brother, stretching his arms out wide. 'There were lots of people all sat down and playing together nicely like – all in 'armony.'

'Er...the many gifts and ministries' thought Victor.

'Well! I've got some liquorice allsorts here,' said another brother, jumping up and producing a paper bag. 'This one's solid liquorice. Mmmm nice!' he said, popping it into his mouth. 'Ah! Now this one is all soft inside!'

'I wonder what gift he's moving in,' thought Victor, smiling to himself. By this time, most people were looking enthralled – and hungry.

'But we need them all!' the brother continued. 'We can't go it alone. Each one here's special. And, what's more – there are no wrappers on these!' He grinned and popped a coconut sweet into his mouth. 'I'll tell you what the Lord is doing with us – he's taking our wrappers off. Yes! Taking them off! And mixing us all up.'

Tears of laughter were streaming down Paddy's face.

Victor smiled at Sheila. He remembered his longing for community after he'd first been baptised in the Spirit. Now God was restoring that vision. All sense of isolation melted away as he moved on into worship.

A lad in the next seat started to groan. 'I think he needs

healing for his stomach,' thought Victor, as the groans increased. Suddenly there was a blood-curdling scream. Two brothers pounced in and nearly knocked Victor off his chair. The demon vacated the scene and the worship continued. Sheila gripped Victor's hand. This was different from Sunday School in Taunton.

At Malhamdale we considered how to work the vision out. Many who lived outside Bugbrooke considered moving in to be where the action was. There were schemes for bulk buying, for a second-hand clothes store, and for sharing lists of needs and gifts. A 'Love Community Fund' was also to be set up. As we lived more cheaply, so money would be released to meet needs and buy houses. Already there was a target of £50,000 for the Housing Association.

Three types of community homes were envisaged. Jesus Family Homes would be simple extended families. Jesus Welcome Homes were to be larger frontline houses for evangelism. Jesus Central Homes in the Bugbrooke area would be at the heart of things to train Christians within community.

Underlying the practical plans was the grand theme of the restoration of God's house. We had a song based on the New Testament: 'We are being built into a temple'. But it wouldn't be easy, as I'd already found. God was not constructing a theological castle in the clouds, he was cementing together human lives, and that meant pain. Our independence was deeply ingrained. Only by embracing the cross could unity be established.

'Individualism has been the bane of the churches,' wrote Michael Harper.[23] The Redeemer Church had confronted this problem and got down to the nitty gritty of committed relationships. We read of how they cut down their activities, entered a phase of building and got criticised by other Christians for being introverted.

In Britain, too, the charismatic scene was muddled about commitment. 'The movement is robust, but amorphous,' observed Michael Harper. 'It majors on individual piety and spiritual drive rather than the creation of a new corporate dynamic.'[24]

The first Christians were 'one in heart and mind' (Acts 4:32), standing 'firm in one spirit, contending as one man' (Phil 1:27), and 'with one heart and mouth' they glorified God (Rom 15:6). But in our day independence prevailed and many of us were coloured by it.

Were evangelicals overbalanced in their emphasis on a 'personal relationship' with Jesus? Did books idealise individual success stories? Did too much stress on grace lead to lawlessness and lack of authority? The problem taxed our hearts at Malhamdale. For many it was a case of 'blood, sweat and tears'. New converts faced less of a problem. They jumped in at the deep end!

In community the self-life gets exposed. Reserve, self-righteousness and self-love are painfully revealed. Love of possessions and the insistence on personal guidance, worldliness, insensitivity and lack of submission to the church — all these harm the life of the spiritual family and have to be faced up to.

At Malhamdale there was a prayer room where some had real dealings with the Lord. Val felt she ought to buy a house on the estate in Bugbrooke. Already she was travelling six nights a week to chapel. Once on the estate she would be putting people up every weekend, ministering late at night, or even cooking for the Almond Close brothers! There would be much commitment, little privacy and fewer visits to her family. After a struggle she abandoned herself to God's will, and rushed out of the room laughing for joy!

For Victor and Sheila the atmosphere of love was a whole new world. In Taunton Victor had engaged in duties, but here was life. Once he had been open to the world, but now he was open to his brothers. He had heard about the need to be 'covered' — to come under the mantle of the body of Christ. That's how it felt — secure and in place. As the strain lifted from his mind, Victor felt enfolded in God's love.

They all came back from Yorkshire to a greater or lesser degree transformed. Happily, I had found some encouragement from God and was around for another try. We were moving on explosively with frequent demonic manifestations in chapel. It was not uncommon to have the preaching interrupted by screams and flying hymnbooks, and Kelly leaping into action from the platform.

On one occasion a man with a violent demon was taken into the vestry behind Noel. A scuffle went on and we could hear the sound of breaking furniture, while the cross on the wall swayed from side to side. Noel continued to speak with a calm smile. He didn't overemphasise the demonic.

In Northampton the two Jesus homes at Argyle Street and Harlestone Road filled up. The weekly notice sheet got longer. 'Is This Your Ministry?' it said on the back. 'Help needed for decorating...Someone required to organise bulk buying...Lawns need cutting...Sister wanted to type new chorus books.' The *Love Community News* section included all sorts of jottings: 'Ralph is working as odd job man...Alan is available to dig gardens...Please bring surplus fruit, veg and clothes to the chapel...Dave and Karen have room for two single people...'

In September I went off to Plymouth for a breather to do teacher training but news of Bugbrooke followed me there. A friendly but extravagant article appeared in *The Daily Mail*:

> More than 200 people in a village of 800 have dramatically dedicated their lives to Jesus. Nowhere else in Britain has experienced such a concentrated surge of religious fervour. So many want to be part of the Bugbrooke Miracle that some travel for miles almost every day to attend prayer sessions...So much was written about the Jesus Freaks. But the pattern here, though similar, is dramatically different. For this extraordinary revival slashes through all barriers of age and background.[25]

Our fame spread. 'What Wesley did for gin, the movement does for drugs,' reported *New Society*. We were wary of publicity, but there was no holding back the secular media. Television companies got wind and Thames Television began to film a documentary on how *The Lord Took Hold Of Bugbrooke*. Community was in vogue at this time and a team from Redeemer Church arrived in England. There were many ventures in communal living and some declared that this was God's contemporary word to the church.

At Argyle Street, conditions were primitive. Victor went to live there for a few days and insisted they make no special provisions for him. They didn't. When he arrived Ralph had ripped out the kitchen and Victor helped wash up in the bath. Floorboards in the lounge were missing, windows were out and the holes covered with sacking. Jess and French Mary cooked chapatis over an oil stove in the lounge and they all sat round on milk crates and chairs from the tip!

Victor sat down to table. They thought it was marvellous – this straight coming to live with them and share their brown rice! They hugged him and welcomed him home. Rufus's bright eyes fixed on Victor, looking for some fatherly lead.

'Well,' coughed Victor, 'let's say grace.'

'What an amazing idea!' they thought. Alan grabbed his busking guitar. Rufus fetched his bongos. The rest reached for spoons, pans, teapots – anything. As the half hour 'jamming' session took off, several of them sang their heart out spontaneously while the rest accompanied on the cutlery.

Victor enjoyed this 'psalming' and felt years younger.

After the meal they sat round talking. Some of it was hilarious. Alan and Rufus were great extroverts. Then the music session took off again with great gusto and shouts of 'Glory! Praise the Lord!'

Life generally at Argyle Street was no less zany. It was a legendary era. With a light-hearted Alan around it was difficult for anyone to stay in the 'poms' (poor-old-me's)! By comparison, Sunday mornings at chapel were rather tame, and they didn't bother going – at least for a while!

Victor had a great week and the hippies were touched by his humility and warmth. Not everyone was as willing as Victor to lose their pride and melt into the pool of community. Christians can be tough old nuts! But God was cracking us open.

Away at Plymouth, my attempts at teaching were a disaster. When my motorbike blew up in the middle of Dartmoor, I threw in the towel, came home, and dived in.

8

Mud, Sweat and Tears

1974

Rodger laughed so much, he fell on his back! He hadn't always been so liberated, but that spring evening he, Pete, and I had come home inebriated – spiritually. It did us good. We needed loosening up. I was into prayer and fasting, Rodger was into logical thinking, and Pete, a guitar teacher, was into sleep and cream buns! They called us the three stooges: two Oxford graduates and an amateur philosopher. I now worked as a school technician and we all shared a flat in Northampton.

Like us, more and more were coming together in some kind of community. Couples opened their homes to singles and some, like Val, moved into the village. Community was now the emphasis. Evangelism took second place but newcomers kept appearing. We concentrated on being a people for God and this caught the public eye. 'Following The Instructions Of Jesus – To The Letter' was an article in the local press. 'This is communism that works,' Paddy comments, 'because it's based on love.'

In June Thames Television screened *The Lord Took Hold Of Bugbrooke*. In one shot Paddy washed the same dishes six times over, while Alan told his story. In chapel cameras zoomed in on tongue-speaking worshippers, but it wasn't unpleasantly sensational. The crew were impressed and frustrated – impressed by our love, changed lives, and liberated worship (some tapped their feet to the choruses); impressed when we ministered healing to the producer; and impressed with words of knowledge concerning them; but frustrated when a demon was cast out. They had taken the afternoon off!

The film was followed by write-ups. 'Spotlight On Bugbrooke' was an excellent article in *Evangelism Today*. Amongst the secular press was 'Our Own Bible Belt' in *The Daily Mail*, 'The Bugbrooke Phenomenon' in The *Northants Evening Telegraph*, and 'Bugbrooke, Where Alleluias Come Bigger And Noisier!' in *The TV Times*. Some comments were amusing, like this in *The Daily Telegraph* under the heading 'Rolling In The Aisles – A Proven Success':

> Abandoning orthodox practices, the minister presents his flock with a form of worship compounded of American-style hot gospelling, a British-style knees up, total immersion, and a few gimmicks of his own. Among these are 'speaking in tongues' as related in Acts of the Apostles...It is difficult not to be impressed. Above all there is an air of total innocence which does not always attach to the more extravagant religious sects. Bugbrooke may not be up front in the intellectual stakes, but it seems a reasonable bet that they have spread more happiness than harm.[27]

In fact, the church was in danger of being overrun by the intelligentsia. Students and professionals swarmed in like bees around a honeypot, but in God's wisdom the pace was set by the locals and the converts. There was some depth behind the raucous brotherhood of Argyle Street, and we all learned to live from the heart. 'Out of your belly,' said Jesus, 'will flow rivers of living water' (John 7:38 NKJ). In the atmosphere of released emotion and spiritual worship, many hearts were inspired and lifted.

Spontaneity, though, needed the balance of discipline. Many drifted in and out, flirtation between the sexes was a danger, and there was a need for holiness. We sought to be more accountable to one another and taught biblical discipleship and commitment. Some resented this and Noel replied with a rain of heavyweight quotes on the notice sheet from men like Tozer and Nee. Cross-bearing, brokenness and death to self-living, became the themes of the day.

The Lord now began to say, 'Take my people deeper!' Deeper into God and deeper into his kingdom. As the word of God's kingdom was proclaimed, I felt I was watching the parable of the sower in action. My spirit was excited (I'd found out where it was!) and I soaked up the vision. Some of us felt we had stumbled upon treasure and wanted to give everything to gain it.

But not all responded this way. 'Life's worries, riches and pleasures' (Luke 8:14) choked some lives, and slowly the summer crowds of 1973 thinned out. As we moved on into 1974 two ugly giants reared their heads – worldliness and independence.

They had one effective cure – the cross – and it came in many shapes and sizes. For some it was the loss of worldly interests. The Spirit wasn't keen on aspects of our old life. Apart from smoking and drinking, it was entertainment, television and secular music that gave way. When we were lukewarm, these things seemed all right, but in revival these amusements were hindrances to spiritual power.

The Lord challenged me, too. Heavy metal wasn't my problem, but giving up my stereophonic Sibelius was painful. I heard the call of Jesus to forsake everything and ditched my pipe and herbal tobacco, too! Many of us parted with relationships, possessions and pursuits that, though not sinful in themselves, hindered us in our quest to travel light and love God supremely.

The cross cut us away from worldly opinions. By now

MUD, SWEAT AND TEARS

we'd had enough of Christmas. Apart from the New Testament stance of avoiding 'special days and months and seasons' (Gal 4:10; Col 2:16), such so-called Christian festivals seemed full of hypocrisy. In family life, too, we gained a vision of loving authority, and determined to rear our kids for Christ. All this invited criticism – and got it!

The cross was reducing middle-classness to ashes as we took hold of a new lifestyle. It was breaking down the aloofness bred through education. We saw clearly that 'What is highly valued among men, is detestable in God's sight' (Luke 16:15).

The cross crucified our independence. Meeting so often didn't leave too much time to do our own thing. We moved in togetherness and opened our lives to input from others. Paddy and Rufus were exercising leadership within the Jesus houses and a male ruling authority was taking shape. That in itself was a cross for some.

Worldliness, too, was a headache. Here we were also fighting the contemporary Christian emphasis on liberty and anyone who found our commitment too taxing could always cry, 'Legalism!' Many who didn't hold our vision were keen to put us right. But we pressed on and ploughed our own furrow. Prophetic voices and prophetic churches were scarce enough.

As Tozer once wrote: 'We desperately need seers who can see through the mist – Christian leaders with prophetic vision...And if they come, we will no doubt crucify a few of them in the name of worldly orthodoxy.'[28]

Separation from the world and brotherly sharing were becoming our hallmarks. It was time for the Jesus Fellowship, as the chapel congregation was now called, to move deeper into community.

Bugbrooke Hall, just up the road from Verna's cottage, had been empty for two years. Now very run down, it was due to be auctioned in June. Built by a rich squire in the early nineteenth century, this old rectory lay on the southern edge of Bugbrooke in thirteen acres of parkland – an imposing Georgian house of pale yellow brick, standing with its long annexe like a stately liner in a sea of grass. To the back was a courtyard complete with stable block and grassy cobbles. All around stood great trees of copper beech and oak, whilst a strip of woodland flanked the stone wall down to the pond.

It was going to be pricey, but if we could raise the 10% deposit we would be in with a chance. It was a risky venture of faith, and felt like crossing a rickety bridge over a wide river. But on the other side was a new land. After a time of discussion, Cyril, who was an architect, summed up the general feeling at the leaders' meeting: 'Cor! We can't afford to miss this!'

Two examples inspired us as we turned to the Scriptures. One was Joshua taking the Promised Land through conquering faith. The other, in Acts 4, was how many in the Jerusalem church sold their possessions and 'put [the money] at the apostles' feet' (Acts 4:35). Our giving increased and people sold things off. Rings and jewellery were handed in. We had also begun buying in bulk and living more economically. One or two couples pledged their houses, desiring to move into the large home. Others gave or loaned their savings.

There was a tremendous sense of expectancy. Together we circled this 'Jericho' in faith. Some gave themselves to prayer and fasting, recognising that this was a spiritual battle. The Lord gave a word from Isaiah 1:19: 'If you are willing and obedient, you will eat the best from the land.'

The day of the auction came. Cyril sat at the front while Noel was at the back praying. The reporters watched Noel like hawks but soon directed their attention to Cyril who continued bidding. He'd hoped for a ceiling of £55,000 but stuck with it till they all dropped out at £67,000.

Rodger and I were thrilled when we heard. Pete drove us into the Hall grounds that summer evening, and I leapt out of the minibus and did cartwheels over the lawn. To me the parklands were like paradise and the Hall was New Jerusalem! Pete was more realistic and saw what was coming.

The battle of faith continued. We had the deposit, but where on earth would we find the rest? Everyone we approached turned down our application for a mortgage until one friendly bank manager pointed to the ceiling and said, 'Well, if him up there is on your side, I'd better help!' It wouldn't be the last time God would touch the hearts of influential people when we needed it.

In July Dave Lantsbery and Steve, a converted young drunk, took possession of the old rectory – at two o'clock in the morning! The owls screeched all night as the pioneers tried to sleep in a dusty corridor upstairs. Dave was soon on holiday from teaching and went round the auctions for furniture. Lots of people offered them stuff – boxes of crocks, sundae dishes and lemon squeezers – most of it useless! But we were in and the adventure had begun.

In July 170 of us left for Ashburnham Place in Sussex. God was taking us deeper, and it was here we all learned to 'meditate'. Or, at least, tried to!

Early one morning I stepped on to the lawn and headed for the woods. It was only six o'clock and the sun was drawing a haze from off the lake. At last I was alone with God. Gently I sang in tongues and felt my desert boots soaking up the morning dew. The donkey brayed noisily, but I kept my distance. (The animal was notorious for biting Christian retreaters!) Otherwise the silence was delicious. I sang out the interpretation and prophesied, then, turning off the path into the woods, I poured out my heart to God. I felt he had become my friend, and I found myself crying as I pondered his goodness towards us. As I walked along the lakeside a chuckle rose from deep within and I jumped into the air. A quick look to see if anyone was around, and then, 'Praise the Lord!' I shouted till my voice rang over the lake, and the donkey screamed.

My days of academic introversion were over – well, almost!

Lots of us had been wandering round the grounds trying to 'prepare [our] minds for action' (1 Pet 1:13) and commune with God. It was a funny sight. Some walked through the woods musing and muttering while others sat on the grass and prayed.

One afternoon we had an hour of silence everywhere so we could listen to God. But the evening meeting was more liberated than ever because we'd been working hard to know and hear God ourselves. A Malaysian student recognised one tongue of praise as Mandarin Chinese and shouted out that the interpretation was correct. Many were sensing their spirit in new ways, ministering or psalming in the assembly.

A fascination with God developed. Corporate worship brought a sense of his presence, but listening to the 'still, small voice' was our need. So much knocked us off balance – our bodies so tuned to the senses, our souls so full of thoughts, feelings and desires. We needed to know God deep in our spirits, to leave behind spiritual adolescence and press on to maturity.

Community without spirituality would be disaster, and we determined to pursue God and follow the Spirit. Already fans of Tozer, we picked up his admiration for the mystics. 'True worship,' he wrote, 'is to be captivated and charmed and entranced with who God is, and struck with astonished wonder at the inconceivable elevation and magnitude and splendour of Almighty God. To love God with fear and wonder and yearning and awe.'[29]

The desire for God consumed other passions. The call was to union with God and 'perfect love'. We became aware of the stages of growth that Christian mystics spoke of – desire, discipline, conflict, purging, sweetness, illumination, and union. (And for some of us, the 'dark night of the soul'.)

It sounded grand, but we were a long way from being little mystics. Bible studies were optional. The campers spent most of their time drying off after the frequent downpours, and many stayed up late chatting or went out looking for glow-worms. Some lay in bed in the mornings and we spent the afternoons walking, swimming and visiting the seaside. The donkey was a distraction, too. It nipped a few fingers and ran off with Verna's handbag.

Community was excellent for birthing inspirations and for earthing them, too. It was good to have people around to tell us we didn't need to fast for forty days or that we weren't quite ready for apostleship!

Ashburnham left a hazy memory of idyllic scenery, new horizons, meditation, tremendous praise and deepening brotherhood. But some remembered it for the mud, sweat and tears. Mud – for the campers in the rain; sweat and tears for the many experiences of the cross as we surrendered our lives to God.

Also that fortnight it dawned on some that they were to be shepherds of the flock. The sadness of our evangelism was the drop-out rate. Few of the early bikers were around and some of the hippies had fallen away. The problem was that these young sheep were not being shepherded enough. Often the wolf picked off the solitary sheep who had been isolated and made vulnerable.

1974 was a year when the concept of shepherding was much abroad. Good shepherding was to bring depth and cohesion to the growing charismatic churches. We needed men we could follow. A group were maturing among us who carried particular wisdom and love, and we felt the time had come to recognise elders. Clearly God placed in the church 'some to be apostles, some to be prophets, some to be evangelists, and some to be pastors and teachers, to prepare God's people for works of service' (Eph 4:11–12). These ministries were emerging and we needed them desperately.

We hadn't recognised elders yet – those invited to the elders' and deacons' meeting assumed they were either deacons or awed spectators! A number of originals went, including Verna and Miss Campion. We realised that not everyone who attended had pastoral gifts. We needed to restructure the leadership without giving offence.

The solution was simple. Our fellowship began to plan a breakdown into shepherding groups – mid-week regional gatherings of up to thirty, designed for fellowship, caring, and ministry. During the Ashburnham retreat, we formed the groups and laid hands on the new leaders. A senior brother was to be assisted by two others in pastoral leadership. That was roughly ten 'sheep' to one 'shepherd'.

We now had a male eldership whose authority was publicly recognised – and frequently forgiven! (They were an immature bunch.) I remember being annoyed at Pete for being an elder when I wasn't. I also remember Pete regularly handing in his resignation! Being a shepherd was no joke. You were pushed up to the front line and from then on you were supposed to be a guardian of others and a fount of wisdom. The qualifications for eldership in 1 Timothy and Titus were enough to make anyone quail (1 Tim 3:1–7; Titus 1:6–9). But at least we weren't into wine and brawling!

In community houses, being an elder meant continuous responsibility. All sorts of people came round and looked to the elders as examples of godliness. The shepherds learned to cast themselves on the Lord. They had to.

God gave us much wisdom about what it cost to be a shepherd. One picture was of a flock of sheep protected by a strong wooden fence. All over the fence could be seen the claw marks of the wolf. The sheep were safe, but the shepherds who protected them would suffer fierce attack. In another picture the true leader was seen as a servant with a mop and bucket. Another scene showed a garden with flowers and trees while in the corner lay a heap of rich manure that the gardener used to nourish them. What was that? The leaders, of course!

Mud, sweat – and tears! A year ago, Malhamdale had been visionary, the first real sight of community. Since then, the cross had bitten deep and some were running from it. The self-life got us into trouble and messed it all up. God's word had to penetrate 'even to dividing soul and spirit' (Heb 4:12) and reveal our true motivations. Altars were built. Tears were shed. Sacrifices were made. Some were captivated by Jesus and considered remaining single for the sake of his kingdom. 'How few are the enraptured souls who languish for love of Christ,' wrote Tozer. 'The sweet "madness" that visited such men as Bernard and St Francis...is scarcely known today.'[30]

Wandering through the woods and lakes of Ashburnham, we paused, took a deep breath, and gazed into the heart of God. I was aspiring to be a charismatic mystic or an evangelical contemplative. But I came home to dig out sewers and rub shoulders with the drop-outs, ex-bikers and teachers. Our hearts were in heaven but we found our feet planted firmly on the ground!

9

New Creation Chaos
1974–75

Arriving back home at the Hall, Dave got a shock when he flushed the loo. The lead pipes had been ripped out and stolen while we were away! The lead had also gone from the roof and the rain came in. Nevertheless, we had big plans for this 'discipleship centre' and people were coming from all over to visit the Jesus Mansion at Bugbrooke.

Mark was an ex-biker who'd been converted from the Cheltenham drug scene. There he kept getting an impression of a large house with a veranda where Christians shared together. Not having a clue where this was, he made his way to London. After a few weeks he told the Lord he would have to give up his search, but that afternoon he met a girl who told him about a chapel near Northampton that sounded interesting. Mark rang the police. It was his last 10p.

'Oh, you mean Bugbrooke!' they said, and gave directions.

Soon he was sitting in chapel, pony tail, earring, large ginger beard, and all. After creating a disturbance in the meeting, the likeable roughneck was prayed for, delivered from a demonic power, and settled in at the Hall to join Dave, Steve, and Malcolm's physics teacher. A few days later Mark walked across the back lawn and his eyes nearly popped out. There was the veranda!

Rodger, Pete and I came from the flat to join the pioneers at the Hall and were closely followed by John Cornish and Ian, a law graduate from my old college. Our numbers quickly increased. Mark went into town and accosted a drunken vice-president of the Hell's Angels, who looked twice as fierce as Mark. Mark spoke to him about Jesus and stuffed an invitation card into his jacket. The 'Angel' soon turned up and moved in.

We were an odd bunch: ex-bikers, hippies and graduates, plus an ex-lay-preacher and her daughter, a pair of village newlyweds, and a Christian family who'd exchanged their council house for a 'mansion'! Life at the Hall was fun, chaotic and rough. We didn't care. If there was any time to lose our comforts, it was now. What we lacked in competence we made up for in enthusiasm. God was real and we were discovering brotherhood and sisterhood.

The house had wet rot, dry rot and woodworm. One bedroom was called the green room from the colour of the fungus where the rain trickled down the wallpaper! At weekends the place was packed out with people on the floors and there was a queue to move into community. If only they knew what it meant!

The Hall needed restoration and redevelopment. (That was also true of its residents!) We formed a building team that summer. Kelly knew the elements of building and Alan the busker had done some bricklaying. It was a beginning. We had to lay new sewers quickly so Pete and I helped dig the trenches. I nearly cut Kelly's finger off with a spade.

We got a grant to convert the house into flats, which gave the families some privacy. Everywhere there was reconstruction. It seemed to symbolise what God was doing with us. In the chaos we were losing grip on our private life and possessions. Often we moved rooms. The building team advanced through the house and grounds leaving a trail of trenches, wreckage and rubble. Kelly's office was the back pocket of his jeans.

Pete was a guitar tutor and hunted for the place of least dust and noise. It didn't really exist! We would arrive home from work to find dust everywhere – or worse. It could be a hole in the wall and bricks on your bed. Alan wasn't too concerned about the niceties of fine living. The motto of the building team was, 'It's slow – but it's rough!' Pete painted his favourite text on the wall:

'Do all things without murmuring or complaining!'

Every Friday night, we swept the place for the weekend, but the dust from upstairs fell downstairs through the cracks in the floorboards. At one stage there weren't any floorboards, and one sister had to walk the plank to get to her room! The fun was when it rained. We would all be crammed into the dining room, perhaps, and at the sound of rain we would each grab a container and scatter. When the building team left a hole in the roof, we rigged up a contraption with a polythene sheet and drainpipes to direct the water through a bath and out of the back door. It all took the intensity out of life.

As the months rolled by, we formed friendships and often stayed up late talking. Sunday morning was a large breakfast time when John and I served as house deacons and prepared the scrambled eggs and porridge. Washing up was memorable. The cold tap gave a mild electric shock, sprang out from the wall, and showered us with water. If you stepped back you got stuck in the floorboards!

And then there were people. Everywhere. People milling around like sheep. Some you knew very well. Some you didn't get on with. Some you'd never seen before. And there were some who frightened you to death! I'd often go out for hours meditating in the fields, just to get away. Then there were Family Days when the whole church gathered on the Hall lawn. Some thought it was idyllic. Others disappeared up to the cafe for a long lunch.

That summer, I formed an unlikely friendship with Mark and often we would go for a walk and share our hearts. This was brotherhood, and it enriched us beyond measure. Kelly led the shepherding group at the Hall and one evening he shared this wisdom with us: on a large metal tray, there were some candles of different shapes and colours. A flame appeared underneath and melted them into one pool. That was a picture of unity. But the wisdom showed something more profound. The pool of wax reformed into many multi-coloured candles. Each individual was enhanced by his brethren.

At the Hall we saw this happening in front of our eyes. Far from losing our identities, we were gaining richer personalities as we came out of our shells and flowed together. We shared our gifts and inspirations and worshipped around the meal tables. Even work breaks were times of singing, prophecy and wisdom. Being together daily broke the barriers between the natural and the spiritual. Instead of being meeting-centred we became kingdom-of-God-centred, and our talents came into play. Helps ministries, administrative abilities, practical and caring gifts all mingled with spiritual inspirations.

Most of us worked for outside employers, but some began to work for the housing association as plumbers, decorators, builders or carpenters. A community Foodstore was established in the Hall stable block and this, along with the garage, employed people full-time.

We were finding our niches. Dave and John planted an orchard and estabished the bee-hives, whilst an ex-hippy tended the garden and concocted some rather suspect herb-drinks. Another brother converted the cellar into a second-hand clothing store. Then we pooled our books and I became the librarian. The tomes poured in till we had twenty copies of *Pray In The Spirit!*[31] and fifteen *Nine O'Clock In The Morning's!*[32]

In the new year John Thom came to live at the Hall with his group of brothers and warmed the place up by installing a central heating system. We spent all morning rigging up an old boiler with pulleys to lower it down the cellar steps. But John forgot to attach the ropes and the monstrosity went hurtling down. The house shook but the Hall and the boiler survived, and there were no casualties.

Cyril, the architect, was trying to direct the exploits of the building team. They were young and zealous and did everything with abandon. At times he was desperately worried. One day he was discussing the new heating system with John Thom. Cyril asked him where he'd learned his plumbing. 'I never learned it, bro!' said John. 'I just got a book out of the library.' Amazingly, it worked!

People kept coming. Car loads of students visited from Oxford, among them Piers, my old friend from the Zoology Department, now doing a PhD in dung beetles, and Mike Farrant, Ian's old 'prayer partner'. Talk of Bugbrooke buzzed around the Oxford colleges, especially after one girl prophesied in a prayer meeting! Some of the Christian Union thought we were great. But not all the executive were so keen when students disappeared off to Bugbrooke for the weekend.

Another set of visitors was a group of girls from Wimbledon. Liz and Janie had already lived in a community in Coventry, founded by the Redeemer church. Now Liz, a secretary, and Janie, a teacher, had gathered six other girls with them and were working out the principles of discipleship and community. They were attracted by the fellowship and within six months had moved up into extended families.

One family came from Aylesbury. 'Here, read this, Mum,' said Maurice, one Saturday evening, tossing a copy of *Nine O'Clock In The Morning* on to the table, 'I'm off to Bugbrooke.'

NEW CREATION CHAOS

Mum read it and was enthralled. 'Lord,' she prayed, 'We've been seeking this for years!' The following week Marion and Lionel, her husband, drove to chapel with their two sons. All of them were baptised in the Spirit that night.

Maurice's brother, Steve, was a bit of a lad with red hair and a cheeky grin. When the family were baptised, they received many words of wisdom and encouragement, apart from Steve. All he got from the Lord was a picture of a brown parcel inside which was a golden crown. Only later did we understand. Steve was enthusiastic and motored up on his bike through all weathers to the Hall. It wasn't long before he moved in.

There were now about thirty of us squeezed into 'New Creation Hall', and many others at the Welcome homes in Northampton, in extended families, or at Verna's and Kelly's cottages at Great Lane (now with shared courtyard and duckpond).

We called the community aspect of the fellowship the New Creation Christian Community. New creation was the theme and a distinctive 'kingdom culture' began to take shape.

We took a newspaper, but there was no place for television or radio in our community houses. We didn't go out for our entertainment either. There was enough at home! Some of us became more creative, learning instruments, and writing poems or journals. Pete enjoyed painting, wrote songs, and was occasionally seen up a tree practising the violin. We couldn't stand the noise of it in the house!

We began to share more of our things. Guitars, tape recorders, and even cars were pooled. God was telling us to live more simply. Giving away your best shirt could be quite sacrificial and deepened friendships. Sometimes we had 'honouring days', when some unsuspecting brother or sister would be showered with gifts, sweets, pictures, poems, prophecies and lots of love and esteem.

At the Hall, we often had four brothers sharing a large

room. Sometimes we welded hospital beds together into bunks – all of seven foot high. Fortunately, I was athletic. At weekends we rolled out the spare mattresses and often guests would end up snoring away in the library downstairs. We thinned out more after the courtyard wing was converted, but such 'close fellowship' encouraged a great sense of brotherhood.

There were frictions, of course. One brother wanted to be reconciled to a fiery Scotsman, so he took a bowl of water to wash his feet. The argument broke out again so he tipped it over his head and ran!

John Thom was keen to start up a common bank account. Noel counselled caution at first, but most of us at the Hall were young and zealous and convinced that the common purse was an example of Jesus we needed to follow.

By the spring of 1975 we were pooling our income (before that we had paid rent). A common purse deacon collected the money every week and put it into a household account. When Mike Farrant moved in from Oxford with a flair for administration and a degree in philosophy, politics and economics, the large tea pot in which we'd collected the money was replaced by a wall safe and an accounts book. We went to Mike for what we needed and, apart from a little pocket money, were expected to produce receipts for all we spent.

We were keen to nurture an atmosphere of the Holy Spirit and encouraged one another along the way of discipleship. I suggested to Pete that perhaps we shouldn't stop off at the pub on the way to Oxford. As for money-bags Mike, I thought he needed to be more heavenly-minded and got him to rise up early to pray, and to meditate daily on the Song of Solomon!

In many ways sisters surpassed brothers in their enthusiasm and devotion to God. They were prolific in songs, poems, embroideries, tapestries, paintings – and cakes! Single sisters lived mainly at Verna's and Kelly's cottages at Great Lane, at the Harlestone Road house in North-

NEW CREATION CHAOS

ampton, or in various extended families, mainly on the Bugbrooke housing estate.

Up on the estate, the villagers were getting worried at the prospect of a Jesus People takeover! Among others, Lionel and Marion moved there and shared a common purse with Val next door who was now married. Victor, Sheila and their kids also moved in from Northampton and extended their house to take in brothers.

Most of the single brothers were thrown together at Argyle Street or the Hall where they had their rough edges knocked off. The cross often came in little things – like living with someone who reads late into the night while you're trying desperately to get some sleep. Or it might be the irritating brother who's always quoting Scripture at you, or the boisterous teenager who gets your neck in an arm lock and says, 'Are you all right, bro?' when you're pondering on some deep things of the Lord!

For others, the cross might walk in as the dear sister who has as much concept of the 'meek and quiet spirit' as Queen Boadicea! Or the brother who comes to 'tell you your fault' with the sympathetic understanding of a bulldozer!

Community living took 'The Spirit of the Cross' out of the pages of a book and made it a necessity for survival. If we had any illusions about community being a quiet haven away from the storms of life, we soon lost them. We discovered it was in these 'courts of the Lord', not in the world, that the old nature faced up to its crucifixion!

In fact, some left us and the original families at the Hall eventually moved out. But most of us wouldn't have missed that era for anything. It was immensely fruitful and strong characters were chiselled out of community life.

By 1975 three things in particular occupied the attention of charismatic Christians around the world – shepherding, community and the kingdom of God. Shepherding had hit a crisis in the States and there was controversy over 'heavy shepherding'. Christians began to view the concept of authority and submission in the church with distrust.

As for community living, the idea was popular but most churches regarded it as a risky businesss and few committed themselves wholly to it. But at Bugbrooke, we resolved to keep our hands on the plough and move steadily forward. Vision was strong amongst us and God was sending us people fast. We pressed on along the 'narrow road' of discipleship, aiming to follow Jesus and 'seek first his kingdom' (Matt 6:33).

Many other churches, too, were gaining a deeper understanding of the kingdom of God. The prophets of Israel had foretold that the coming of Messiah, Christ, would establish the rule of God. But when? Christ had come, but what of his kingdom?

By the time we arrived at Ashburnham in 1975, we, like many Restoration churches, were looking for a kingdom not only in the future, but now – and on earth!

10

Zion, City of God

1975

There is a holy hill of God, a spiritual Zion, a mountain whereupon His house is built, which the wing of the Almighty overshadows; and His sheep feed there.

Isaac Penington (a Quaker) 1676

The evening sun streamed through the windows of the meeting room at Ashburnham as the harmony of guitar and mandolin held us in the presence of the Spirit. John Cornish and Pete sat on the floor amidst 200 worshippers and led us in a holy jamming session. We lifted our hearts in the spiritual song and the praise took us higher. New tongues harmonised like threads in a tapestry. The instruments joined in and a group of sisters danced before the Lord. The gathered church did feel like a holy place. The 'wing of the Almighty' was overshadowing us and the atmosphere was rich with God's presence.

Young Darren weaved through the assembly and plonked

himself on my lap. I looked over at Kelly. His twelve-string guitar hung across his chest as he pursed his lips and looked contemplatively at the ceiling. What a sight! Kelly was a guy you learned from. No frills – just spiritual reality. 'Once you were not a people, but now you are the people of God' (1 Pet 2:10). That was his favourite scripture.

It had been a fascinating year at the Hall. New friendships were a tremendous inspiration and my path to spirituality was no longer a lonely road. Most of all we were a people. As the worship faded into silence I looked around the room. Victor was still lost in worship. He loved the silent times. A great contentment came over me. I'd come home to 'Zion'.

From the corner of the room a squeaky voice began to sing: 'Out of Zion, our God shines forth.' It was far too high and the assembly dissolved into laughter. Verna came to the rescue on the keyboard and the tambourines started up.

'We are his Zion, perfection of his beauty, radiance of his glory, bearers of his name.' The song came to an end after the fifteenth time and we erupted into loud cries of Jesus! Bless God! and Hallelujah!

Some of the Ashburnham staff crept in and lined up along the wall. They exchanged glances and smiled. Noel stood up and swept his greying hair off his forehead.

'Ashburnham 75,' he began quietly, 'is radically different from '74, because then God established a structure and now he is building on it with his goodness, his sweetness and his life. Before us lies the task of perfecting the beauty of Zion. We sing from Psalm 50: "Out of Zion...God shines forth." Now some are using the word "Zion" a great deal nowadays to describe the church. Zion was one of the hills of Jerusalem. We read in 2 Samuel 5:7 of how David captured the fortress of Zion. Zion was associated with all the glory of David's rule, when God was with his people and Israel was a light to the nations. But for Israel there was eventually a judgement. Zion's temple was destroyed and they were scattered.

'Beloved, is this true of the church today? Are the "precious sons of Zion" scattered and in exile? Or is the church a nation set apart? If not, then may God call her back to her identity, and cause her to be a city on a hill.

'Brethren, it's time for Zion to arise and conquer! She must stand up and express what God so burningly longs for, and what our hearts so desperately need.'

Noel paused to look around. Most of us were gripped, but his eagle eye spotted some nodding heads.

'Wake up, beloved! Wake up!' he shouted. 'Let's not be duped any more. The world may hate us, as we emerge from its stranglehold. But may it never say with scorn, "Is this the city that was called the perfection of beauty?" (Lam 2:15). There are songs going around – "When the Lord restored the fortunes of Zion", and so forth. There's a movement abroad in which God is restoring glory to his church. The call is to be his Zion. We have heard that call and it has taken us into community.

'Now the Jews lost Zion, but their prophets spoke of a King who would restore her and establish the kingdom on earth. This anointed one, this Messiah, was the hope of Israel. But when he came he was crucified and rejected.

'Beloved!' said Noel, 'Jesus told his disciples that some of them would not taste death before they saw the kingdom of God come with power (Mark 9:1). It came! At Pentecost it came! In the power of the Spirit it came! Look at Acts 2 and 4. Here is a nation born in a day! Here is the new Israel. Here is the kingdom!'

Noel paused and leaned forward, as if to impart some secret. 'We who believe in Christ, as Paul says, are now the true "Jews" and the spiritual "circumcision" (Rom 2:29; Phil 3:3). These are now the "Israel of God" (Gal 6:15, 16). We need to stop behaving as if we were the world's people. We are not! We are God's people. God's Zion.

'"See, I lay a stone in Zion..." the apostle quotes – let's turn to it in 1 Peter 2. "As you come to him, the living Stone...you also, like living stones, are being built into a spiritual house to be a holy priesthood..." (1 Pet 2:6, 4-5).

'Brothers and sisters, we give ourselves to the perfecting of this Zion. We have barely skimmed the surface. Zion is holy. Zion is distinctive. Zion is beautiful because it is magnificent with God's presence and power.

'This is the good news we are seeing. Personal salvation? Yes! But with it the gospel of a new kingdom. Leaders like Ern Baxter and Arthur Wallis are now proclaiming this. You see, the church is to inherit the promises. She is to herald the ultimate kingdom. In our brotherhood, in our distinctiveness, in our freedom, we are prophesying a new order. Zion is a foretaste of the new earth.'

The atmosphere was charged. We sensed something of awe and destiny in it all. Noel was fired with a vision and we were catching hold of the prophetic word.

He spoke of the maturity of such a Zion; her simplicity and peace and the beauty of her strength and righteousness. Zion, the city of truth, was defiant and secure, a place of joy and creativity. Like a precious jewel she shone in all her colours and distinctions. But only through the cross could such a beauty be born.

In the afternoon we walked around in twos and threes. Here in sunny Sussex was an opportunity to get to know one another more deeply. 'Let us open up ourselves to one another, without fear of being hurt or turned away,'[33] was the theme song of the fortnight. Friendships deepened as we confessed hidden faults and fears. Hopes and aspirations were shared and we exposed the real 'us'.

God showed us that we were like a broad river flowing along. All looked well, but below the surface were dividing partitions. The river moved on to a waterfall where it cascaded down a cliff and was dashed on the rocks below. In the turbulence, the partitions were broken up and then a swift, strong river began to cut its course down the mountainside.

So we, as a body, were to experience a new 'brokenness' bringing oneness. We were a remarkable mix of straights, freaks, professionals, and village folks. God was determined to break down any remaining barriers. Class divisions were now a thing of the past and there were some hilarious attempts to prove it! Rufus came in one morning sporting a jacket and tie, while Victor followed in a boiler suit! Jessie appeared in a tweed skirt. She'd lent her hippy cheesecloths to Val the schoolteacher! Whether freak or straight, biker or Beethoven addict, we let these things go and joined the flow!

Noel stood up in the morning meeting and there were a few more smiles – he was wearing an orange kaftan!

'We are revolutionaries!' he declared. 'What then are we to become? The answer is simple – I just don't know!'

We all laughed. Noel smiled and picked up a book.

'Let me quote from *Dust Of Death* by Os Guinness. He refers to the fact that since the war there has been a great radical outcry – a lot of communism, hippies, anarchists and so on. Now this desire is a right desire although it springs from a wrong spirit and has wrong results.

Os Guinness says, "The day the radical falters is the day the Christian radical must demonstrate his staying power. If reformation does not come, then the Christian community must assert its regained integrity in being a loyal remnant."[34]

'We radicals, then, amidst a basic Christian culture which has gone phoney, should be a godly remnant, a people of God who show his holiness and love, a people who will not sink themselves in the dereliction of our society.

'"Such people," says Os Guinness, "may be a spearhead in a new reformation, but let them have no illusions about what will be involved."[35]

'No illusions, brethren! We shall be mocked. The church, as well as the world, will point the finger and say "They are extreme!" Don't be alarmed. I am sure that if Jesus came to Britain, as he did to Palestine, he would be in some cruel fashion rejected. He would not be acceptable. Few churches would welcome his radical lifestyle. It is a shameful thing that the radical, seeking, idealistic heart is so readily turned off by our churches.

'Os Guinness continues: "We must engage in a rigorous

practice of truth."[36] We are doing it. It's uncomfortable, isn't it? The overturning of all the selfish thought pushed into us from birth. Truth? We are naturally false. We are naturally superior and selfish. Truth? We hate it! Knowing the truth about ourselves can be awfully painful. Some of you are going through it here as God's searchlight explores the very fabric of your lives. You see, the truth of God is active in our hearts! The rigorous practice of truth!

'Brothers and sisters, Zion is the "city of truth". Only truth will be attractive to those who are searching for an answer. They are looking for a people of truth and equality.

'Dare we be that? Dare we set ourselves against the current of the world? Dare we be a holy people? Dare you join us in what your heart so desperately longs for, but what your flesh shrinks from? Jesus did it. He practised truth. He practised love. It brought the resurrection. But the cross came first. The rigorous practice of truth!'

Noel's voice had faded into a whisper.

'Brethren,' he continued, lowering the book, 'if you cannot receive this here, you'll never apply it there. This retreat is as close to community living with all its beautiful outflow as we are likely to see for some time. With all the pressures on you back home to conform to the world, unless you are prepared to be real now, the devil will lead you a dance.

'Now Os Guinness remarks that the early Christians faced a twofold cultural threat. They acknowledged neither the Lordship of Caesar, nor the wisdom of the Greeks: "They refused to be classified. They were neither Romans, nor Greeks, nor Jews, nor Gentiles, nor masters, nor slaves, nor rich, nor poor. They were a healing community, they were one in Christ. They were a third race."[37]

'Now, my brethren,' said Noel, putting down the book and looking intently at us, 'this is not an easy road. But Jesus trod it and we must follow him. We Christians must become a force declaring something new. Remember, when Luther stood up for truth, it was as if he got hold of a rope connected to a great bell that rang all over Europe. Beloved, our nation is ripe for a radical demonstration of Christianity. Only that will save the day.

'We are to forge a holy Christian culture such as is rarely seen. Our worldliness is against it, and our flesh will scream in pain. Are we willing to be such a third race? Or would we rather stay in the establishment? People's minds have been so brainwashed today that they think the way British society runs is somehow righteous. Do you really think it was ordained in heaven? What utter nonsense! Are we then going to be trapped by the greedy urges of society? No!

'Now the Hebrews have a word *shalom*, which means peace, harmony and completeness. It is such an atmosphere of fulfilment and simplicity that we desire to create.

'Let me quote an Anglican bishop. "We need a new kind of monastic movement," says John Taylor, "to include simplicity, non-violence, and community."[38]

'You see we are going to refuse the world's pressure! We are getting off the treadmill. We are regaining our creativity. The drives of materialism are moving against human fulfilment. All kinds of things are taken for granted that are dehumanising man. I hate it! We must say "enough is enough"! We pursue this old way no further.

'Consider how Jesus lived for his Father's will. How completely wholesome he was – how he rejected the treadmill of his age. Jesus created a new society!

'Now a last word from our bishop friend before we go to lunch.' (The gong had gone ages ago.) '"We must live by the divine contrariness of Jesus...We need an increasing minority that will call the bluff of the trendsetters".[39]

'Brethren, we move into holy abnormality. We rediscover the joy of living. You see, so many people are sick of what they are into. Prick the surface and you will find a desperate sense of unfulfilment. "Our need," says John Taylor, "is for men and women who are free with the freedom of Christ, free to come up with the answers no one has dared to give."[40]

'God is setting us free. Free as a people. Free to be what we long to be. Christ's kingdom is the answer. A people cleansed by his blood! A people of one heart! Beloved, this is the city of light and truth. This is the new creation – this great harmony with God, this harmony with angels and with creation, this brotherly love, this beauty, this creativity – this Zion!

'Let's stand,' said Noel as he raised his hands in the air, beamed contentedly and looked heavenward. Together we praised God. The vision of Zion had been set ablaze in our hearts. For many of us it seemed everything we had desired. We were coming home – to Zion.

In Bugbrooke, the chapel was changed to allow an overflow into the side room and upper lounge. A few left us after the challenge of Ashburnham, yet the vision of Zion was drawing people. One of the Ashburnham groundsmen returned with us starry-eyed. The Hall now had brothers living in the downstairs rooms and people were streaming on to the estate.

'Israel is gathering!' we sang. 'Come and make music on Zion's height!'

We had left Ashburnham with a zeal to 'take the land'. Cyril found some actual land, two miles from Bugbrooke – a large farmhouse with outbuildings and acres of orchard and fields. 'Oh no!' said Noel 'Not farming, bro!' But Cyril was undaunted and the leaders were soon enthusiastic.

Meanwhile, the Hall was our community showpiece. During the summer months we held Family Days, and gathered with visitors to celebrate 'with gladness and thanksgiving, with cymbals' (Victor), 'harps' (Alan and Kelly on the twelve-string), 'trumpets and lyres' (or, to be more accurate, Paddy on the bottle-top shaker). We sat in groups, drank tea, consumed sandwiches and cake, stretched out on the grass, and 'fellowshipped'. They were hot, gregarious, outdoor-praising times – idyllic or difficult according to the state of your soul.

Favourite songs carried into the village. 'Let's call our

walls salvation!', 'Zion is restored' and 'Arise! Shine! for your light has come!' We danced. We were festive, confident – excited at what God was bringing to pass.

After tea we would make our way to chapel, continue our worship, and listen to the preaching of the kingdom gospel. Isaac Watts inspired us with his songs of Zion as did Wesley's hymns, hymns like, 'Happy the souls who first believed'.

> Propriety was there unknown,
>   None called what he possessed his own:
> Where all the common blessing share
>   No selfish happiness was there...
>
> Oh what an age of golden days!
> Oh what a choice peculiar race...'

We were entering into rest. Driving evangelistic fervour and independent action were being replaced by the peaceful, attractive power of Zion. As we were pleasing to God, he would bless and increase us. The church was for the Lord. It was his people, his temple, his bride.

11

Take That Land
1976

John and Dave rushed out of the house as flames leapt up and licked under the oil tank. Then they ran back for a brother sick in bed and hurried him out into the night. The biting air would kill him or cure him! The Fire Brigade hurtled up the long drive and Dave greeted them with an embarrassed grin. Within minutes a hose was rammed down the grating and the cellar flooded. Steam, smoke and an acrid smell of burnt oil wafted up. Meanwhile Dave explained how he had set fire to our latest community house. Fortunately New Creation Farm survived.

John was out early next morning. He looked up at the large red brick farmhouse with its tall Victorian chimneys rising into the dawn. Beyond it a line of poplars stood guard on the orchard and broke the skyline. He blew a cloud of breath into the air and considered the days ahead. 'Is this really happening to me?' he thought. It was just three years since the Jesus People had walked up the steps of All Saints and met him and Paddy. Now he was a leader in a Christian community. Amazing!

A train thundered down the line at the bottom of the hill. John turned. It was a beautiful view. The sun had risen through the mists turning the canal blood-red as it glistened in the frosty fields below. He spotted the trees that sheltered the Hall in Bugbrooke. Beyond lay a hazy Northampton, the distant rumblings of the M1, and the wooded hills on the horizon.

John 'Gentle' was a key man. ('Gentle' was the 'virtue name' we gave him to distinguish him from all the other Johns). He was a guy you wanted to be with – natural, easy, and gentle – a good support to Dave who'd now abandoned teaching for farmwork. Steve 'Faithful' and another brother had accompanied John and Dave from the Hall to the newly acquired Farm. On the sisters' side they were joined by Irene (a Norwegian), Liz and Janie.

With this nucleus, plus a friendly rat called Walter, a new era began. The Hall carried on its chaotic way as the Farm took brotherhood deeper. There was so much enthusiasm around. It was a mixture of fun and togetherness; of cold and primitive living conditions; of meditation in the fields; of late nights and discussion round the lounge fire; of hard work and quickness to sacrifice.

Noel frequently stayed overnight. 'There are five new arrivals at the farm,' he said in chapel one Sunday morning. Everybody looked puzzled. Who could they be? They were the first five sows! Steve had done a course on pig breeding, Noel was brought up on a farm, and Dave had plenty of theory. But all this wisdom failed to get Wilbur the boar off the Transit. He wouldn't budge for an hour!

Whether charismatic community or pig farming, it was all new to us. The locals smiled and gave us six months at the most. But we had a will to win, and soon the brothers were sitting up all night for the birth of the first piglets. They all came out to greet the first batch of hens, too. Generally if one person did something, six others did it with them!

Noel planned to move in and asked Rufus and family to join him. 'We can't leave the lads, bro,' was the reply. They had quite a scene going at Argyle Street and weren't interested in breaking up.

'Well, bring them all then,' said Noel.

'Bro's!' shouted Rufus that night, banging his fist on the table. '...we're all moving to the farm!' An uproar of shouts, hoots, yells and hallelujahs followed as the cutlery went flying. (Argyle Street was still working on 'the beauty of restfulness'!)

Soon Rufus and Jess with their two kids and the seven brothers turned up at the farm and, following the word of Jesus, (John 13:14) their feet were washed as a token of brotherly love. God joined these two 'families' together and 'the lads' looked to John 'Gentle' to take them deeper.

Shortly after, somewhat apprehensively, Noel moved in and filled his little room with books. Surprisingly, he didn't take over! Noel had a great respect for Rufus' inspirations. Dave 'Elder' Lantsbery began pastoring the sisters and John led the brothers.

Noel wound up his business partnership and transferred the proceeds to the community. We leased a shop in Northampton and divided it into a jeans shop and a health food store. Together with the farm, these formed House Of Goodness Ltd., our first community business. Noel acted as farm manager, and was often seen in his battered cloth cap walking behind the tractor or overseeing the birth of piglets.

Lunch round the farm kitchen table was memorable. Steve 'Faithful' slouched between Noel and Kelly, who'd come fresh from the building team and now expounded deep insights in scruffy jeans. The pigman and cattleman grunted wisely whilst John 'Gentle' pondered the state of the brothers and Steve 'Stalwart', the farm mechanic, quietly tucked into his soup. What a heavenly bunch! Conversation ranged from potatoes to personal hygiene – from holiness to the moods of Wilbur the boar! Meanwhile, the weather-beaten Dave would be looking after visitors in the dining-room.

During the evening grace times Noel would sit back and enjoy the ministry of his brothers and sisters. It felt good to be part of such a family and he sought to hear the wisdom of God through them.

Community life required mutual submission. The lie was that independence brought fulfilment. It didn't. Community brought fulfilment. But, boy! Some of us struggled! Rufus went through it! He had a big ego and was used to his own scene. Now he was one of four leaders and learning to work with them.

We saw submission taught in the Scriptures: 'Submit to one another out of reverence for Christ' (Eph 5:21). As we learned to move in unity as 'one new man' (Eph 2:15), we touched the very heart of Zion.

John and Steve were drawing the brothers together. They were all very real as they opened their hearts to each other, and discipled one another fearlessly. Above all, they made brotherhood enjoyable.

At New Creation Hall, Pete was producing paintings of community life and writing songs from the Scriptures – 'We know love by this, that he laid down his life for us, and we ought to lay down our lives for the brethren' (1 John 3:16).

Wesley's hymns also expressed our heart:

> Mollify our harsher will,
> Each to each our tempers suit...

We valued individual character and refused the trend towards unisex, which we saw as unbiblical and psychologically off-beam. Equality between the sexes wasn't the point. Rather, it was being the personality God intended. Women began to enjoy their femininity more and developed a strong sense of sisterhood. Brothers found that their manly sharing produced manliness and appreciated the friendship and reality of brotherhood. 'As iron sharpens iron,' said the wise man, 'so one man sharpens another' (Prov 27:17).

There were outward changes, too. Brothers lost their flowing locks and some grew beards. Sisters let their hair grow. Biblically, it spoke of their 'covering' (1 Cor 11:3–11). At Harlestone Road the sisters converted their jeans into denim skirts. One sister felt the Lord telling her to get a dress, but couldn't afford one. Out of the blue her mother gave her £10. 'Polly, I'm sick of seeing you in jeans,' she said. 'Go and get yourself a dress!' Dresses were made from corduroy, denim or even patchwork. With long hair and flowing dresses some of the sisters managed to extend the hippy era for a few years!

Make-up vanished, too, as sisters applied the word from 1 Peter 3:3–4, 'Your beauty should not come from outward adornment ...Instead, it should be...the unfading beauty of a gentle and quiet spirit.' We had some very enthusiastic sisters who saw the preciousness of all this and sought it. Others were at first reluctant, but when they let go of their natural assertiveness, they 'found themselves' in a new way, and entered into a deeper relationship with God.

Indeed, once the trauma of rediscovering our identity was over, a new sense of security settled over the whole community. Men took up their leadership, and husbands brought a godly authority to their families. The sisters were beautiful in their loving support and made way for the men to find their strength and potential. So much sprang from sincere love for Jesus and an innocent conscience.

Much care was put into children's upbringing. The young soul needed protection, training and nurture. Children should be surrounded by holy influences, creativity, love and discipline. The question was always there too: would the next generation maintain our radical vision? We held to the promise, 'Train a child in the way he should go, and when he is old he will not turn from it' (Prov 22:6).

That year saw the establishing of divine order in our

relationships. Far from being 'under law', this was grace bringing together the beauties of Zion. Of course, there were conflicts and some tendency to overbalance. But we felt we were unearthing precious truths and when we saw something in God, we went for it.

We saw simplicity, too, as one of the 'treasures of the kingdom'. Jesus lived simply and possessed little. We wanted to follow him along this path, and agreed to spend as little as possible. We began to cut down on our wardrobes and eat more simply. Fashions were passed by, and we made more use of our second-hand clothing store. We made our cars last longer and cut each other's hair. We saw so much wastage and fussiness around – leaving food on the plate and so on. These were all areas for embracing discipleship.

Chinese take-aways and fizzy apple drinks breathed their last. We cut out costly spreads like honey and peanut butter (for a while), stopped drinking coffee and gave up sugar in drinks (guests excepted). The chapel tuck shop substituted nuts and raisins for sticky chocolate bars, but soon disappeared altogether!

Expensive and gimmicky toys gave way to creative, constructional things. We realised the danger of being 'lovers of pleasure rather than lovers of God' (2 Tim 3:4), and determined that the ego-boosting competition of sport, as well as the indulgence of worldly entertainments, were not for us.

The common purse had been a watershed and paved the way for deeper unity in the Spirit. Many found they could go the whole week without money. It seemed strange at first, but was a blessed release. In little things we realised the grip of self and in little things we proved our love for Jesus.

My parents often visited us at the Hall: 'Well, you're bound to love one another now, if you share everything,' my dad remarked. He was right. We were dependent on one another. 'Do not be afraid, little flock,' Jesus had said, 'for your Father has been pleased to give you the kingdom. Sell your possessions...Provide for yourselves...treasure in heaven' (Luke 12:32, 33).

We were doing it. All over the community Zion was putting on her beauty and her lifestyle was characterised by modesty and simplicity.

'They've really gone off the rails this time!' people said.

'They're even dressing differently now!'

Yes, we were becoming different! We had quietened down. Paddy's bottle-top shaker disappeared and Rufus' African drum was laid to rest. Percussion was replaced by gentler music: violins, recorders and clarinets. The racy choruses slowed down and the heavy beat was turned off. We wrote songs and hymns that were deep and prophetic and sang more of Wesley, Watts, and the old worthies.

Fluorescent stickers were removed from cars and clothes and we changed the colour of the Oxford minibus from bright orange to tasteful blue. The modern trend was too flashy for us. Purity and sobriety weren't exactly 'hip' words in the charismatic scene, and some visitors felt less at home. 'Show me as my soul can bear the depth of inbred sin,' wasn't quite what they were used to. Why did we talk so much about Zion and holiness? It all smacked of legalism, they thought. Noel's application of the Scripture, far from being entertaining, was cutting, commanding, even humiliating. And then all this stuff about discipling one another! Bugbrooke had definitely gone off the rails!

Despite the objections, we continued enthusiastically to forge a kingdom lifestyle. Some found the modesty of our life beautiful – a place to open up and find godly friendships. Others found it dull and boring: 'What! No tellies! No alcohol! No football! No going out for a good time! No holidays abroad...!

'Man! What do you do? Just pray and talk to each other?'

As we passed through this almost legendary era, our sense of identity sharpened up and Zion became less a concept and more and more 'us'. A patriotic zeal for our church arose that broke the chains of public opinion. Confidence replaced timidity as we felt our unity and strength. The danger, though, was the arrogance of youthful zeal. As God

TAKE THAT LAND
123

led us along this radical path, it would be easy to feel that we were somehow special.

Indeed, the move into community had precipitated a new culture. Now that we had the farm, just being up there on a summer evening picking gooseberries together left us with heartfelt gratitude to God and a great love for this Zion.

By the time we were at Ashburnham again, we were determined to explore more of 'the beauties of holiness' – and the bite of discipleship!

'The Lord has delivered me from all my fears! Amen!'

A high-pitched voice echoed over the lake, and trailed off into an embarrassed giggle.

'And again, Yvonne!' shouted Liz from across the water. 'And with the emphasis on *all*.'

'The Lord has delivered me from *all* my fears!' she shouted.

'Right!' echoed her friend. 'Now jump up and down, praise the Lord, and say, "I'm a super sister!"'

'Oh no!' thought Yvonne. 'Not this! What have I let myself in for now?'

Just as Yvonne was poising herself Piers crashed through the undergrowth, followed by a line of six brothers. 'Praise the Lord for the trees and grass!' he shouted.

'Yeah! Thank you Lord for making me a new creation!' yelled another.

'I'm a king in Christ Jesus!' croaked an academic voice.

'And bless God for that sis over there!' someone laughed from the back. Yvonne watched the line of 'liberated' disciples career off into the woods.

'They've all gone mad!' she thought to herself, and smiled.

It was a hot, dry, afternoon half way through the Ashburnham retreat – though 'retreat' was hardly the word. Noel called it a spiritual outward-bound course!

Gut-level reality at the farm had paved the way. The elders were finding their godly authority, and throughout the fellowship there was a growing accountability to one another. But we needed many more pace-setters – visionary men and women who could train others. *Disciple* by Juan-Carlos Ortiz was bringing the same kind of vision to the churches generally.[41]

Three hundred of us gathered on the lawn and Noel asked us to call out the names of the most esteemed brothers and sisters. Some had a shock! Irene went white, and Marion tried to make a getaway! They were quickly surrounded and pushed out to the front! Soon fifty had been thrust forward and were surrounded by their friends. With a bit of reshuffling each 'discipler' had an instant 'disciple band'.

The bands majored on openness; second, came 'liberated worship'. We lost a lot of prayer-group piety as we leapt around, shouted and sang, danced, played guitars, and shook tambourines and maracas. Thirdly, the disciplers taught from their experience – but no soap boxes were allowed!

Correction was a fourth element. Most of us were keen to have our faults pointed out, and we would assess one another's strengths and weaknesses. This was very constructive but revealed some self-righteousness and self-justification. With a skilful leader, a punch-up could be avoided!

The fifth area was meditation and prayer. We would go off alone to ponder on Scripture or pray and then regather to share what the Lord had shown us.

Then there were 'discipline activities'. (St Francis, too, practised 'holy obedience'.) The discipler gave the band 'disciplines'. 'Faith confessions' were a favourite and Yvonne had to sing hers every hour! ('I'm free! I'm free!' she squeaked in the middle of Noel's teaching.) Leaders received their own medicine, too. Liz had to spend time with the sister she found most difficult. It all produced rapid growth.

The last point was ministry activity. In a group of five friends it was easier to launch out in spiritual gifts. We learned to speak in tongues, interpret, prophesy, or sing out spontaneous 'psalms'. We prayed for healing, wrote songs or brought out wisdom.

The bands were to meet once a week. Once the leaders had lost their nervousness and delusions of grandeur, the bands became very precious to us. Most members didn't live in community houses and disciple bands brought something of the reality we knew at the Hall and the Farm.

Living at the Farm had made an impact on Noel. He admired the reality of the relationships among the brothers and realised his own reserve. What did being 'members one of another' (Rom 12:5, RSV) really mean? Were we of one heart?

As Noel spoke on the 'beauties of Zion's maturities', he became more pointed. The previous Ashburnham retreat had been visionary, and now the truth had to be applied in every area. If we were to 'love one another deeply, from the heart' (1 Pet 1:22), we had to lose our pretensions. We needed a deeper experience of the cross to produce a character that was not only strong and stable, but able also to flow in brotherhood.

The theme song for Ashburnham 76 was Pete's: 'Now we are the body of Christ...If one member suffers, all suffer together, if one member is honoured, all rejoice' (from 1 Cor 12:26). When the second week arrived, John 'Gentle' and Steve 'Faithful' had to go back to the Farm, and as we gathered round their minibus we sang this song. Many broke down in tears.

Amidst all our attempts to perfect one another, the theme of the one heart emerged as the Lord's word to us. God gave two sisters some wisdom which was read out in the meetings. The first picture was of a maypole. The maypole was the Lord; the dancers members of his body. Each was joined to him by a coloured thread which spoke of an individual walk with God. The dance began and the threads were woven together. As hearts were entwined, all got closer to the Lord.

The second picture was an aerial view of a transparent people. Their hearts were small and their eyes lifeless. But as they worshipped they came alive, and upon their hearts appeared words like love, joy, loyalty. The more they sang, the larger their hearts became. Eventually these all joined to form one great heart with the words: 'The Fulness of God'. The people now laughed and wept freely together. Some crept to the outside but those of the one heart drew them in and knelt at their feet. Some of these joined the oneness but others fled away into the darkness.

The Spirit was working in our depths. Many who once felt rejection and loneliness now wept it all out. It was hardly surprising that the jazzy choruses were giving way to gentle worship and songs that expressed the longings of the soul.

At Ashburnham, the instruments would lead into spiritual singing. Then individuals sang or improvised on their instruments. Alan's old busking partner would pour his heart out on the electric guitar. Once he'd lived like a tramp, addicted to cough medicine. Now he sang in the courts of the King. At times a sense of the preciousness and depth of Zion spread over the assembly like liquid gold. We were learning to break open our hearts and release the fragrance of Jesus.

But what did the staff at Ashburnham make of it all? For one young woman, meeting the Jesus Fellowship in full flight was quite an experience:

> What struck me was the difference. It wasn't just a conference. It was more like a life force! These people just flowed out. I felt I was coming in out of the cold and suddenly there's this massive great bonfire. And I was being slowly defrosted! I stopped swearing and forgot to use make-up. But the biggest surprise was when it suddenly dawned on me that I wanted to be holy. Needless to say, I moved up to Bugbrooke as quick as I could — on my motorbike!

During the time at Ashburnham, we realised that 'Zion' was becoming a place of green pastures and refreshing streams. A word of prophecy came: 'Your pastures are too plentiful.' God wanted to send us others who were hungry for the reality of community living. Indeed, we sensed that throughout the country God was gathering his sheep together. The frustration and loneliness of Christian individualism was giving way to the strength of brotherhood.

The full import of what God was about was dawning on us. Arthur Wallis had said: 'Find out what God is doing in your generation and throw yourself wholly into it!' That was our spirit. We were taking risks and moving fast to keep abreast of what God was saying to the churches. There was an awesome sense of destiny and we felt we were becoming a prophetic people – hence the hymns and songs, the authority of the word and our provocative stance towards the low level of church life we were emerging from. Our confidence took wing; we were coming of age.

It seemed that God was preparing his church for spiritual warfare. The nation was speeding towards moral disaster and the powers of darkness were on the march. Charismatic adolescence was okay, we had needed it, but now was the time for charismatic manhood. 'We proclaim him,' wrote Paul, 'admonishing and teaching everyone with all wisdom, so that we may present everyone perfect in Christ' (Col 1:28). Discipling one another was to make us fit for battle. At Ashburnham, the Spirit confirmed this to us through prophetic wisdom:

> An ocean liner was plying through a calm sea, and there was a relaxed, festive atmosphere on board. Then the skies darkened as it headed into enemy waters. The word went round to prepare the ship for action. The crew had been trained to play their part in enemy encounter and the liner soon looked like a battleship. Some of them thought this was all a bit intense and went below deck to relax, play cards and have a good laugh. When the battle was engaged they were taken by surprise and in panic turned on the rest of the crew.

Everyone needed to be functioning, and ready for battle. Amongst us, most were keen to move on in ministry and were prepared for change. Moving into community had been a big step in discipleship. Living together, we had to walk in the light. All was revealed: the good, the bad, and the ugly.

Jesus Homes were training leaders, and new people were arriving all the time. Over a hundred people were sharing in the common purse and the farm, health food and building enterprises were growing, too. New Creation Hall was so full we had two portakabins in the courtyard. There was a lot of interest among students in Britain. A number of Dutch people moved over from Holland, and one girl came all the way from the Australian outback! Four large houses were now established and over a hundred of our people now lived on the Bugbrooke housing estate. Most of these, intending to move to large community houses, were keen to leap out of the frying pan into the fire!

On the last day at Ashburnham we stood and sang to the Lord, 'for the one I love a song about his vineyard' (Is 5:1). With eyes open, and appreciating one another, we worshipped in tongues. Many such moments would linger – not the least when a bashful Marion sang to us from Psalm 16: 'As we dwell here in your presence, there is such peace and security.'

We paused and took stock. Three hundred peculiar people being knit together in one heart – what a task! But we were confident and felt ready for anything. On that hot, dry, summer evening we sang a new hymn:

> His great power increasing we shall know,
> Although days of battling lie ahead...

Little did we know the storms prepared for our Zion battleship.

12

The World Strikes Back

1976–77

Trouble was brewing as the enemy launched a counter-attack. The devil is always keen to offer a substitute for what is lacking in the church. When Christians are worldly, his alternative is the mysticism of the east. When they refuse the miraculous, he summons the occult. Likewise discipleship and devotion to 'the apostles' teaching' (Acts 2:42) are replaced by the idolising of cult leaders.

The cults proliferated and the devil made use of their mimicry of the truth to harm and shackle the witness of the radical churches. Hare Krishna, the Children of God and the Moonies captured the public imagination and engendered fear and suspicion. In some minds our church got mixed in with this rag-bag of cults and those who couldn't fault our doctrine were critical of our practice.

Evangelicals at Oxford were cautious of our influence amongst the students there and the mother of one girl involved with us feared that her daughter would be subject to brainwashing, low-protein diet, sleepless nights and religious fanaticism.

So Mum came to a chapel meeting with a tape recorder. The worship was charismatic. That was bad enough. Then Noel preached on repentance and whole-hearted following of Christ. The man was obviously some kind of dictator, holding people in sway by his hypnotic personality!

She decided to bring along a GP and a psychiatrist friend, and as her daughter was just under twenty-one, they were able to get her provisionally confined under a section of the Mental Health Act. But after psychiatrists could find no evidence of brainwashing, the matter was dropped and she returned to us. It was an isolated incident, but a pointer to the misunderstanding and persecution that lay ahead for us.

From within rose some disunity. Brian, who had been a key figure from the early days, struggled with our lifestyle now his family was at the Hall. The radical lifestyle, challenging enough for us singles, was a culture shock for the average couple. The self-contained flats provided privacy for the nuclear family but some found it hard to integrate into the rather motley 'family' at the Hall. Brian and his family began to withdraw from the life of the house. We found this isolation difficult to accept and Ralph and others gently entreated him. But the gulf widened and eventually the family left. It was a great loss.

Another brother had recently joined us. We took him rather quickly into leadership, despite his strong opinions. He enjoyed the charismatic worship but found our radical principles hard to stomach. When we encouraged him to be an example to the flock and open his large home to the brethren, he refused. He soon left and, unlike Brian, became very critical of us for a time.

Loss of these leaders and confusion with the cults were two aspects of the battle. The third was more poignant, and followed the death of a brother.

David was a gentle young man who had recently transferred his job as articled clerk and moved up to Victor and Sheila's house on the estate. One Saturday in December he took his Bible and went for one of his 'prayer walks'. It was sunny but very cold and frosty and Dave had no coat on. When he didn't appear after lunch, Victor sent someone looking for him but without success. As the day drew in, he grew uneasy and organised a proper search. By seven in the evening we left off to attend chapel but continued afterwards. Perhaps he'd gone off somewhere on impulse, as he'd told us he was prone to do.

A time of great anxiety followed, especially for David's parents and for Victor's household. The next week, a villager walking his dog found his body in a strip of scrubland. Next to him was his Bible and, strangely, his neatly folded shirt, socks and vest. Accidental death from hypothermia was the verdict of the coroner. One symptom is the feeling of being hot and confused and this probably explains why David removed some of his clothing.

The tragedy caused us to see afresh the preciousness of each brother and sister. Dave was 'with the Lord', but his death was an untimely loss. It was a particular grief for his parents who felt we must be to blame. Local newspapers, though, reported the coroner's comment that he could see no reason to blame the church.

However we sensed the spiritual battle was increasing as false rumours, accusations and opposition now mounted up. Some of the stories were silly, ranging from Swiss bank accounts for Noel to cold showers for erring members! It was inevitable. Quakers, Methodists, the Salvation Army and the Pentecostals had all received the same treatment. So had the early Christians. 'In fact, everyone who wants to live a godly life in Christ Jesus will be persecuted,' wrote Paul in 2 Timothy 3:12.

Some Christians, too, thought us arrogant, purposely isolated in our 'Zion fortress' in the Northamptonshire countryside.

'Bugbrooke think they're right and everybody else is

wrong,' they said. 'If you watch telly you're a spiritual moron. If you don't live in community you hate your brothers. If you play tennis you're in love with the world. And if you criticise them you are a tool of the devil! – Just who do they think they are?'

'Bugbrooke' became a worry to the world, an irritation to the evangelicals and an embarrassment to the Baptist Union. But we were confident of the leading of God and the radical message he had given us to proclaim. As Arthur Wallis wrote:

> We have overlooked Christ as the revolutionary teacher, the controversialist, the provocative preacher, the man who disregarded convention and protocol, the implacable opponent of the religious establishment, the leader who associated with all the wrong types and seemed intent on provoking rather than placating his critics.[42]

We felt we were pioneering something that God was trying to get across – holiness, brotherly love and kingdom culture. It was all part of what any church should be – Zion, a prophetic people, a city on a hill.

We received sniping and suspicion, but our community houses were open to visitors and our meetings public. Our message was pungent but our hearts warm. True, our style of worship was more sober and, though some groups were inspired by frequent visits to us, we rarely ministered in other churches. Not that we got many invitations! We determined to follow God's call to build a strong fellowship. Like some of the new churches, we were pioneering within the radical tradition and seeking to rediscover the fullness of New Testament truth.

So we dug in our heels and reached for our prophetic guns. Each week the chapel was packed out for the Saturday night shoot-out as we urged Christians to full sharing and brotherhood. Noel was convinced the charismatic renewal movement was losing steam for lack of radicality. Restoration leaders were in agreement and from within the renewal movement came the cry: 'Where now?'

Many came to us disillusioned by sloppy Christianity in the churches and hungering for clarity and commitment. Like Victor, quite a few had felt a desire to live in community when they were baptised in the Spirit. Jesus had practised the common purse, and after Pentecost he had given the apostles clear directions to teach all nations 'to obey everything I have commanded you' (Matt 28:20).

Our heart was to accept Scripture. It was painful, but swept away confusion. The temptation was to accept some biblical teaching and put the rest to one side. In *Disciple*, Juan-Carlos Ortiz wrote: 'If you want the gospel of the kingdom, go back and read the verses you never underlined, because that's the truth you lack.'[43]

The New Testament told us that: 'All the believers were together and had everything in common' (Acts 2:44). Acts 2, we found, was a bitter-sweet pill – best swallowed whole!

Around the country we heard of semi-renewed churches, often with denominational restrictions, within which small charismatic groups struggled without leadership. Little was built, hearts grew sick and the fires dimmed. It was sad to hear the tale again and again. Where were those who grappled with the vision and brought it to pass? Where were those who did not shrink from proclaiming 'the whole will of God' (Acts 20:27)? 'The dearth of its prophets', wrote Michael Harper, 'is one of the saddest failures of the renewal.'[44]

Was the problem lack of vision or failure in courage? Either way, the climate seemed unfavourable to the root changes that prophetic ministry demanded. Evangelists and healers were acceptable. Prophets were not. Those with vision often moved out into the house churches.

'Lifestyles change when they embrace the prophetic vision,' Terry Virgo was to write. 'Many churches are beset by layers of tangled undergrowth. The prophet cuts through. Sometimes his message will appear unkind...but it comes from a heart burning with zeal for God's church.'[45]

Jesus called the people of his kingdom 'the salt of the earth'. We recognised that if we were to be such kingdom salt we must never yield up our radical discipleship – even if that meant being salt in the wounds of a lukewarm Christianity. We were to sharpen our prophetic edge, not lay down the Spirit's sword.

We were fleshing out the vision. We had set up common purses, discipling bands were in progress and people were finding their ministries. Businesses were established and the church and community were growing. The Farm was expanding, with cattle and new land. We now bought Shalom, a farmhouse over the hill from the Farm.

Many have patronised the Jerusalem community as an 'experiment', but amongst us we were seeing the outcome of what Jesus had promised: 'No-one who has left home or brothers or sisters or mother or father or children or fields for me and the gospel will fail to receive a hundred times as much *in this present age* (homes, brothers, sisters, mothers, children and fields – and with them persecutions) and in the age to come, eternal life.' (Mark 10:29–30, italics mine).

We certainly had the persecutions, and we were finding more brothers and sisters, with already well over a hundred children!

By the spring of 1977 we had opened two more community homes. One was in Daventry and consisted of three houses in a row. The other was in a village just over the A5 from the farm. Sheepfold Grange, as we renamed it, was beautifully situated on a hill and overlooked a valley dotted with sheep.

Sheepfold housed about twenty. There were single brothers and sisters, marrieds and single-parent families, with a real sense of homeliness. Kids were everywhere!

The household (which included non-residents) was led by Pete and Carol, whose liberated 'tribe' of children was regarded as a fairly good example of community life. 'Welcome to the families of Zion, Lord,' wrote one sister,

'...holy, happy children, strong in character...' – though sometimes more strong in character than holy!

Sheepfold wasn't perfect, but from this inspired little community house issued a stream of life, wisdom and hymns. Pete had a prophetic spark and sang of the vision of a holy Zion:

> Zion, the city of pure gold,
>   Is holy, righteous, pure in heart.
> In awesome reverence we behold
>   No spot or stain in any part.

It was our vision of holiness that united us with the dissenters, trouble-makers, and martyrs of the past. Since the decline of the early church, a persecuted remnant has always stood bravely for the practice of biblical truth. Through such pioneers God has been gradually restoring New Testament radicality to the wider church.

'Pioneers, shock troops, are always necessary for God's movement in history,' says Roger Forster. 'They are to fulfil their true calling which is ultimately to bring blessing to... God's people.'[46]

Just as the Reformers recovered biblical saving faith and the Nonconformists, the independence of the local church, so the Methodists restored the blessing of holiness and the Pentecostals opened the way for the charismatic movement. Who, then, were God's pioneers in this generation? It could only be those who built on all this and pressed on.

But was there more to be recovered? 'Yes!' We felt. 'Community of goods!' That, if anything, was surely a lost jewel of the evangelical church. In Acts 4 Luke records that after the outpouring of the Spirit, 'All the believers were one in heart and mind. No-one claimed that any of his possessions was his own, but they shared everything they had.' (Acts 4:32). This was no 'experiment'. Community of goods sprang from hearts on fire with love. It was a master move of the Holy Spirit and was followed by 'much grace' and miraculous power for healing and salvation.

There was a move towards community living following the charismatic outpouring of the early seventies. In that decade community came within the charismatic compass and was featured in prominent Christian magazines. Many had heard of the Church of the Redeemer, and by 1977, to our joy, we were discovering that similar communities had sprung up throughout the world.

However, in general the community revelation was now being passed by. Some had experimented unsuccessfully with extended households, and larger ventures had faltered. Few were founded on radical principles and fewer still on the common purse. There was talk of alternative lifestyles, but it was rare to find churches teaching and embracing community.

In Britain the 'Jerusalem model' was dropped in favour of a moderate version of 'community lifestyle'. Arthur Wallis wrote: 'The world is waiting to see God's alternative society...the spirit of community living is being restored.'

We felt that was great! But speaking of the early churches he qualified it: 'This is not to suggest they...had extended households...Nor did the sharing of possessions mean that they necessarily relinquished possession of their goods.'[47]

It was true that not everyone outside Jerusalem was so radical. Not only did slavery and persecution hinder community, but the early churches had their difficulties. The fact that Paul could write, 'everyone looks out for his own interests, not those of Jesus Christ' (Phil 2:21) indicates a key problem – the waning of first love.

Some have said that the church has enough problems without adding community to them. But we felt immeasurable richness was lost by this stance. As others took one pace back, we found ourselves fighting a lonely battle.

However, church history was ablaze with 'pilgrims of the common life' and we took heart from their example. Generations after the apostles, Justin Martyr wrote: 'We who formerly treasured possessions now hand over all we have to a common treasury.'[48]

In the deserts, communities arose that housed thousands and were centres of power. One old saint wrote: 'We thank God for the sweet fragrance of submission and true sharing. We have surrounded ourselves with the wall of salvation which is love for God and the call to community, that we might walk on earth according to the ways of heaven.'[49]

They too got a lot of criticism. 'A time is coming when men shall say you are mad, you are not like us!'[50] wrote another.

Many in the Catholic tradition have favoured communal living as a good soil for spirituality. But it was persecuted pioneers like the Anabaptists of the sixteenth century who really stood out for truth, especially for baptism, separation, brotherly love – and community.

The Hutterites were Anabaptists who lived simply and gathered in large numbers with their families and children. They were skilled in crafts and trades and even had their own schools. Hutterite evangelists moved in power throughout Central Europe and huge numbers were martyred for their radical word. One of them wrote from prison: 'Whoever wants to join himself to Christ must forsake created things. This is why the Holy Spirit began community in such a glorious way at the beginning.' Knowing that some conditions favoured community more than others, he added, 'If anyone should say "It only happened in Jerusalem", it doesn't follow that this should be the case now!'[51]

The Hutterites found that heretical groups spoiled their reputation. Anabaptists were the cult scare of their time. Nonetheless, they insisted that community was the 'highest command of love', a treasure for which a man gives, not a tithe, but all that he has.

We came to Ashburnham 1977 inspired by the example of these radical brethren. We, too, had an identity and a 'Zion culture' to be grateful for. Noel outlined our position as a radical church and dealt with the matter of private ownership. Our community lifestyle was built on personal sacrifice and leadership of the church could only be entrusted to those who had renounced all. Many, desiring freedom from personal ownership, put their homes in pledge to our Jesus Fellowship Community Trust. Heart purity, we felt, was easily marred by possessions.

Much of the fellowship now expected to move into community. Many of the estate households had clustered together to share in common purses, practise discipleship, and foster the community vision. Victor and Sheila had already moved to the Hall and, whilst retaining their family identity, thrived on the closer fellowship. It was quite something for the four children, too: lots of others to play with, thirteen acres, and all those big brothers and sisters! Extended families were good, but large houses provided more opportunities for growth, ministry — and death to self!

We intended to increase the number of large houses and to expand the businesses, allowing more to live and work in community. Some of us chuckled as we imagined hundreds of us working together on a community production line, and there were also howls of laughter when Noel outlined the possibility of a holiday school at New Creation Hall. It was difficult to tell who looked more horrified, the poor teachers, the hard-worked Hall sisters, or the kids themselves! It happened too, and continued for some years. The Fellowship kids had the Hutterites to blame for this one!

Our understanding of covenant deepened as we saw that in biblical revelation God dealt with a 'gathered people'. The Reformation had emphasised personal faith but was inclined to open the floodgates to individualism and even anarchy. God's covenant was with Christ and a people. Just as the Passover lamb had been slain to take a people from Egypt, so Jesus had covenanted in his blood to take a people from the world, and make them one heart and soul.

One old hymn became a favourite at this time: 'Twixt Jesus and the chosen race, Subsists a bond of sovereign grace...'

'You know, bro,' said Pete Matt to Noel one morning, 'when I see these young folk singing old hymns about the covenant – the amazing thing is, they understand them!'

It was true. The freaks had come a long way from Jesus shouts, long hair and hippy placards. The straights had come even further from their British independence! We were discovering the powerful realities of covenant brotherhood. Towards the end of the fortnight we stood up to pledge our loyalty to God and one another.

'Let King Jesus reign!' we shouted, echoing the cry of the Scottish Covenanters. We admired their zeal for brotherhood, but not for war! We determined to follow God, and stand for the precious truths of covenant and community.

By November we had purchased a builders yard in Towcester and created Towcester Building Supplies. Another house was opened in nearby Pattishall and renamed Festal Grange. We were in a confident mood. Steve 'Faithful's' dad, Lionel, captured these events in heroic metre:

What promise lies within this regal place?
   This home of kings, this 'palace' of God's art,
Where each true member of this chosen race,
   Will, for his brother, purify his heart.

Our life is 'now', eternal on the earth,
   Although our steps much higher still will roam.
Why not then let your brother see his worth?
   Don't let us wait until he's been called home.

1977 had seen conflict, but we were winning. The enemy was on the run. Many more had caught the vision and joined us, and opportunities for outreach were opening up. There was even talk of planting a daughter congregation somewhere not too distant. The new year was going to be a victorious outflow to the regions, bringing the message of salvation and brotherhood in Jesus.

By February 1978 we were in Leicester, holding a series of meetings of 'worship with the New Creation Christian Community'. The trumpet of the kingdom was set to our lips – or so we thought. But God had other plans to deepen and sweeten our brotherhood. And oh, the cost! The third meeting at Leicester saw a church stunned and broken in heart.

13

My Friend, My Brother
1978

Steve 'Faithful' sat in chapel one Sunday evening in February and grinned at his mum and dad from a distance. Though only nineteen, he was a strong man. His ruddy face and thick auburn hair gave him a youthful glow. Steve was quite a nature lover and enjoyed being out on his tractor. Blunt, honest and unpretentious, his sober face would break out in a warm grin that betrayed the softness of his heart. He and John 'Gentle' were close and their boisterous friendship was a focus for the farm brotherhood. Steve had won a place in Noel's heart, too, and was unafraid to turn his cheekiness in that direction! 'Noel gets in the flesh just like us!' he used to say – usually after Noel had corrected him!

That February evening Noel spoke from James: 'What is your life? You are a mist that appears for a little while and then vanishes.' Steve knew it. He was no yokel. After a day of mud, sugar beet and potatoes, he would go off to meditate in the fields or cross over the railway track to the canal.

The quotes in his diary from Faber and Fénelon were an indication of his inner life with God. He loved community and, with a twinkle in his eye, determined, with Andrew Murray, to 'look upon every man who vexes you as a means of grace to humble you'!

The next morning Steve was up bright and early and made the sisters a cup of tea. There was a freshness on him and at lunch he breezed in from the fields, flung his slippers across the floor and grinned.

When the elders arrived at the Farm for their meeting that night, Steve joked with some of them. Then, after spending some time mending his wellies and chatting, he donned his donkey jacket and went out. As evening wore on, some of the brothers began to wonder where he was, and when he hadn't turned up by midnight they went to see if he'd fallen asleep in a hay loft or something. They checked the farm buildings, and searched as well as they could in the dark. When daylight came, his brother Maurice and a friend looked all round the farm for him. As they walked towards the canal, there in the dawn light they saw the remains of a body on the railway track. The red hair was unmistakable.

An awesome silence brooded over the farm that day. Some of the brothers were notified and came home from work. They sat together in silence or wept. Down at Shalom farmhouse Kelly was working with the building team when the phone rang. 'Bro...I have some sad and glorious news for you.' It was a subdued Noel. '"Faithful" has been killed. There are a lot of brothers up here who need you just now.'

Kelly walked slowly back to the tea break. Alan, Rufus and the others were larking around but the look on Kelly's face brought instant silence.

'Bro's,' he said, '"Faithful's" been killed.' The words hung in the air. No! It couldn't be true. Not Steve. Then the truth sliced into their hearts and they all burst into tears, grown men just weeping helplessly together. By the end of that day the whole church had heard and a hush crept over all the

MY FRIEND, MY BROTHER

homes. 'Faithful' was in heaven – it was almost unbelievable. Four hundred people were in mourning.

Investigations were made. Evidently he had been struck down around eleven at night by a goods train travelling from London. As a railwayman explained to us, Steve couldn't have been lying down because his body had been knocked between the rails. We discovered that two trains passed each other around 11.00 pm at the point where Steve was killed. Possibly he was returning from a walk by the canal and as he waited in the dark for one train to pass, he was struck by the other.

The funeral could never be forgotten. Any grief that had been bottled up now flowed out as tribute was paid to this lovable young man. The hearts of the Farm family were cracked wide open. It was an amazing and awesome time to live through. Heaven came close. Pride was shattered, and a new love blossomed, as tough young men sobbed their hearts out together. The brother who took over Steve's job mounted his tractor and wept. How could he ever live up to Steve's example of diligence?

Some of the brothers and sisters struggled with their first experience of grief. Noel was heart-broken, but clung to grace, stood like a rock, and led them through it. A ring of brotherly love so encircled the farm family that for years no one would move elsewhere.

Steve by his death had drawn many others into the heart of brotherhood, and a softness and tenderness spread over the whole church. His dad Lionel, with Marion standing strongly at his side, picked up his pen once more in elegy:

No more shall breezes waft his auburn hair;
   No more the air from field and pasture breathe;
No more the earth to furrow with his share;
   No deepened ruts his tractor wheels shall leave.

His face no more we'll see within these walls,
   His earthly voice no more shall praises sing,
But sweeter still is echoing through the halls
   And palaces of his beloved King.

Steve had gained his crown. For us, the plough had gone in deep for a richer harvest.

Kelly had often worked with Steve on some farm project. They had shared easily as men do when they work hard together. A warm regard bound them in heart, but the younger disciple had 'outrun him' and was home.

The impact upon Kelly's household was immense. Verna, Kelly, Norma and the ten sisters found a new depth of oneness, as they realised afresh the preciousness of each individual; it was an esteem, almost a reverence, for one another. As one sister wrote in a song: 'My heart is your heart. Your heart is mine. Our heart is one heart – Pure love! heart divine!'

In the throes of this delicate oneness, they moved on from their cottages at Bugbrooke, taking with them Snowy the aloof cat, and a lovable, but senile dog called Goldy. To this refined and tenderhearted group were added two rough breeze blocks from the Hall – Ian 'Courageous' and myself.

In the new house at nearby Flore we gained a deeper experience of community – and discipleship! For us it was a fresh start and we felt honoured to learn at close quarters from Kelly. Our diaries made fascinating reading!

'So this is it,' wrote Ian, 'we are in! I got my first correction from Kelly about driving fast on the gravel. I was freaked out at the mealtime. It's so quiet! Often there is only one conversation.'

The house was built of blocks of golden sandstone and was overhung with purple wisteria and honeysuckle. Above the door was a motto chiselled in Latin: *Dare To Despise Riches*. From the french windows a sunny patio overlooked the lawn and at the back the shady cobbled courtyard was home for Kelly's ducks and geese. Down in the paddock, we dug out a little pond for the ducks who got some 'heavy shepherding' from Mildred the hen! On a spring morning the air was fragrant and many were the sun-drenched teas on the patio. It was, to quote Isaac Watts:

A little spot enclosed by grace,
> Out of the world's wide wilderness.

'People reckon this place is a pretty good do,' Ian recorded. 'It's called the House of Living Stones – but I haven't the nerve to tell anyone at work yet!'

The honeymoon lasted about a week. Kelly sussed us out and brought 'the faithful wounds of a friend'.

'Kelly's so austere,' I complained, 'and Ian has the insensitivity of youth. Oh for my friends at the Hall!'

'Kelly hammered Simon (graciously),' Ian revealed. 'He told him he's arrogant towards the sisters.'

'I feel like the bottom of my life has fallen out,' I wrote, 'and all my spirituality is a load of rubbish.'

The process of being fitted into the 'spiritual house' continued. 'I'm writing this in the bathroom,' Ian records, 'cos "you know who" can't sleep with the light on! I react to Simon a lot over little things. He said I need to be more of a friend to him. I felt quite touched really.'

The 'sandpaper ministry' continued its painful work and slowly our rough edges got worn down – a bit.

The gracious sisters, nurtured by Kelly, befriended by Norma and mothered by Verna, seemed to love the cross, and to be constantly turning out deep wisdom, beautiful songs, and lovely paintings. In company they were as demure as fragrant flowers (most of the time). But the noise and laughter that reverberated from the sisters end and down the elegant staircase told a different story! Those who were intense, or 'in the flesh' were surrounded and sung to! They weren't perfect but they'd got it together.

We saw the preciousness of genuine love, and our own need for a serving heart. I started to make the tea for them all, but holiness was a still a long way off!

'I'm failing to manifest the sweet disposition of Jesus under trial,' I wrote.

'Simon said he felt like thumping Kelly!' was Ian's rendering! Kelly was quick on the draw and our pride got riddled with holes.

In the summer, a pentecostal brother joined us from up north. Kelly thought he was wonderful – he was actually humble! Wilf fell in love with the place immediately.

'When I got here,' he said, 'it was like our 'ouse. It was where I belonged – despite the fact there were umpteen sisters I was terrified of. They all seemed like Mother Teresa – junior corps – and I felt like the little boy in short trousers! But it was so homely and inspiring. It was all the clichés you can imagine. It was like that to me – heaven on earth!'

'Wilf's just moved in,' wrote Ian. 'We spent the evening gooseberry picking, which was fun. By the way, we've bought another house. It's called Vineyard and Mike Farrant is moving there from the Hall. Its got six acres and some fallen down outbuildings...I beat my discipler up this morning! He lost again. I'm glad our relationship is not all wishy-washy. I reckon, on the whole, all things considered – he's all right.'

Gradually the tensions mellowed and friendships grew. Wilf's positive happiness was infectious. He would come home from work with a big grin and gleaming gold-rimmed spectacles. 'Eh, it's good to be back in Zion!' he would exclaim in his Chesterfield accent, as we sat against the window seat, playing guitars and chatting. Kelly put his 'smoking guns' back into their holsters, and filled up our 'appreciation buckets'. Ian perked up, too: 'We went for a walk in the wind, then sat round singing songs with the sisters. It was a good scene and Kelly called me an amiable twit!'

Church week came round again and as Ashburnham Place couldn't squeeze any more of us in, we met in Northampton and enjoyed the time off together at home. During the school summer holidays I worked on the Farm. It was hot, hard, wholesome work. From the top of a strawstack you got a tremendous view of the blue skies and the open countryside. Such freedom and purity! Goodbye to the school laboratory! Babylon had fallen – well, at least, for seven weeks! Laughter, sharing, and closeness to creation – it was a great opportunity for friendship, whether chatting, lying exhausted on the stubble, or hurtling down the A5 on the tractor and trailer!

In the evenings we sat around talking – of diggers and breakdowns (Ian and Kelly), of sanctification and the new earth (me and Wilf), of gaining hearts, of submitting our spirits one to another, and the nature of the Lamb.

I looked around and thanked God – for Kelly, troubleshooter and peacemaker, for Verna with her never-failing supply of compassion and cakes, for the sisters with their inspirational unity. Despite the occasional tension, it was, without a doubt, idyllic. When I got back to my laboratory in the autumn I penned a hymn:

> Happy the days in Zion's fields
>   Enclosed away from Babel's strife;
> Beneath the Father's open sky
>   We feel the Spirit's fertile life
> Unfold the beauties of our heart,
>   Breath holiness through every part!

As I considered all that God was doing, and all the self-sacrifice, meekness, and love for Christ – the nobility of it swept over me and I was supremely grateful for Zion;

> Once we expected ne'er to see
>   This kingdom glory here on earth;
> Or such a heaven here below
>   Or such a home for pilgrim faith.
> Yet here we taste, and here we feel
>   A foretaste of Christ's final rule!

Two more brothers, Steve and Dave, moved in, and the five of us grew to appreciate one another. Vision for holiness and revival inspired us, and the subject of entire sanctification even appeared at the breakfast table!

Ian was gaining spiritual perception. He wrote in his diary:

> I was painting at home, and could hear the sisters working. I was amazed at their natural holiness. To find sisters like Pat just serving and serving with a contented heart when once she was a self-made women – it's just amazing! I doubt if there are many places around where there's such unity, caring and concern.
>
> As for Steve, he seems always willing to go the lowest way, not as some high flyer desperately trying to get on. He has silently followed the Lord with no real thought of self and is gaining the immeasurable quality of a heart that delights in God...
>
> When I ponder on the inward foundations of Zion, I feel a warm delight. It seems as though in all those who are growing there is, deep within the heart, an altar. And daily to this altar is brought all self-interest, and there it is burned. Though hidden from the eyes of men it fills the soul with a fragrance that the noblest virtue of Adam could never match.

He was grateful for correction too:

> I find the 'kingdom heart' a precious but painful expression. Once I sat on a stool with a smug smile and a self-congratulating heart. Then the Lord came and kicked the legs away! If it wasn't for the reality of discipleship, I could imagine puffing up to the throne with a box of diaries and a heart untouched by the cross.

Brotherhood was meeting our needs. Kelly's love reached us, and as we esteemed him, we grew like him. Often he would come home weary from a demolition day on his digger, flop against us as we sat by the window seat and breathe a great sigh.

I glimpsed something of the friendship of Jesus with Peter, James and John, or David with Jonathan. Holiness was warm, human and brotherly. It 'fleshed out' the kingdom of

God, and branded me with a love for Zion that could never be erased.

About this time Kelly called the house together. 'Ralph is "getting related" to Clare,' he announced. That meant they were considering marriage and would be spending time together. Ralph would be around Living Stones more often to see Clare. They would be going out for walks together and sitting with each other in some of the meetings. It didn't sound too romantic.

We had kept a degree of segregation since first establishing mixed community at the Farm and Sheepfold. Men shared their feelings mostly with men, and women with women. That encouraged depth and avoided the subtle dangers of flirtation. We mixed together in company but avoided being left alone together. Romantic inclinations stirred under the surface, of course, but we were open about these with our friends and were determined to tackle our feelings in a mature way. Community could so easily be littered with gone-wrong relationships.

So over the years we gradually developed our community 'relating procedure'. When a brother wanted to approach a sister, her pastor would find out if anyone else was interested and she could choose which brother to get to know first. This all helped to remove the pressure to flirt.

In Ralph's case, he was keen on Clare and felt marriage was his calling. So he spoke to Kelly, who asked her for her thoughts on the matter. She was unsure and Kelly suggested that she and Ralph spend some time together. As it happened, they both felt that their marriage would be of God and would enhance their ministry within the church.

At one time Clare had considered remaining single for God. We were becoming very positive towards the single state and were well aware of Paul's advice: 'Are you unmarried? Do not look for a wife' (1 Cor 7:27). We saw that the teaching of Jesus in Matthew 19:11–12 also indicated a gifting either for marriage or celibacy. 'Not everyone can accept this word, but only those to whom it has been given. For some are eunuchs because they were born that way; others were made that way by men; and others have renounced marriage because of the kingdom of heaven. The one who can accept this should accept it.' Unlike the common attitude of today, the New Testament seemed to hold celibacy in high regard. In fact, Paul had said, in effect: 'To marry is good. Not to marry is better' (paraphrase of 1 Cor 7:38).

Janie from the Farm was now a leader amongst the sisters. She'd considered celibacy before but it was unheard of in the circles she'd moved in. After joining us, she soon found a deep fulfillment in community, took hold of the celibate gift, and sought to live 'in undivided devotion to the Lord' (1 Cor 7:35).

Piers was another enthusiastic advocate of this path:

> To me celibacy was the highest way according to Scripture, and I didn't want second best! I reckoned I could handle it temperamentally, so I laid it before God. Shortly after that I was struck by an article in *New Wine* magazine about being single for the Lord and I knew God was telling me to 'Go for it!'

Increasing numbers among us were finding the celibate gift and making lifelong vows. Piers became a celibate leader at Sheepfold — and a useful contrast to Pete and Carol with their growing family! Piers wrote: 'I didn't want to get bogged down in the cares of life. I never regretted it or hankered after marriage. I just wanted to follow Jesus and travel as light as possible! Time is short and there is so much to do. Celibacy is priceless! It's pure! I love the freedom it brings.'

In prophetic wisdom we saw celibacy as a precious gem covered over by a cloth of fears, reserves, and general disapproval. As we took the cloth away, God polished the jewel and set it once more in Zion's crown.

Celibacy of course was nothing new. Jesus was the supreme example. Paul was also unmarried. Mystics like Augustine and St Francis who were great builders of brotherhood, saw chastity as an heroic virtue. The example, too, of people like David Brainerd and Amy Carmichael urged us on to higher things. 'If I had a thousand lives,' wrote the dying Brainerd, 'I would gladly lay them all down for Christ.'[52]

We needed firebrands like these who were recklessly in love with God. As Watchman Nee wrote of one celibate woman who had greatly influenced him: 'Immediately you detect a sweet savour of Christ...something has been broken and you smell the fragrance.'[53]

Celibacy was no easy road but as celibates knit themselves together into strong, deep friendships they brought a groundswell of vigour and inspiration to our church. They were worth their weight in gold. Unlike many charismatic scenes, among us it was the celibate brothers and sisters who began to set the pace.

Our leadership included increasing numbers of men like Piers who were 'travelling light' and ready for battle. Indeed, throughout the church we had little intention of settling down to a fossilised lifestyle. As the year came to an end, vision increased for church planting and evangelism.

Zion had awoken. God had made us a people. But now the cloud was moving on.

City on a Hill
1979–1983

14

The Cloud Moves On

1979

The church buzzed with excitement and rumours flew from house to house. We really were going to expand the community outside Northamptonshire. This was new. Who would go? And how would they cope being away from the centre of things?

Actually, it was Sheepfold Grange that was losing some of its key people. Pete and Carol, as well as a new young leader, Mick 'Temperate', were bracing themselves for the unknown. There was a great farewell at the house with an abundance of gifts, people and tears. That night Pete Matt couldn't sleep and Mick was up early to pray.

The winter dawn was breaking over the hills as he stepped into the garden. Mick would miss that view across the valley. Sheepfold had renewed him. It had been a wonderful experience, but now they were moving on.

He reflected on the past. Ten years had passed since he'd been baptised in the Spirit. After leading his college

Christian Union, he'd thrown himself into youth work, and considered being a missionary, but the fires had dimmed until he'd only been happy when out rock-climbing.

Mick remembered how stunned he'd been in 1975 when he saw the change in his sister. After moving to Bugbrooke with her husband, and then discovering the Jesus Fellowship, she had bubbled over with enthusiasm. So Mick had visited the chapel and found God again.

How he'd wept with remorse when he looked at his expensive climbing gear. Jesus had been pushed into second place – but no longer. Mick tried to bring the community inspiration to his church in Leicester but after eighteen months of frustration he left for Bugbrooke.

'You'll never look back now,' the Lord had whispered as he drove down the M1. 'This is the road to maturity.'

Mick smiled as he remembered. It was true. He hadn't looked back. As he watched the morning shadows creep over the frost, he thought of teas on the lawn, the bleating of sheep, learning Pete's songs, community lettuce-planting, and meditations in the garden. He'd shared his inspirations, his trials, his tears, his life. Now they were off to Warwickshire.

The previous summer we'd received prophetic direction from Isaiah 54: 'Enlarge the place of your tent...lengthen your cords, strengthen your stakes' (Is 54:2). We were to spread abroad, and bear 'sons and daughters'. We'd received wisdom about 'Mother Zion' and recognised, as Paul wrote, that spiritual Jerusalem is our mother (Gal 4:26). In the atmosphere of love many came to spiritual birth amongst us. 'More children!' we sang from Isaiah. 'All your sons gather and come to you...[they] will yet say..."This place is too small for us; give us more space to live in"' (Is 49:18: 20; also see 60:4, 66:8).

Our little 'Zion' was expanding. With 400 members, the chapel was ready to burst and the bustling balcony worried Cyril the architect. For some Saturday night meetings we now hired halls in Northampton or Rugby, whilst every

THE CLOUD MOVES ON

fortnight the mid-week gathering was broken down into 'area assemblies' where we could stretch our wings and allow new ministries to emerge.

New Creation Hall and the Bugbrooke estate, the Farm, Shalom, Sheepfold, the Daventry houses, Festal Grange, Living Stones and Vineyard were all filling up and in December 1978 we took over Cornhill Manor, a mile up the hill from Bugbrooke. The old hotel, still reeking of beer and cigarettes, provided space for sixty people, and some of the families from the estate, including Lionel and Marion, moved in.

Local villagers wondered what was coming next and were relieved when they heard of our plans to spread elsewhere! Our vision was to stay in the countryside but to spread out. We pulled up the stakes and extended the 'tent'. It was only an extension, as we intended to remain a single church. Central 'Jerusalem' (as we called the Northampton area) was putting its feelers into surrounding 'Judea'. (We weren't ready for the 'uttermost parts of the earth' yet!) And so our Zion fortress spilled over into Warwickshire.

In January we commissioned the twenty pioneers: Mick 'Temperate', Pete, Carol and family, the newlyweds Ralph and Clare, plus those studying in Warwick or Coventry. Eathorpe was a village twenty miles north west of Bugbrooke and within easy reach of Rugby, Coventry and Warwick. Our new home was a converted motel standing next to The Plough pub. We called it Harvest House!

The Harvest household travelled down to the meetings in Northampton, while we from 'Jerusalem' went up to encourage the family in 'Judea' and give them lots of pictures, prophecies, cakes, and so forth. I was learning to drive at the time and swerved through the country lanes, Toad of Toad Hall fashion, in a borrowed three-wheeler. Twenty miles seemed a long way! For many years people had come to us but now the church was flowing out to them.

Mick led an evangelism team to the 'Uni' disco in Coventry, and we held large gatherings in Warwickshire. We also invited folk to an informal time on our own ground at Harvest House. Many who came were interested Christians.

Along with the new churches, we were accused of 'sheep stealing'. It would be wrong to say we didn't want Christians to join us. Rarely, though, did we go out to find them. They came by word of mouth. Occasionally we visited Christian festivals to share with the unconverted, the searching or the backslidden. It was often a case of finding lost sheep.

The extent of backsliding amongst Christians shocked us and we saw many wrecked, frustrated lives. It was the acceptance of worldliness that seemed to open the door to disaster. One brother returned from a Christian event and sang out his heart in chapel:

If you could hear what they're saying in Christendom,
It would bring tears to your eyes;
Tears to your eyes and a weeping to your heart.

For many, community was the answer to a real longing. Graham was one student who joined Harvest House. He first visited us in 1977 as a frustrated Christian, and was bowled over by the brotherhood at the farm. He helped on the straw-carting and joined in the gooseberry pick. He wasn't used to openness, but, to his surprise, it came easily. He enjoyed the strength of fellowship and began to seek God.

Graham was mad on flying (his grandfather had been a fighter ace), but when someone in chapel gave a word of knowledge about aircraft, he saw that for him flying was an idol. At that moment he let it go and was filled with the Spirit. He went home, turned down an RAF scholarship and at eighteen joined the farm family.

In chapel one evening, after a Family Day on the Hall lawn, he shared some wisdom. A grassy hill towered over the valleys. This was Zion. A noon sun blazed down, the atmosphere was peaceful and upon the hill were hundreds of sheep, quietly munching in twos and threes.

'Brethren,' said Graham, 'when I consider these pastures, my heart is filled with gratitude. I was a lost sheep. I loved God but other things obscured my vision. Now I've come home. He's making me feed on the richness of his kingdom and I'm finding myself as never before. I believe there are many Christians who long for holy brotherhood. They're tired of straddling two worlds. Here, in Zion, we've so much to be grateful for, so much to offer.'

It echoed the feeling of our hearts. 'Jerusalem is our delight,' sang Mike 'Rockfast' Farrant in his new hymn, 'And we who mourned in Babylon, now cry aloud for joy!'

What we had was rare. Together we had discovered rich truths. Together we had honoured New Testament revelation and together forged a new culture. Insularity had been inevitable, but now we wanted to open our hearts.

Some Christians in other churches were enthusiastic but many were increasingly suspicious. Tensions at Warwick University highlighted this. Someone told the President of the Student Union that we were like the Moonies. When Graham tried to hire a room for a small student meeting, he got a grilling. The Christian Union were also nervous of us and felt we were too elitist. We seemed to insist that lifestyle was inseparable from the gospel. Indeed we did. Lifestyle was the issue.

As we moved around with our 'Jesus is Lord' assemblies, some ministers were annoyed because we hadn't consulted them first. Others renewed their criticisms of us. It seemed that the quiet days were coming to an end.

In *The Daily Star* an article appeared: 'CULT CRAZY – The Facts Behind The Mindbenders'. After mentioning the Jonestown massacre, it lumped us with Scientologists and the Children of God. Our mysterious sect shunned the outside world and lived the spartan life; Noel fancied himself as a latter-day Wesley; the men were bossy; the kids beaten; and the women (including doctors and teachers!) were chained to the kitchen sinks. It was all gross distortion. Noel replied with statements of orthodoxy on the notice sheets and added this:

> By dictionary definition every church is a cult. Jesus, his disciple band, and the early Jerusalem Church, would, in modern Britain, be greeted by the shrill cries of the anti-cultists. The Methodists were scorned for their perfectionism and for their joyful convicting faith. We too must carry the reproach of the cross.

We saw the spiritual battle and rejoiced. We had entered the arena. But the fact that fellow believers could oppose us was an indication of the state of Christianity in Britain.

'Britain accepts religion, uses it, and self-righteously flatters it,' wrote Noel. 'The rich strength of a gathered brotherhood it patronises with smiling indifference or attacks with false accusings. Western Christianity is an impure, materialistic, self-centered version of New Testament faith. It is Christianity without regeneration, without separation, without the Spirit of love, without the cross, without communal life.'

Noel's words sliced into unreality. At the same time we yearned for the disappointed. Britain was littered with Christians who'd hoped for much but seen little. We felt we should, like the Good Samaritan, pour in the oil of grace, share our lives with them and bring them the vision of a restored Zion. The keynote of our meetings was the restoration of Christian lives, and hymns like Wesley's 'Weary of wandering from my God' were sung with tenderness.

We knew from experience that it was only when believers had entered into the rest and enjoyment of God's kingdom that they could make it attractive to others. Those who insisted only on aggressive evangelism, wrote Noel, were often restless, dissatisfied, and rarely successful: 'To be effective light in this nation, God's people must enter the Sabbath rest of kingdom life, and the Jubilee that God has provided.'

At Harvest House Mick 'Temperate' was keen to reach the unconverted.

'I want you to lead Zion's evangelism,' the 'still small voice' said to him one morning.

'You what, Lord?' he thought. 'Me? Oh well, if it's of God it will come together, and the brethren will confirm it.'

Mick led some informal 'new life' meetings at Harvest House. A few Christians soon joined us, but more and more his burden was for the lost. One day, while praying, he saw a golden city. The gates opened wide and a band of glowing figures descended into the valley below, where they mingled with the wounded and brought some back to be healed. A sister had similar wisdom of golden doves flying out of Zion with the message of peace despite attacks by the black crows of the world.

In August Mick took a team to the Knebworth Rock Festival. They parked their converted ambulance, and soon a young man pitched his tent nearby. He made friends with them and marvelled at their message. Their gentle vibe of love contrasted with the heavy beat that throbbed into the night. He threw his cigarettes away, stuck with them, and gave his life to Christ.

A few days later Mick was listening to Noel at the elders' meeting. 'Of course, there's nothing very difficult about being celibate,' Noel remarked at one point, 'you just receive the grace.'

Some of us, who felt we were passing through the agonies of Gethsemane, grinned!

'That's for you,' the Spirit whispered to Mick.

'I want you to receive this.'

Mick sat back in the armchair. 'All right, Lord, I take it now.'

On the way home he felt as if he was taking off in an aeroplane – a great lift in his spirit. He got home at one in the morning to find he was locked out. Mick climbed in through one of the bedroom windows.

'Graham! he said, bubbling over, 'I've received the gift of celibacy!'

Graham flashed an angry, bleary eye and snorted. Their friendship had often been a bit stormy.

'Oh! Go to bed!' he shouted, and turned over.

By September the Farm had begun evangelism at the Leicester University disco. Noel and others waited up into the early hours to welcome the team home and hear reports. One evening they had been followed round by a demoniac girl.

'You can help me! You can help me!' she had screamed.

'You should have done!' said Noel, and ticked them off for their lack of courage.

The disco was a heavy scene. Bikers, prostitutes and drug dealers were regulars, and only a few students set foot down there. Mick's team joined the farm brothers and sisters in Leicester and used a house rented by our girl students. There a group of intercessors, welcomers and cheese-on-toast makers created a good atmosphere to bring people back to.

One night they met a young man who'd become a Christian in his early teens. He'd been baptised in the Spirit, but his church rejected charismatic gifts and he was put off. His family were into the occult and it wasn't long before he fell away and became a heavy drinker. When he met us, he'd been in a car accident, and though his leg had been healed by spiritualists his vision and hearing were still impaired.

Frustrated and aggressive, he had come for an argument, but he soon calmed down and they invited him back for supper. Simply talking to them made him feel different. That week he stopped drinking and the next Friday went back to the Farm for the weekend.

As he sat on the wall, looking over the valley, memories of a holiday with Christian friends returned. 'If only we could live together like this,' he had thought. He felt the presence of God again, and his leg shot with pain as the spiritualist healing vanished away. The brothers prayed for him, broke the occult power, and he was healed in the name of Jesus. Back in Leicester, he woke up on Monday morning to find his hearing had improved. Within weeks he'd moved in to the Farm.

Pete 'Valiant', our Dutch medic, joined the team at the 'Uni' disco. He flopped on the seat, wincing as the heavy metal blasted his eardrums. The rest of the team were lost in a haze of smoke and coloured strobes, and a heavy smell of cigarettes, dope and patchouli oil filled the basement. It was hard going. Pete couldn't wait to get back to our Leicester house.

'Lord,' he prayed, 'you'll have to bring them to me.'

Pete was a straight, and most took him for the drug squad and avoided him. When they found he was a Jesus Freak they avoided him even more! Eventually a group of girls sidled up.

''Ere!' said Vikki. 'What are you lot into, anyway? I heard you took Olly and 'is mates down your place last week.' Vikki looked menacing.

Pete smiled and said, 'We're just here loving folk and seeking to bring them new life in Jesus.'

'You're a load of nutters!' said another, and giggled. 'You don't think you're going to convert us lot – do ya?'

''Ang on, Luce!' said Vikki. 'Give the bloke a chance.'

Vikki was interested. She'd watched the Jesus People moving around – right out of place! She was into the occult and fascinated with spiritual things. Perhaps they had something. Pete spoke seriously to them but the girls got silly and he told them off, which annoyed Vikki, though she liked the way Pete seemed to care for them.

Pete invited them back to the house and after a rowdy journey on the minibus, Vikki found herself munching cheese on toast and talking to a sister who had been a medium. Vikki liked her and they prayed together. In the next room the guys got wild and abusive, so Vikki went in and gave them a telling off! That put her on our side.

Later that week a brother visited their squat and sat around playing his guitar. 'Somethin' moving in my heart,

Jesus, Jesus,' he sang. It was his latest song. They chatted and he left a box of groceries.

Soon Vikki got evicted. As she was obviously responding to God, they invited her down to the Hall. She had no deliverance ministry or dramatic conversion. She just decided for God and stopped smoking and swearing. It was a new life – quaint, but clean. Vikki was impressed by the sisters at the Hall as they went round singing and making marmalade in huge pans, so she got herself a dress from down the clothing store and joined in!

Some travelled a long way to worship with us, including a small fellowship from East Anglia. One of these brothers had grown very discouraged and spent most of his time in his pottery studio which happened to be a converted bank vault. One day he was in desperate need of £50 when a friend walked in saying he felt the Lord telling him to give him £50 and also to encourage him to go down to Bugbrooke.

The following Saturday night at Bugbrooke he was in chapel listening to the words of wisdom and knowledge that God often revealed during the worship. 'I can see a strongroom door with a big brass handle,' declared Alasdair, one of our doctors. 'It's either in a bank or on a ship, and I can see a brother closing the door behind him. I feel that God is calling you to close the door on your present life and to move in a new direction.'

The brother concerned was very shaken, and touched by God's care for him. It wasn't long before he and his wife knew the call of God to join us in community. On the next visit down he made a bee line for Alasdair. 'Hey, bro,' he grinned, 'I do my pottery in an old rented bank vault. It's got a big brass handle on it and it's in Ship Street!'

Soon almost all that little group moved down and joined the church. They weren't all spoken to so dramatically, but they were drawn by the reality of God's presence amongst us.

'Substitutes for God's presence are many,' wrote Noel, 'jazzed-up choruses, shallow praise, liturgy, an easy gospel, drama, beautiful music, youth clubs etc. Our real need is for the glory of the Lord to fill the house.'

The Fellowship was attractive to those who sought a radical path, but as we entered the eighties they were increasingly hard to find.

15

Into the Eighties

1980

As the church in Britain entered the eighties, many felt that the renewal movement had lost steam. The charismatic ship launched in the sixties was running aground in shallow waters. Enthusiasm had waned and pioneers had become settlers. 'Have all dug in?' asked Arthur Wallis in *The Radical Christian*[54]. The renewal began to reflect on itself and look for direction. Clearly the church needed to rise up and go on the offensive.

'There is a scent of spiritual warfare in the air,' wrote Denis Clark in *Renewal*. 'Only now is the concept of God's people being an army taking on proper significance. Psalm 110 could become the vital focus for the eighties:

'"The Lord will extend your mighty sceptre from Zion; Your troops will be willing on your day of battle."'[55]

But denominations seemed weighed down with the armour of Saul. Vigour and vision lay with the radical churches, and they began to get the flak we had experienced.

The house church movement grew stronger and the Dales Weeks became a force to be reckoned with. 'Gird up your armour, ye sons of Zion!' the thousands sang enthusiastically. The Spirit had come to prepare an army for God. The nation was in an alarming decline and unless the churches rose up to confront the prophets of Baal, Britain was on course for disaster.

Encouraging voices declared that revival was on its way. Many converts had slipped through the net in the early seventies, but God had been restoring the churches – mending the nets for a larger catch. The fruits of past revivals had often been lost for lack of radicalism. Thousands were converted but little was built.

Wesley had made no such mistake. 'Souls awakened under Wesley's ministry, he joined in class, and thus preserved the fruit of his labours,' wrote his friend George Whitefield. 'This I neglected to do, and my people are a rope of sand.' Both were great evangelists but Wesley was also a builder.

We, too, heard the call of God to build in the eighties, but success would depend on the church being a holy, alternative society. We agreed with Ern Baxter, a popular speaker at the Dales Weeks: 'When I see Babylon falling, I am looking for Jerusalem to emerge...I expect us to return to the simplicity referred to in Acts 2. There we find loyalty, integrity, covenant relationships, community'[56].

Like the Methodists we imitated the 'love feasts' of the early Christians (Acts 2:46; 1 Cor 11:20). Once a week we sat around our 'Agape' meal for a few hours, eating, worshipping, and sharing the bread and wine. 'One heart and soul' was the theme. There would be reconciliations and sometimes we washed one another's feet. Finding unity could be painful, but covenant brotherhood was the only ground of hope for revival. Covenant was the foundation, and for us, loyalty meant we intended lifelong commitment.

In America, the charismatic leader Don Basham defined Covenant Community as: 'A community of redeemed people, bound together in covenant love, submitting to compassionate authority, and manifesting peace, holiness, and family fidelity...A community where loving correction and instruction produces maturity; where dedication to excellence produces the finest results in arts, crafts, trades, and commerce...where all life is inspired and directed by the Spirit of Jesus Christ and is lived to his glory as a witness and testimony to the world.'[57]

It was an excellent definition, and Noel reproduced it on our notice sheet. Cautious of prosperity teaching he added: 'And the "prosperity and abundance" are to be shared in holy equality as God sends the needy to find his just society.'

We entered the decade in a confident mood. A kingdom feast was spread and the prodigals could come home. Backed by intercession, we emerged to fight on the world's ground, and went into the streets, pubs, discos, and clubs. Meetings were booked in Rugby, Coventry and Leicester. *Now to Live His Triumph!* was the motto, as we exalted Jesus as Lord, proclaimed his kingdom, and called disciples.

In Warwickshire the work was none too dramatic but was growing. We bought a country house near Rugby, a few miles from Harvest House, and Mick's sister and family left the Bugbrooke housing estate for Stockton House, with its trees and lawns. They were joined by Dave 'Resolute', one of several Oxford graduates whose abilities were coming in useful.

As we became well-known, people wanted to know where we stood theologically. Were we orthodox? Did we have pet doctrines? Also, how did our church work? And what were members committing themselves to? Noel worked with Dave on a Statement of Faith and Practice. He also joined Ian 'Insight', the solicitor, and Mike 'Rockfast', our treasurer, in mapping out a new Church Constitution and a Trust Deed that dealt with the administration of New Creation Christian Community.

Our basic theology had already been summarised on the church notice sheets:

INTO THE EIGHTIES

> This church upholds orthodox Christian truth, being reformed, evangelical and charismatic; practising believer's baptism and the New Testament reality of Christ's Church.
>
> We believe in God, Father, Son and Spirit; in the full divinity, atoning death, and bodily resurrection of the Lord Jesus Christ; and in the Bible as God's word, fully inspired by the Holy Spirit.

We were card-carying, Bible-waving, charismatic evangelicals – despite the nasty rumours! The full Statement, which ran to forty articles, was checked by theologians from Oxford University and London Bible College.

The public reading in chapel was moving and some aspects were a little controversial:

> We believe that God's purpose is to gain a people...God made covenant with Abraham, and the promise finds fulfilment through the New Covenant, in which both Jews and Gentiles are of the true Israel, the church of the living God...
>
> We believe that God's covenant people are called to be separated to him from the spirit of the world. They are to bear prophetic witness to the Kingdom of God as a visible expression of the Lordship of Christ. They are thus the City or Zion of God, His temple and dwelling place...
>
> We affirm the call of Jesus to renounce all other things to be His disciple...not that this requires rejection of the nuclear family or any strict exclusivism. The regenerate, as may be possible, shall voluntarily have all things in common, but we do not make this a condition of membership...
>
> We affirm that male and female are equal in status, but we hold the scriptural distinction...that men differ from women in role, appearance and dress. We regard the keeping of special days and seasons as unwarranted by scripture...
>
> We also hold that believers are to bear their cross as Christ's disciples. The world must persecute us...

Three days later a headline appeared in the *Oxford Journal*: 'MP URGED TO PROBE RELIGIOUS SECT. An Oxford couple have accused a religious sect of splitting their family.'[58]

Their son, who had maintained regular contact with his family, was in fact a twenty-eight year old teacher with a PhD! Within weeks the *Baptist Times* had grieved many of its readers by reproducing this headline on its front page.

Lewis Misselbrook from the Baptist Union headquarters was a friend of ours and replied, 'Bugbrooke is a member of our fellowship of churches. I hope our Union will never become a dull uniformity where great experiments of this kind are feared...'[59]

Lewis visited us and prepared an article which later appeared in the *Baptist Times*:

> When I arrived, Noel was out in the fields working. He came in, mud all over his gum-boots, and gave me the shy, welcoming smile I remembered so well...He is still the same quiet, deep man, but one held by a vision that by the Spirit the church is to be a visible and powerful expression of the kingdom of God...
>
> Most of the criticism of the community has been unfair and uninformed, and some has been malicious. Bugbrooke is not perfect. Noel Stanton is not always right. But it is a bold venture of faith...
>
> First, it is a genuine effort to express the Gospel in practice...
>
> Second, it is a lay movement...every member plays his part...
>
> Third, it reveals the kingdom of God as a true alternative and revolutionary society.
>
> Fourth, for the Jesus Fellowship, mission and community are inseparable...
>
> Fifth, it is a dynamic and ongoing movement...
>
> At last week's Baptist Union assembly it was said that God is doing a new thing...If we are not too afraid of change to lift up our eyes to see, we may well be considerably enriched, whether we follow the Bugbrooke pattern or not.[60]

Dave 'Resolute', who was becoming our PR man, went round visiting Christian leaders like Arthur Wallis, Roger Forster and Gerald Coates. One day Dave and I sat down in Gerald's home at Cobham. His openness impressed me and I smiled at the NOT UNDER LAW plaque above the tray of assorted wines!

'You're pioneers,' Gerald told us, 'and pioneers exist for

the sake of others.' In his eyes we were a bit legalistic, but had a lot to offer – if only we could communicate.

We certainly wanted to. For us 1980 was a year of expansion, public relations and bridge-building. Bank Holidays were billed as Community Open Days, when friends, relatives, and interested Christians came around.

Lewis Misselbrook spoke at one special meeting at Cornhill for local church leaders. We also advertised a conference in magazines like *Renewal*. We called it *A City To Dwell In* and invited Christians to stay for a weekend in August and sample community. Worship and teaching went on in a marquee on Cornhill's lawn and indoors we held 'share groups'. Six panels answered questions on areas such as administration and business, marriage and celibacy, evangelism and church building, and household life.

Dave's team dealt with theology and included Trevor Saxby, who was finishing his doctorate and writing *Pilgrims Of A Common Life*[61], a history of Christian community. They all wore glasses and looked studious, apart from Andy, a sausage packer with a degree from London Bible College!

When I arrived with Jim, a guest at the Hall, the questions had already begun: 'So you practise rebaptism then?'

We turned our heads and noted a provocative looking chap at the back. Dave grinned. 'Over to you, Trevor.'

'Thanks!' said Trevor. 'No we don't. Most Christians who come to us have been baptised as believers and are happy about their baptism. But we do get a few who feel that in the light of the New Testament theirs wasn't a valid experience.'

'What about lifelong commitment, then? Is it biblical?'

'Well, we shall always be members of Christ and his body,' said Dave.

'And it's a big worldwide Body!' was the reply.

'This guy's interesting,' whispered Jim.

'But it's only real at a local level...isn't it?' Dave grinned.

'Yes?'

'Yes!'

Our heads swivelled to follow the ping-pong.

'In the early church, they were a covenant people. There was one local body, and you were either in or out!'

'Fair enough!' he smiled.

There was a brief silence.

'I bet he's got one about community,' I said.

'Do you think community is for everyone?' he asked.

'Trevor!' said Dave.

'Umm,' said Trevor. 'Well, let me see...the Hutterites called it the "highest command of love". If you follow the biblical teaching to "renounce all that you have", "love your brother as yourself", and "come out from amongst them", where does that get you?'

'Not under one roof!' exclaimed our friendly critic. Everybody laughed.

'Not necessarily,' agreed Trevor, taking off his glasses, 'but the common purse does strike at the root of selfishness.'

'Ouch!' whispered Jim.

'Let's get out of here while the going's good,' I said.

We walked into the crammed Octagon. Jim chuckled at the posh decor we had inherited. (I assured him that even with our 'mansions', we were poorer than the average Englishman.) Pete Matt, our family spokesman and holiday-school headmaster, was holding forth and soon the questions turned to discipline. Carol smiled sweetly as one of the children tugged at her hair.

'Yes, we do train our kids quite carefully,' she said. 'Pete and I find that our children need the security of being under our authority. They need a lot of love and care and we try to spend as much time with them as we can. Of course, love means that we sometimes have to discipline them.'

'Yes, said Pete: 'Proverbs 29:15 says, "A child left to himself disgraces his mother." I think society is quite blind in this area, and we see the fruit of it on the streets.'

'What about toys?' asked another.

'Ugh!' said Pete, 'Consumerism gone mad!' We like simple creative things like Lego and Meccano...and word games.'

'And pots and pans!' added Carol.

'So why don't you have your own school?' asked one person perched precariously on the window seat.

'Too expensive and too much hassle!' said matter-of-fact Pete with a twinkle in his eyes. 'Apart from which they need to handle the world. We're not a desert island, you know!'

'Look!' whispered Jim, 'I've got some questions for the admin group.'

'Hang on,' I said, 'they all change soon.'

Afterwards, we moved next door to one of the old bars where Ian 'Insight' answered Jim's questions about joining.

'People join us because they like our vision,' explained Ian, 'and we receive them with baptism, if needed, and "the right hand of fellowship". Not everyone enters community and we have many non-residential members. Families often first move into the Bugbrooke estate and later join a large community house.'

'So how do the community finances work?' asked Jim.

'Over to you, Mike,' Ian nodded.

'Right,' said Mike. 'New friends, as we call them, pay board and lodging, if they stay around, but members share income through a common purse account. Any surplus goes into the Community Trust, which also receives capital from members over twenty-one who have completed a probationary period of at least six months.'

'And where does it all go?' Jim smiled.

'Not on holidays in the Bahamas!' Ian chuckled.

'Seriously, chaps,' said Mike, 'none of it is money in the bank! It's all tied up in our property and capital goods, like cars and furniture. The accounts are open to members, audited by outside accountants and presented at the annual church business meeting.'

'What if people want to leave?'

'Well, the Trustees are empowered to return their capital. If they'd had nothing to contribute, the Trust normally makes a payment to cover immediate expenses.'

As we walked back to the Hall, Jim mentioned a few criticisms he'd heard.

'Some people say the Fellowship is legalistic,' said Jim.

'All holiness depends on the baptism of the Holy Spirit,' I explained. 'That's how it all started, when the life of God was poured into thirsty hearts. Then the Spirit led us along the way of the cross and that meant deliberate choices. What does it say in Titus 2? "For the grace of God that brings salvation has appeared to all men. It teaches us to say 'No' to ungodliness and worldly passions, and to live self-controlled, upright lives...".'

I was getting inspired. 'Well, grace did teach us! And purify us! And bring us together as a people for God! Grace gave us a heart to practise Christ's teachings and we began to cleanse ourselves from the spirit of the world. Our whole lifestyle was shaken up! Leaders began to lead. Brothers and sisters discipled one another. Men and women found their true identity. All the time grace was telling us to lay down our lives for the brethren and giving us the vision of a holy Zion...'

'Yes, yes, I see that,' he said. 'I'm not supporting worldliness. But isn't it easy to become a people of rules?'

'Well, of course it is! And that's the fate of so many moves of God – the wine is gradually lost till only the wineskin remains. So we've got to keep thirsting after God, seeking a deeper purity and a greater love. But a holy people are a different people – and the world rejects them. That's the issue, Jim, not legalism!'

Our attempts at bridge-building made some headway, and within the next two years we had received visits from a number of Christian leaders. One surprise visitor was Ern Baxter. From the top of a strawstack I watched him walk, tall and frail, up the Farm drive. 'We are the world's last hope,' he had said at the Kansas City Shepherds' Conference. 'We must bring the sheep into a community of power and compassion that will attract the world to an alternate society and a counter-culture and a way of life that they are looking for.'[62]

Gilbert Kirby paid us a visit, too. He was then General Secretary of the Evangelical Alliance. Michael Harper also came and asked Stanley Jebb, the minister of New Covenant Church in Dunstable, to write an article on us for *Renewal*.

Stanley Jebb attributed our comparative success to strength of leadership and careful shepherding, to the application of the Scriptures, to holiness and to covenant loyalty. The criticism, he reckoned, stemmed mainly from gossip and ignorance of the real facts. 'The church is orthodox in doctrine. Being different is not the same as being heretical...' he wrote.

He saw the danger of the Jesus Fellowship becoming isolationist. But he said there was also the 'danger' of 'having our way of life challenged, our horizons widened, and our understanding of Scripture tested, if much contact is made with the Bugbrooke Fellowship. Some are not willing for this, so they stay away.'[63]

By the autumn we were evangelising in Milton Keynes and had bought Promise House in Coventry, and Faith House in Leicester. The Fellowship was on the move and becoming increasingly public. Dave 'Resolute' was now editing our magazine, *Newness*, which explained our biblical basis and conveyed our radical vision to others.

Arthur Wallis and Gerald Coates were amongst those who called in. Our bridge-building efforts had broken the ice, but where larger, more visionary men saw in us a venture of faith, many still treated us with caution, or even contempt.

Dave wrote in *Evangelism Today*:

> Once our charismatic worship was misunderstood. Now it is our lifestyle and our emphasis on holiness. Many find this unusual, even controversial. But we rejoice in what God has done in forming a 'people for his own possession'. Our vision is to be a 'city on a hill'.[64]

City On A Hill was an ITV documentary on us and was a fair representation of where we stood. 'Of course some will misunderstand and oppose us,' said Noel at the end, 'but we believe our testimony will win through!'

As the year came to a close I was needed back at the Hall. I left Living Stones with tears: Kelly, the hero, and Norma; the brothers who were my friends; the graceful sisters; the irreplaceable Verna; Goldy, the very senile dog; Snowy, the more approachable cat; the ducks, the geese, the memories. I wrote a farewell hymn:

> How rich these years in which we spend
>   Our lives in mutual love entwined;
> Such gracious times are rarely found,
>   But here, on Holy Zion's ground.

Zion was precious indeed. But her peace was coming to an end, and a valley of humiliation lay ahead.

16
A Crown of Thorns
1981

Despite our attempts at bridge-building, we encountered growing opposition from some quarters. When the Christian magazine, *Buzz*, visited the community in the autumn of 1980 they found us 'hospitable, welcoming, and helpful', but came away with 'a distinct unease'. Over-modest women seemed to hover in the background. 'They wear long dresses, no make-up, no jewellery, nothing that can possibly be seen as allowing a woman to make the best of herself.'[65]

Buzz disliked our caution about over-familiarity between men and women, and criticised Noel's authority. 'The result of his teaching', they complained, 'is that the whole community acts as one.'

Unity was bad enough, but we also took the biblical command, 'Love not the world' too seriously. 'So there is no TV, radio or pop music. Nor are there the basic social pleasures that make up a full and balanced life – outings to the cinema and so on.'

We were on different wavelengths. *Buzz* mourned the loss of worldly influences and called us isolationist. Noel, on the other hand, felt it was 'important to maintain our holy identity'.[66]

Buzz concluded: 'The Fellowship has a commitment to their understanding of community being an essential part of New Testament Christianity. And this divides them from their fellow Christians.'[67]

Buzz set the tone amongst Christians. At the Greenbelt Festival our presence was unwelcome and we were regarded as independent, legalistic – even dangerous! Already the Greenbelt organisers had given a general warning against 'sheep-stealers', and one leader, engaged in anti-cult work, distributed a leaflet. Our name appeared in it!

Another document had been circulating for a couple of years from an anti-cult body called FAIR – Family, Action, Information, Rescue. This 'unfair' document passed between angry parents and critics, and became standard press material. It was inspiring, even entertaining – and libellous!

> Their ethos is modelled on the Anabaptists, who believed the only valid baptism was of adults who experienced new birth. Turning from the broader base of established Christianity in the world, they followed a narrower, purist creed, taking Scripture as their authority...The Hutterites maintained a high standard of morality, [and] practised community of goods...The Bugbrooke Fellowship aims to emulate them. Their... fellowship is real and warm. Their adherence to traditional Christian values of selflessness and self-discipline is essentially beyond criticism.[68]

That was inspiring. Their portrait of charismatic worship, though, we found hilarious.

> Members go into a trance-like state, sobbing, muttering, and swaying with arms outstretched. Stanton preaches for two or three hours. The rest of the time is given to violent rhythmic singing, prayer, and individual rambling outpourings. This

creates a state of emotional climax and abandon. Combined with late hours, poor food, and lack of normal emotional outlets, the members are continually swung between deprivation and ecstasy.[69]

It was a strange caricature! Noel (unbeknown to himself!) had been to the States, the hot-bed of cults. The plebs suffered from a lack of veg and a surfeit of spuds. Members were pasty-faced and overweight. Children were subdued (ho! ho!) and undersized. We shared all our clothes and had little idea where our money went. All in all we had a 'fanatical desire to reach perfection at the cost of our normal equilibrium' – in other words, we were religious nutters!

There were deplorable references to the deaths, several years before, of Dave and Steve. Parts of the document were savage.

Individuals bent on our downfall were delighted with such material. One local woman was particularly virulent and a local pentecostal minister was obsessively anti-Bugbrooke. Together with a few disgruntled ex-members and irate parents, a web of opposition was spun.

In April the *News Of The World* produced some priceless journalism: 'How Hardline Noel Beats Out The Devil!'[70] The photo of 'sect hysteria' featured one of our leading couples with quaint smiles, and on the point of nodding off! The elders were Noel's 'spy network', a gang of Gestapo heavies bent on 'cracking' the flock! Force-feeding carrots was one method. Sharing dirty socks was another. With an iron fist Noel ruled a fanatical colony of brainwashed zombies! In worse taste was the false account of Steve's death, and his family was made to grieve yet again.

Our enemies egged on the press, using the FAIR document as fuel. In reality, however, evangelicals on the FAIR committee had been duped. No one had visited or asked for information. So we spoke to the co-chairman, a college chaplain. He listened to us and when he saw how unbalanced and inaccurate the criticisms were, he apologised, regretted the cult link, and promised to withdraw the document. But the damage had been done.

By June the pentecostal minister had gathered those who were opposed to us and held a meeting where they spoke against the Fellowship. The only way to get people out of Bugbrooke, one said, was to send in a helicopter! It was all very silly and unhelpful. They made a tape of the meeting which was circulated widely. The smear campaign put us all in a defiant mood and I wrote a hymn:

> Brethren we stand and here defy
> > The world and all its darkest power!
> Pure love and brotherhood now wins
> > This evil day, our finest hour!

Noel added some verses.

> Though false religion speaks against
> > And carnal Christians run to oppose,
> These brethren stand, in Jesu's name
> > In faith and love, and bless their foes.

However, even the apostle Paul didn't find blessing easy. 'Alexander the metalworker did me a great deal of harm,' wrote Paul to Timothy. 'The Lord will repay him for what he has done' (2 Tim 4:14). But persecution was a must and we needed to rejoice in it. Indeed, of the early church it was said, 'people everywhere are talking against this sect' (Acts 28:22).

The hornets were stirred. We had defied the worldly spirit, and as the devil wouldn't take it lying down, we entered a new phase of spiritual warfare. Noel was a particular target of attack and felt the criticism keenly. It was all the more painful because of the genuine attempts we were now making to open our hearts to Christian brethren. Many seemed ready to kick us down, but few to stand with us.

'Zion "rules in the midst of her enemies",' wrote Noel,

referring to Psalm 110:2. 'They attack us with bitterness and slander, and refuse to forgive. They reject open-hearted communication. We go to them once, twice, more; but they reject our brotherly appeals. But we must rejoice and stand firm, knowing that in suffering we shall find meek and softened hearts. "No weapon that is fashioned against you shall prosper" (Is 54:17, RSV).

In the midst of such trial we sensed God's purposes. At the July church week in Northampton we received a word of prophecy: 'I have raised up this people in this nation at this time, to bear witness to my holy name. Rejoice in the opposition of Satan! Conquer with the blood of the Lamb, binding him in my name and living in the righteousness of my Spirit! Rejoice in your heritage. Hold fast what you have that no man take your crown!'

The moral emptiness so evident in the nation was creating a hunger for the gospel. Before the Evangelical Awakening in the eighteenth century, it was poverty and desperation that ploughed and prepared the country for revival. Now the time of the poor and needy had come again, and God was raising up his people 'for such a time as this' to reap the harvest.

Noel read out a letter from Mick 'Temperate' in which he expressed his weeping heart for the unreached thousands of Birmingham. Compassion grew amongst us, and our focus began to shift towards the inner cities. These needy, 'forgotten people' would respond to the love and equality that we offered.

Amidst the opposition, God reminded us of the winning power of brotherhood. We were proud of what God had done, and were grateful for such clarity, devotion, and unity. Indeed with 600 in residence and 70 leaders, we had established what was probably the largest Christian community in Europe. Our businesses were expanding and there was an advance in evangelism.

But we felt the strain and were being worn down by persecution and discouragement. It was a year for courage. We needed to endure through the 'darkest hour'. 'It's easy at the start,' we sang, 'with hearts aflame with zeal...It's now the second watch and the night is dark and cold...'

The evil day was a time to stand together, and the word came through clear – 'Hold on to what you have!' (Rev 3:11). As evil powers put a cloud upon us the temptation was to compromise or desert. But the vast majority clung to covenant loyalty. We were determined to retain our depth in God, and let 'no one take our crown'. But somehow the crown was tarnished. Something of the glory was passing away.

In September, prophetic wisdom was given that sounded the alarm. A group was seen standing in a circle facing outwards ready to go and welcome in the lost. But at the very centre was a dark cloud where the enemy had gained a foothold.

Could it be true? Had 'the flesh' gained ground amongst us? Had we become lukewarm? Our growth rate was slow and our evangelism disappointing. Was this a sign of our decay, that our arteries were hardening, that spiritual death was creeping over the church?

We faced up to the possibility of God's judging hand upon us. All was not well. The converts we did gain, like Vikki, often split off. We were making little impact on the educated and professionals, and few Christians joined us. At home, our teenagers were difficult and some quite rebellious. Holiday school was a strain and had to be abandoned. Our standards were slipping, people were uninspired and enthusiasm for self-denial had abated.

Noel urged us to take the 'central ground' or we would be defeated. The drift had to stop. We refused the downward trend, and took measures to deepen our spirituality. We held short 'brotherhood times' before going to work. The Agape meal was set apart for members only, and there we reaffirmed our covenant, bared our hearts, and discussed weekly Bible readings round the tables. More prayer was urged upon us and shepherding groups were split down for closer reality.

The drive was on! Some felt secure within a stronger framework, but, of itself, it couldn't get to the root of the problem. In our zeal for outward holiness we had cooled on inward experience. 'Lord can it be a church should die through loss of first fraternal love?' asked one brother in his hymn. The answer was, 'Yes!' Form without power was useless.

Now that I was back at the Hall, I realised that the deeps of brotherly love were not over-common. Away from Kelly's wing, I discovered Zion's problems. She had plenty of spots and warts. The Farm bristled with young men 'being themselves', while the Hall, with its families and older characters, seemed a little reserved and institutional. Either way, a spiritual dullness had settled over many parts of the church.

'Do we really want the presence of God?' I wrote in my journal. 'Would it be too troublesome? We've got it nicely wrapped up. We are a well-ordered community. Rushing wind and tongues of fire? The awesomeness of God? Oh no! We're content to know him in a relaxed way; you know – the "still, small voice". And so the Bugbrooke revival becomes the Bugbrooke "denomination" and dies in the midst of prosperity.'

We were making outward changes – but where was the power of God? The joy and spontaneity? The miracles? The surprises of the Holy Spirit? 'Things have become routine,' wrote Mike 'Rockfast' in his diary. 'We have almost succeeded in eliminating the unpredictable and taming the Holy Spirit.'

We put on a brave face. People learned the ropes and were loyal. But there was unreality. Also some of the originals like Paddy, French Mary, and Alan had found the going tough. Paddy and his family had left the church, Mary had split off for a long while, and Alan and his family, though still loyal members of the church, had moved out of community.

The church had moved deeper since the early days but somehow we had 'matured' out of praise, and the innocence of first love was tarnished with self-righteousness. We needed a touch of the divine, the supernatural.

Mike 'Rockfast' expressed his feelings as he wrote short stories about the 'little people of Kingdomland'. The children at Vineyard loved them, but they carried a serious message. The tale of 'The Great Dam' was prophetic as the sudden turn of events amongst us was to prove.

To start with it was just an idea.

'Why don't we build a dam across Eternallife River? Then we can make it go wherever we want it to!' They got to work with plans and diagrams. At one time you would have seen bands of merry little people singing and dancing in the morning sunlight as they drank from the river and gathered fruit from the hedgerows. But now they were far too busy.

Soon the dam was finished and they were proud of their work. Even visitors from Sinfulgloom came to admire it. The little people settled down to cultivate their own plots, and were glad they didn't have to dance to the river any more. So they all got fat! What's more, they built houses to keep themselves warm. (Once they just huddled together.)

But some got sick, and arguments broke out about who owned what. Then the water became stagnant and a film grew over their eyes. The leaders were very worried and as they discussed it together, there was a knock at the door. The Ruler of Kingdomland stood before them. How had they managed to forget him? A silence fell as they gazed into his face. He was angry, but there were tears in his eyes.

'What have you done to my beautiful land?' he asked quietly. They bowed their heads in shame.

'My little people, I fear that the blindness of Sinfulgloom has come upon you.' His words made them sad, and before long they were all crying. As they wept, their eyes became clear again. 'Now see what I will do! Gather everyone together on the highest hills!'

The tears flowed into the night as the little people came

together and looked on the land they had spoiled. Then suddenly the night sky was torn by great flashes of lightning. The rains came down, and the channels swelled, until with an almighty crash the dam burst open and the swirling torrent swept everything away before it.

As the morning sun crept over the land they saw it was beautiful and fresh as once before.

17

Dambusters!

1982

Entries in my journal for 1982.

Sat. 18 Jan. Things have changed. When God works, programmes go out of the window. There are long times of prayer and we sing 'Bend me lower'. Weeping and confession of sin have replaced teaching, and Noel just reads from the Scriptures. We want the Spirit to move. Expectancy is in the air and we hear the rumblings of spiritual upheaval.

Sun. 19 Jan. Wilf saw a river as in Ezekiel. He went in ankle deep, then knee-deep, then further in. Some stayed on the edge, fearful of abandoning themselves, but God is swelling the river. The morning meeting was spontaneous. A brother stood and asked his shopmates to gather with him and pray. Many houses and groups gathered together to seek God. Tears were shed as we confessed faults and embraced one another.

Thank God for all this. We want his presence. But if he is to 'rend the heavens and come down' he must first bring conviction. The Hebrides Awakening began when a man confessed his sins. In the American revivals Finney thrust in the sword before pointing to the Lamb of God.

'Too many souls,' wrote Frank Bartleman, 'are dragged from the womb of conviction by force. They have to be incubated ever after.'[71] This is why we lack power. Repentance is shallow and we are plagued by the self-life. It needs burning out.

Tues. 21 Jan. All around Britain we hear of grace but who speaks of the fear of God? Entertainment replaces awe. Peace! Peace! they say, and the wound is healed lightly. We want the mountain tops but refuse Gethsemane. 'Don't sing!' Evan Roberts would cry. 'It's too terrible to sing!' How easily it thrust away God's presence.

Wed. 22 Jan. How have these recent changes come about? Partly from frustration. We have sought to be the 'friends of sinners'. Many are drawn into evangelism, whether in the front line, in prayer, or as deacons and caterers. Whole afternoons are spent in 'saturation evangelism' when the church is out in force. We bring folk back but few come through. So much travel and energy! The reaping is hard and the church is weary. Our great need is for God.

'Oh that you would rend the heavens and come down!' (Is 64:1). That was the burden of Noel's ministry as we entered the new year. Our hearts leapt as we considered the revivals of the past. Maybe it could happen here. But it had to begin with us. 'Bend the church and save the people' was the motto of the Welsh Revival.

A child went home from our meeting and wrote a song:

The mountains of pride, the mountains of sin,
Shall all flow down at the presence of him
Who comes with fire!

That was our expectation. Revival was the talk of the day. Routine was over and we were moving on.

There were many new faces at the first leaders' gathering of the year as over a hundred of us met at Cornhill. The ministry was on awakening. Revivals, we noted, were short-lived; they ran their course and died. Often it was from lack of commitment, but that wasn't our problem. Over-familiarity with God was our crime.

'This is the one I esteem,' we read, 'he who is humble and contrite in spirit, and trembles at my word' (Is 66:2). Our hearts were searched that evening and there were tears. At midnight we stepped out silently into the cold night, much subdued.

The following Friday the evangelists stayed in and prayed for a mission we were planning to hold the next day in Rugby. There was more weeping and a strong expectancy that God would move among us. In Rugby the ministry was very urgent and the word cut home, exposing our indifference, self-interest and lack of oneness. During the bread and wine many knelt together and wept.

Judgement had begun at the house of God. Programmes were suspended and for two months no notice sheets appeared. The elders' meeting was cancelled and we held a church meeting instead. Noel spoke of revival. Real desire was the key: prayer must prevail, and obedience to the Spirit was vital. In past revivals God used women and children to melt the hearts of sinners, meetings ran themselves and the ministers simply prayed. In Wales the miners would hurry from the coal faces to chapel where there were cries for mercy, songs of deliverance, testimony, tears, hearts poured out in praise and great love.

We needed that. Our large meetings, which were now mainly in Northampton, had lost something of their spontaneity. Now we found that prayers, confessions and simple testimonies carried power. There was a renewed emphasis on the blood of Jesus. We were inspired afresh to proclaim the sinner's gospel, to concentrate on Calvary and trust that a heart for community would arise from deep repentance. Along with our twelve verse hymns on the ways of God and of Zion, we now sang two-line songs on the name and blood of Jesus.

As one meeting drew to a close we sang of the departed saints: 'Come let us join our friends above.' It was very moving but seemed strangely out of the flow. Two days later a brother was killed on his motorbike. It had been his last hymn on earth.

As eternity drew close again, we started revival meetings in Northampton. 'Can you determine when you die?' asked Noel. 'Then let us live for God now rather than for this passing world.' Friends had already died through accident or drugs. We felt we had failed them. The stakes were high, and the young evangelists longed to snatch people out of the fire.

These Northampton meetings ran four nights a week in a small dusty hall above the Co-op. They were serious but not glorious. A local pub lost two regulars and a brick was thrown through the Goodness Foods window. However, a fresh vision for Northampton had arisen, an evangelism team was meeting success there, and many of us now went on the streets.

My little team inadvertently evangelised a local reporter and the teachers at my school had a great laugh as they read about our exploits in the press. The 'anti-Bugbrooke' tape that had been circulated was also local news. Northampton's main youth leader, the Rev Harry Whittaker, sprang to our defence, but the local Archdeacon launched into the attack. One local ecumenical leaders' meeting was taken up with discussions about 'Bugbrooke'.

By April the work in Northampton and Rugby had received considerable impetus, although our expectations of local revival were disappointed. The pattern resumed and notice sheets reappeared. We organised a nurture group for the converts, but they were few.

Most of the fruit was within the Fellowship. Houses were revived, children and teenagers were touched and many found new liberty. Inevitably, the phase of repentance was difficult for some. A few left. Others had to be encouraged not to overdo the groans, sackcloth and ashes! But all in all, the church had been shaken up and the dams were breaking down.

The vision now was for church growth and revival. God-consciousness had been restored and prayer increased. Shepherding groups were further broken down into cell groups of five or six and their emphasis shifted from shepherding to outreach and serving others. All over the Midlands we visited people in their homes and welcomed them into these little 'servant groups', as we called them.

Birmingham, Rugby and Milton Keynes were opening up for us. There were now many cell group leaders, and some brothers also began to lead Sunday gospel meetings in Warwickshire, Leicester and Birmingham. There was more scope for ministry and many of us felt we were getting our teeth into something.

By August we had bought Dayspring in Northampton and Plough Hall Farm in Warwickshire with 120 acres of pasture. Fruit-picking, potato-harvesting, gooseberry-grading, and straw-carting now occupied much of our spare time. We enjoyed it and whistled 'Happy the days in Zion's fields'.

As the year progressed, we were increasingly active in farm work, business and drives towards church growth and evangelism. Lethargy was knocked on the head, and rusty disciple bands were galvanised into action. The good old days of community lounging were over and the church lumbered into widespread evangelism. We sang a Moravian hymn.

> The love of Christ their hearts constrain,
>   And strengthens now their busy hands.
> They spend their blood and sweat and pains
>   To cultivate Emmanuel's lands.

Some of us looked aghast. It was all toil, strife, labour, industry, prayer and burning zeal! 'If you're not Evan

Roberts, you're backslidden!' grumbled one farm brother. As Noel blasted passivity, Zion's dreamers groaned. We were not out of the woods yet. Throughout the church, those who had sat through the repentance time untouched or even cynical, continued deaf to this new call to action.

At the Farm, the 'brotherhood' was at times more natural than spiritual. Cattle-men reacted against the thought of 'more pressure' and some wondered whether it was all worth it. But Noel upheld the vision and refused to lessen our standards of diligence and holiness.

When Kelly lunched at the Farm, he was at times sandwiched between an overburdened pastor and a discouraged brotherhood. Noel needed support, especially in the face of all the criticism from outside. 'No man can take the strain alone and remain inspired,' thought Kelly and urged Noel to lean more on other senior brothers. In July a group of seven were recognised as a 'Covering Authority'.

The spiritual battle was fierce all round, and not just at the Farm. It was the price of moving against the tide. Sniping came from within our own ranks and some of our outside supporters tended to draw back in the face of the constant criticism we received. How long could we go on pioneering?

Many were burdened in prayer. Val would often cry out to God and at times all she could get out was, 'Oh God, save our church!' and then just tears and speaking in tongues.

'The powers of darkness were doing their utmost to destroy us,' she later wrote. 'Our witness was vital and I prayed for our leaders to be men of strength and unity. I was burdened for the state of the nation, and for Zion that she might stand. The future for us and for our children was at stake.'

Mobilising a community of 600 was no mean task and many had settled down. Noel continued to exhort and motivate us fearlessly. At times he roared on the platform and purred at home. At others he purred on the platform and roared at home! Paul's directions were to 'encourage and rebuke with all authority' (Tit 2:15) and to 'help the weak and be patient with everyone' (1 Thess 5:14). The balance between prophetic ministry and the shepherd's heart can be difficult to find!

Whilst some of our leaders were too fond of the rule book and needed bigger hearts, others were all for joy and liberty but needed the balance of holy discipline.

A few felt that Noel's strong ministry was alienating those it sought to reach. Some reacted angrily to his renewed call to 'blood, sweat and tears', and spoke of the need for 'grace'. Noel caught the critical darts, sharpened them, and flung them back in the form of two new hymns:

> I speak of grace to suit my state
> Of natural soul desire.
> 'It's all of grace', I restful cry,
> 'Relaxing' in self's mire!
>
> 'Holy by faith' my nature says,
> 'I need not will at all!..'

The lawless trend needed purging, and after twelve verses of pungent irony, anyone who was into being 'laid back' felt pretty uncomfortable!

Reflecting on this time, Val wrote: 'Often I felt tearfully grateful for Noel, because no matter how imperfect he may have been, he was so devoted. Sometimes it seemed there might be a split between the staunch-discipline, and the grace-allow-people-freedom-to-move leaders. When it came to it, I knew God would always honour loyalty and covenant.'

At the elders' meeting Noel dealt with the critics, and applied the Scripture: 'Those [elders] who sin are to be rebuked publicly, so that the others may take warning' (1 Tim 5:20). It did the trick. The advocates of 'cheap grace' saw the dangers, were humbled, and opened up to conviction.

Noel's ministry now became more visionary. One morning he spoke on identification with Christ in suffering and read accounts of some of the martyrs. 'We will bear reproach,' he said. 'We will never turn back. We will fight and endure hardness. We will win through, whatever the cost!'

I looked at him. He could be stern and perfectionist, but he was an inspiring leader. Not one public meeting had he missed for years. Through sickness and loneliness, through opposition and disloyalty, he had endured. He stood rocklike, visionary and devoted, knowing well that the tide in Britain could only be turned by sacrifice and guts.

At school, I'd been showing videos on the Second World War:

'We shall not fail, nor falter. We shall not weaken or tire. ... Give us the tools and we will finish the job!' That was Churchill. We too were fighting a battle. It was hymn-worthy. We were a people 'adorned with grace and crowned with thorns':

> Despised below, yet loved above,
>   Companions of those men of love
> Who for the truth of Christ laid down
>   Their lives, and gained the martyr's crown.

We began to take persecution more in our stride. It was obviously going to be our lot so we might as well 'rejoice and be glad', and carry on pioneering.

There had been losses. One farm brother who split off became a vociferous opponent. Three or four junior leaders also left us. Even John 'Gentle' had gone off for a breather in Switzerland, though he later returned to us.

The battle had been fierce but God had often given us this word from Isaiah: 'Your builders outstrip your destroyers' (Is 49:17, RSV). Loyalty had won through. Characters were strengthened and roots went deeper. We were a humbler people. Stories of rapid church growth in the third world both shamed and inspired us. We listened to our critics more and opened up to new input.

There were others who shared our ideals. Simple lifestyle was a current theme in Christian circles, and community itself was still attracting interest. In fact, David Watson was about to write warmly in *You Are My God* of his own experience of community and the common purse.[72]

We had, of course, much in common with the 'new churches', and amongst the more radical groups, covenant commitment was being emphasised. In *Restoration* magazine David Matthew likened the radical church to Elijah, with his separated life, unusual appearance and prophetic unction from God. 'Just so, believers today are beginning to live together...in redeemed communities, partaking of a whole new kingdom culture...'[73]

Perhaps we had been treated rather like Elijah. Certainly we had been regarded as 'troublers of Israel' and hounded by a few Jezebels! But we felt we had pulled through. The church had been ploughed up, and now the storms and trials of the early eighties were bearing fruit. God was calling us onward.

18

Visions

1983

> The more I see Christians learning to share their lives, their possessions, and their homes, the more I am convinced that we are coming home to Zion.
>
> Dave Tomlinson, 1982[74]

By the spring of 1983 we had turned a corner. Links with other church communities grew and visitors, ranging from charismatic Catholics to modern Hutterites, came from as far afield as France, Spain and Norway. With all the foreign visitors around, the Farm lunch began to look like the United Nations!

It was a sunny morning in May when Pete the Dutch medic and I took some visitors from Holland on a whistle–stop tour around the community.

A tractor hurtled towards us and screeched to a halt. Pete

'Valiant' edged our minibus past it up the drive at New Creation Farm and waved at Steve 'Stalwart', who was straightening out the railings from a previous encounter! A few sheep turned their heads as Pete changed gear. Passing the gooseberry bushes and apple trees on the right, he parked outside the farm shop.

'Right! Everybody out!' said Pete.

'Hello there!' A lean beekeeper sauntered by and lifted the net from off his face. It was Dave Lants. 'Welcome to the farm. You will have to excuse the smell of pigs!'

As we chatted, an older man stepped out of the farmhouse, dressed in a tatty sports jacket and cap. He beamed benignly and slapped me on the shoulders, 'Bless you, 'Overcomer'! All right?' But before I could answer he had gone.

'Who's that?' enquired Henk, 'The farm manager?'

'Yes,' I said, 'he's also our senior pastor!'

'Really?' said Henk, as we walked into the pig shed.

'Yes,' I shouted above the squeal of piglets, 'I don't know how he does it all.'

''Ow do!' the pig-man nodded, sipping tea from a tin mug. 'Ian 'Honest'!' I said. 'Tell us a bit about these pigs.' Ian stood chatting to us all for a while, and Anneke, a town girl, was fascinated.

'Hey chaps!' said Pete, 'let's keep moving! There's lots to see'.

'Mind the puddle, bro!' he said, as we walked past the muck-heap towards the chicken huts. After visiting the egg-grading shed and the honey room, we walked through the orchard and then piled back into the minibus.

Soon we jumped out at New Creation Hall. 'This is the first big house the Lord gave us,' I said proudly as we stepped inside. JESUS CHRIST IS LORD! The poster in the hallway told you this was no ordinary mansion. The Hall was looking quite respectable now, and Kelly's trenches were a nostalgic memory. On the walls there were paintings and embroideries quoting hymns or Scriptures. We admired one of the pictures, which showed a group of brothers relaxing together.

'Do you get much time to do that?' asked Henk.

'A bit,' said Pete. 'We all work, either in the community or outside, but the evening meal is important for fellowship. The evenings vary: Monday is generally free, unless you're some kind of leader. Tuesday is our covenant Agape meal. On Wednesdays the servant groups zoom all over the Midlands meeting people, and on Thursdays we relax. Some people go evangelising on Friday night, often very late.

'What about weekends?' asked Henk.

'Busy! Most of us usually work around the house on Saturday morning or sometimes at the farm. The afternoon is normally relaxed and we often take visitors round the community. In the evening we either have full church meetings or house groups. On Sunday we have the main meeting of worship in which we share the bread and wine and Noel gives some teaching. After that we invite everybody back to the community houses for a late lunch and an afternoon of fellowship. The evening is for gospel meetings in various parts of the Midlands.'

'A full life!' said Henk, walking into the Quiet Room.

'Your house is with the books filled up,' said Anneke. (Her English wasn't up to Henk's.)

'Afraid so!' I said. 'The library has thousands of them – mostly Christian paperbacks – and we also have a reference section next door on church history, theology, community...'

'The Hall is quite a centre,' said Pete, 'what with the library, the clothing store, the pre-school, the laundrette, and the FDC.

'The FDC?' Anneke looked puzzled.

'We'll show you,' he said, leading them into the courtyard. In front of the converted stable block a man with snow in his hair struggled by with some boxes of frozen meat.

'Hi, Steve!'

'Bless you! Bit cold for May, isn't it?' (He'd just come out of the freezer van!)

'Steve was training to be a vicar,' I explained, 'but joined us instead. He now runs the FDC – the Food Distribution Centre.'

'More like Stephen the deacon, eh?' said Henk.

'That's right!' said Steve. 'Except the stuff we distribute is from manufacturers and wholesalers!'

'How does it work?' asked Henk.

'Well, each house sends us an order for food, clothing and household needs, along with a cheque for the previous week. We try to keep things simple, and supply what's needed...as long as the orders get in on time!'

Steve disappeared into the store room.

'He's busy! Upstairs is the pre-school,' I pointed. 'It's for three to five year olds. Notice the cardboard tractor in the window?'

'Right, chaps!' said Pete. We clambered aboard and headed for the A5. 'There's Honeycomb Grange ahead!' he said, as we sped past the cattleyard at Shalom Farmhouse.

'Sheepfold, Vineyard, and Praise Court are up on the left – Cornhill and Festal are back up the A5 – and Highway House and Living Stones are coming up!

'How much houses are you now having?' Anneke asked.

'Well, there are two more in Northampton, one in Daventry, four in Warwickshire, and one in Leicester...'

'That's ours!' I said, as a yellow tipper went past. 'The driver used to be a guitar-teacher!'

'There's Weedon shop on the left,' said Pete. The visitors just caught sight of a GOODNESS FOODS sign. 'They sell health foods and our bread and farm produce.'

At Daventry we turned into the garage. Outside was a plumber's van with SKAINO SERVICES on the side.

Anneke frowned. 'Skaino is a funny name.'

'It's from the Greek for tentmaking,' I said. 'It was Paul's trade which met his needs but left him free for ministry.'

'Once our businesses are established, we intend to release people regularly for evangelism,' added Pete.

We walked in and stepped over a pair of oily legs.

'Pete "Upright"!'

'Umm?'

'Bless you! He'll soon get that on the road,' I said.

'Hopefully, bro!' answered a muffled voice. We just had time to watch Alan's old busker-friend respraying a car, then Pete urged us on.

'Time for Goodness Foods, chaps!'

The lightning tour continued as we stepped into the warehouse.

'Here comes Mike 'Rockfast'! He runs just about everything in this community!' I joked.

'Not quite, bro!' answered Mike in his quiet, unruffled way.

'Actually, I'm the treasurer of the Community Trust and general manager of House of Goodness Group.

'It all seems very organised,' said Henk.

'Thanks. It needs to – it's all the Lord's money.'

'But how have the businesses grown so big?'

'Well, Goodness Foods started in 1976 when we opened a shop in Northampton. Then we expanded slowly to include shops in Daventry, Towcester and Weedon. In 1980 we took over a village bakery. All this was our cottage industry phase really.'

'It's more than that now!'

'Yes. We began wholesaling from this warehouse in 1981. When we started delivering all round the country it really took off. We've also opened shops in the larger local towns – Leamington, Bletchley, Rugby, and Leicester.'

'And what of Skaino and the builders' merchants?'

The phone rang. 'Excuse me a moment...'

'Yes, earlier this year Skaino Services moved into Unit 14 just down the road. The building side began at New Creation Hall back in 1974, and the garage started in the old stable block there. We launched the road haulage with an old lorry that came with the farm.

TBS began in a builders' yard at Towcester mainly to supply our own team, but it was popular with the locals and has now become quite profitable. They've opened another branch in the warehouse next to ours. We've now appointed executives to manage Goodness Foods, Skaino and TBS more efficiently.'

'Do you pay them differently?' asked Henk.

'Oh no,' said Mike, 'We pay the same level of wage to everyone.

'Then where goes this wage'? Anneke chipped in.

Mike smiled.

'Well, we put it into our house's common purse.'

'And how many work for the community?' said Henk.

'About 150 are in kingdom businesses now.'

'Kingdom businesses?'

'Well, it's all part of kingdom life. It was inevitable that the vision of being a 'kingdom people' would affect our everyday work-life. Businesses support our ministries and provide an atmosphere of discipleship.'

'Yes, it's all one, isn't it?' I chipped in. 'Praying or cooking; evangelising or mucking out the pigs! We're God's people. That's what counts – living for him and displaying his righteousness and love. People may not see the invisible God, but maybe they'll see his city on a hill.'

'That's right, chaps!' said Pete, slapping Henk on the back.

'Apart from which – it's time for lunch!'

As the summer of 1983 approached, everyone was looking outwards. The central ground had been strengthened and many desired to reach out and plant elsewhere. Church growth was vital and we were inspired by Yonggi Cho's 500,000-strong church in Korea. His input of faith, vision and prayer targets came at the right time.

We had heard of other communities hitting bad patches and then losing direction. But as we pressed through, a sense of destiny returned with force. God had shaken us and given us a new vision. Britain was our parish, and our dream was now for revival and church growth.

The push was on for 200 servant groups – a hundred per

cent increase! We visualised them, prayed for them and believed for them. We even sang about them! 'Two hundred servant groups we claim for needy souls in Jesu's name!'

We preached the good news. At one time our message had centred on holiness and 'kingdom lifestyle'. Now, after the trials of recent years, God had pointed us back to the basics – the blood of the Lamb and the love of God. Many found a renewed compassion for the sinful and broken-hearted. 'Feel the flow of Jesu's blood,' we sang tenderly, as all around us we saw a desperate need for the healing touch of God.

God gave us a tremendous inspiration to penetrate the inner cities. Our evangelists in Birmingham were on fire and became examples to the rest of us. They reached glue sniffers, pimps and prostitutes. They often prayed with people on the streets. They were the heroes!

By May we had established Anchorage, a large house in Handsworth, Birmingham. Some moved up to form the new house and Kelly led a church-planting team there for a week to boost the work. God had given us a strong vision for a multiracial church. The team befriended some of the blacks and Asians and soon a converted Sikh girl had joined them.

We were pioneering in other towns too. My own servant group went to Banbury. There we were welcomed by a Christian family, and some of the neighbours were interested. Soon our cell group divided, other groups joined us there, and we had a number of non-resident members.

We began Friday night evangelism on the streets of Banbury, and made friends with some bikers. The sister of one of the bikers found God and was delivered from demons. The bikers were impressed.

I visited them on Saturdays and was introduced to a world of heavy metal, patchouli oil, Newcastle Brown and do-it-yourself tattooing. One wiry lad looked me in the eyes. 'I've just put someone in hospital,' he said, as Iron Maiden throbbed in my eardrums. I felt a long way from home and wondered whether evangelism was really my scene.

I began to write songs for our servant group. The atmosphere of worship and friendship attracted folk and they sensed the presence of God as we prayed with them and sang and spoke of Jesus. We also taught from the Bible, enthused about community, chatted, and passed round the tea and biscuits.

Most groups had targets: Mary to be saved this month; Wayne to be healed; Sally to get a job next week, or Olly to come off booze. Servant groups believed for disciples to join them and households began Covenant Classes for new converts to cover basic teaching and practice.

Our press files for 1983 were all but empty, as we kept a low profile. Noel stopped leading us all on large campaigns in the Midlands. Outreach was personal and grass roots, and we encouraged people who were interested to visit our homes and come to our various Saturday house-meetings. These smaller meetings encouraged expression, and many more of us were actively involved in ministry.

As for Sunday meetings, there was some flexibility as to where we went. A sister from the Hall might travel to the meeting in Leicester because she supported the evangelism there. Many carried particular vision: a 'heart for Birmingham' or 'faith for the skinheads.' With a breakdown of a hundred servant groups, twenty-eight households and four Sunday night meetings, there was scope.

However, the concept of the church 'household' as a distinct unit sharpened up. The church 'household' was a community house family, plus its non-resident members and friends. This increased the sense of belonging and households began to function like little churches. They were expected to grow, divide, and plant elsewhere. At the Farm and Cornhill the larger family sometimes functioned as two households with their own separate meetings, whilst at the Hall, one household focused on evangelism in Banbury, the other in Kettering.

Many were going out in evangelism teams and sang on the streets, whether at Birmingham New Street Station,

Northampton town centre, or Banbury market square. Some were bolder and disappeared into pubs and clubs, whilst others interceded on the spot or stayed home to welcome people back.

Sisters were good front-line evangelists with a heart for sinners – at times a weeping heart. Lesley, who was one such evangelist in Leicester, was a keen celibate. 'Celibacy!' she said, 'I love it! Jesus said, "Seek first the kingdom". I made a pact with God and expected him to meet my needs. Celibacy is like getting into a new car. The sun is shining, God is with you, and you can explore. I gained many hearts because I spent time with people. One girl went through cold turkey – all night. I was exhausted, but she came through.'

Lisa, one of the young sisters at Living Stones, had grown up in Bugbrooke. 'Celibacy is natural and normal,' she wrote. 'Jesus oozed warm humanity. He was so tender, secure and so very liberated that he attracted the common folk. That's my vision.'

More sisters joined the growing number of celibates at this time. We were increasingly aware now of the brothers and sisters who had chosen celibacy and sought to encourage them at special celibate gatherings.

As we became more outgoing sisters began to modify their appearance. They still had long hair and no make-up, but their clothes began to look a bit more fashionable. The meek and quiet spirit was still their vision (in the main) but sisters became increasingly dynamic.

With the fresh thrust in 'friendship evangelism', servant groups were breaking new ground. One group met in a caravan in Coventry. A gypsy had turned up at Promise House thinking it was the doctor's and was pleasantly surprised to hear the sound of Christians singing! Dai invited them to the site and some of the gypsies were converted. Florrie was a real Romany – headscarf, rings and all – and she soon joined us. Tarzan was another gypsy friend.

'How's Tarzan doing?' someone asked.

'A bit up and down!' replied Piers.

There was also a renewed emphasis on intercession. Like the Moravians of old, and Yonggi Cho's church in Korea, we organised a 'prayer watch', aiming for a continuous chain of prayer. (Some gaps in the night were hard to fill!) Many spent an hour a week interceding for the church and its work. Each household had a co-ordinator and requests were fed into the chain at any time. A friend might be seriously ill, a new convert struggling, or an evangelist in a tight spot. Someone, somewhere, would lift the need to God.

The whole Fellowship was mobilised, now, as never before and God was taking us into a new phase of our calling. Our servant group overseer in Birmingham became very interested in William Booth and the Salvation Army. His lamp burned into the night as he explored, read and enthused. Books flew from second-hand shops to Anchorage, and sometimes down to New Creation Farm. Noel read again of Booth and his Army. They knew the power of God! They were persecuted! They loved holiness! They reached the masses!

When we prepared a guide for servant group leaders the General was quoted: 'Give me godly, go-ahead dare-devils, and anybody can have the preachers!' We sympathised with the vision and spirit of the early Salvation Army, and their all-out offensive to rescue the sinful. This was our dream. We, too, needed to be a strong, organised and fearless army of the Lord.

As evangelism team leaders met to discuss strategy, bring reports and inspire one another, town plans and maps of Britain began to appear on our walls. It looked as though the city on a hill was becoming an army on the move.

On the March
1984–1988

19
Jesus 84
1984

'Hey! You guys some bunch of dudes, or sommat?'

We carried on singing, and watched the trouble brewing. A black lad was being hassled, so we walked over and surrounded them. Did we start fighting? No! Singing! Singing about Jesus.

'Hey! C'mon, leave off, man! This nice guy owes me some notes, yeah, and he's gonna be all right see! He's just gonna hand me the notes.' The guy was skint.

We talked to them about Jesus. They weren't interested. Christianity was 'no go.' It didn't work. They were black in a white world. They were resentful and frustrated. Ten thousand words about Jesus wouldn't have made a scrap of difference. They were £15 short. Nothing had been given them but hurts. There was no way they'd forgive this man his debt.

'We'll pay it for him!' We offered them the money.

'Hey, you guys really are a bunch of nutcases. Look, this guy owes and this guy is gonna pay, right!'

'We want to pay it for him. No strings attached.

'Just like Jesus paid our debt,' someone added.

They took the money. They knew we were different. Our words didn't get through. Our actions did.[75]

It was spring 1984. This story was printed in *Jesus People Lifenews*. We were in Milton Keynes, visiting pubs and singing in the shopping centre. The hassler, Nathan, was a black street kid and he came to the Lord. He backslid in detention centre, but the Farm prayed for him, wrote to him, visited him, and he came through. They won his heart.

Who were the Jesus People? The Bugbrooke freaks, of course! Over a decade had passed since we had first been given the name – and it had stuck. Early believers were 'Christ-ians!' Wesley's folk were called 'Methodists!' (and got pelted with rocks and rotten eggs!). We were Jesus People. It was a good name, and we were proud to have it. *Lifenews* was our new evangelistic paper and contained many of our people's stories.

Our outreach was continuing along the lines of friendship-evangelism and church building. We looked for those with an eagerness for discipleship and began to expect the supernatural to follow kingdom proclamation. But we were now entering a new phase as the 'Jesus People' went high profile with stickers, banners, tracts, hand-outs, newspapers, discreet metal badges and not-so-discreet plastic ones.

'This is where I came in!' some of us thought.

'Jesus phones' were set aside in some houses for those seeking help or information. Gold labels adorned our free literature with the slogan *JESUS 84 – God Loves To Save Us!* There were Jesus People colours too: blue (for heaven), gold (for God's glory), and white (for purity), with a red cross. We also bought a coach, turned some of the seats round, added drop-leaf tables, built in a kitchen, and hung curtains. 'Crusader' was painted in blue, white and gold, and on the side, in yellow letters, was *JESUS 84*. Soon we added a smaller bus. Crusader 2 gleamed, but the respray was deceptive – the suspension had died years ago!

This was a campaign with maps and battle plans. Central England was divided into nine areas from Stoke to Oxford. Each had two evangelism leaders, and from spring on ('when kings go out to war') we concentrated on a different area each month, praying for it and joining evangelism forces there.

We targeted for two hundred new members. Many contacted in 1983 now wanted baptism, and there were more converts in 1984. Two hundred committed prayer-watchers helped to fight the battle and they sent in reports to the weekly prayer-letter:

– Prayed for Gill to get a council flat. She did.

– Expecting the Lord to change my boss!

– Prayed for Hannah's meningitis. 100% healing in two weeks

– Since the prayer watch, my insomnia has been healed.

– Finding a new walk with God through this praying.

As *Jesus 84* took off, we hit the press. The *Northampton Mercury and Herald* featured our *Lifenews* paper. HOMESPUN MIRACLES! was their caption, and a photo showed our headlines: GOD LOVES US ALL – HEROIN ADDICT FINDS CURE IN JESUS.

'God healed me of addiction,' wrote Jamie. 'Mind you, life hasn't been a bed of roses since!'

RACISM IS ABOLISHED! was another caption, under which Nathan and a white brother grinned contentedly at the general public.

'Miracles, healing, supernatural experiences, and speaking in tongues – its all part of daily life for the Jesus People of Bugbrooke,' proclaimed the *Mercury*[76].

People had been healed physically but also emotionally from the pains of broken marriages, loneliness and rejection. 'Jesus comes with good news for the poor,' we sang, and other songs began to pour out identifying with people's heartbreak and their need for God's love. Guitars appeared in public again and some of us led songs from the platform. Even Noel wrote lyrics. When twenty songs appeared on the notice sheet it was fun guessing who wrote which!

We launched into praise. Tambourines and banjos were effective for street singing and violins, trumpets, and recorders were also heard (in moderation).

'Shout! O shout! O shout for joy!' we sang. (And was that Rufus back on the bongos?)

'Yes, we'll celebrate Jesus, we'll shout and cheer and sing!' (What! The Jesus Fellowship cheering and shouting?) We loosened up after years of deep, serious community, helped on by songs from *Mission Praise*.

Other radical churches evangelised in earnest around this time. Andrew Walker remarked, 'This first organised assault by the "restored kingdom" upon the secular world was begun only when leaders felt that the kingdom base was now secured.'[77]

Our base was community. Zion was the rock, the central ground, the pearl. Evangelism was exciting, but as one evangelist sang:

> My heart is held and planted in Zion;
>   And world and death and sorrow
> Can never part this bond we have.

Sinners were coming home to Zion and the Jesus People were breaking out! But not without reverence for all God had shown us. Zion, her ways, her very dust and stones, were still our 'joy and crown'.

The results of the new thrust in evangelism were encouraging and of our target for 200 people that year, we gained 175. Joining the Jesus People, even as a non-resident, was quite a turnabout. It was 'the world behind me, the cross before me'. Nurture was all-important, and those baptised entered into covenant, pledging loyalty to Jesus and the brotherhood. Covenant classes extended before and after baptism, and members were expected to be at the meetings, especially the weekly Agape.

Fellowship houses were the focus of our work, though in Oxford and Banbury, where houses were not established, we shared the Agape meal in our non-residents' homes.

Not everyone was ready for residential community. Indeed, for some families and those with unconverted partners it was impossible. Some would be unable to give the practical commitment essential to community living, but we did expect them to carry the Zion vision.

Many did to a high degree, and some of our deepest prophetic wisdom came from non-residents, who were often very grateful for what those in the community houses easily took for granted. They were frequently around, stayed overnight, were active on the prayer watch, and used the Food Distribution Centre. They carried a vision for their neighbourhood, and opened their homes to us. Non-residents were vital.

All new members belonged to a servant group and a discipling band, as well as having a shepherd and a 'caring brother' or sister. They were 'bone of our bone' and part of our 'family'. A smaller proportion fell away than is normal with more impersonal big mission evangelism. After a year some twenty per cent of our new members were not actively with us. Even that was heartbreaking.

We pushed further afield. Stoke was our northern frontier, and Mick 'Temperate' visited two friends there, Pete and John, who had 'split' from New Creation Hall some years ago. Pete's mother hadn't slept properly for two years, but after they prayed, she overslept and was late for work the next morning! Soon Mick had a coach team in Stoke where they met one of John's friends. He sat in the meeting and, when the call to Christ was made, he felt someone jabbing him in the back. He turned round, but no one was there! He was converted that night.

Roy and Maggie encountered the supernatural, too. Roy had been a Christian for twenty years, but felt dry. What's more, he didn't believe in miracles – until he met someone who radiated life and spoke in tongues. He welcomed Mick's servant group to Stoke and was filled with the Spirit. But days later he keeled over and was rushed to hospital with a collapsed lung. They discovered a blood clot.

Roy was in a bad way, so Maggie rang her friends and alerted the prayer watch. In a couple of days he was sitting up in bed and grinning at the doctor. The X-rays and tests showed perfect blood and his high blood pressure had disappeared.

Soon there were four servant groups in Stoke. The local Teen Challenge used our *Lifenews*, but a pentecostal deputation warned them against our 'heretical' practices. We carried on undeterred and John's little house in Stoke soon became a sanctuary of friendship, praise and chip-butties.

In May we established the 'Eagles Wings' household at Milton Keynes. Apart from the lovely gardens, the house had gold plated taps in the bathroom and goldfish in the pond! The following month we bought another substantial property, 'Firstfruits', in Nottingham.

Servant groups extended our work. 'Search groups' roamed free and 'Strike groups' aimed at distant towns. We followed any lead. One day two of the Farm teenagers vanished with a tent and were soon relaxing with their ice creams on the east coast. Eventually some brothers came to collect them, but on the way home they had a clear prompting to evangelise in Yarmouth. As a result, two people showed interest and the next week there were three more. All these were converted and began to visit the Farm. Thus was born the Yarmouth household.

One team went to the Glastonbury Festival and pitched their tents. As the heavy rock pounded day and night, they moved amongst crowds, chatting with people and sharing the gospel. A Christian lady who lived nearby met them while she was walking her dog. She thought they were marvellous, and opened her home to them. On the last day she gave a farewell buffet where Jesus People, punks and freaks were served cakes, trifles and strawberries by a team of genteel Anglican ladies!

In Birmingham there were plenty of stories and unusual encounters. One was reported in *Lifenews*:

> It was an ordinary flat, but the couple were not alone. Milk bottles would fly around the kitchen and there were knocking noises. The water heater and cooker would be turned on. An apparition was seen, and visitors were fearful. So we went to the flat and commanded the evil presence to leave in the name of Jesus. Now it's a place of peace.[78]

Birmingham was still central to our vision. We held missions in the city and in the autumn bought Cofton Hall, an historic mansion, which stood in fine grounds below the Lickey Hills. At 'Cornerstone' there were shades of the pioneering days at Bugbrooke. It was large, cold and empty, and needed a lot of repair. When Skaino Services got to work, the brothers had to sleep in the baronial hall with its old oak rafters and stone walls. The place was spooky – you half expected an ancient butler to come downstairs and croak, 'You rang, Sir?' But after they had all gone round the house shouting the name of Jesus, the atmosphere changed.

One person at Cornerstone saw an angel standing at her bedroom door. Another night, a new convert came home drunk and discouraged. 'God,' he said, 'if you're really there, why don't you make a tree fall down or something?'

The night was calm, but the next morning he wept when he saw a huge tree sprawled over the lawn.

In Birmingham they met homelessness, poverty, violence, addiction and loneliness. One woman, whom they were seeking to lead to Christ, died drunk in bed. They saw afresh, as Booth once did, how an army of Christians must arise to meet the need. The powers of darkness were rampant, the occult ran wild, and a great heartcry rose up from these inner cities. The evangelists wept at some of the things they saw.

They saw riots, race-hatred and unrest. We longed for a

multiracial church, and were saddened by our slowness to reach blacks. Maggie from Liberia was one who found our friendship. 'My life was very sinful,' she wrote in *Lifenews*, 'and I had reservations about a white church anyway. I made sure I was out when they called, but they caught me unawares! What really surprised me was that they didn't mind me being the only black. After that God worked in me, and I became like one of the gang. I knew I belonged.'[79]

In Britain the harvest was ripening. We spent eight months of mission work in central England, on top of a busy working week. 'God is keeping his soldiers fighting,' we sang from the Salvation Army song book, but with such a full programme and the huge increase in raw converts many of us were getting worn down.

Steve 'Genuine', the farm strong man and kiddies' hero, went through a crisis at this time. Once he had 'seen the kingdom', Steve had sacrificed his nice background, Christian ambition, and degree, for tractors, straw-carting, and cattle-rearing. He scorned false spirituality, but now had lost his inspiration. In his own words, he was 'the farm slob'. In frustration, he decided to 'split', but his mates pleaded with him, and he had a change of heart.

Steve began to pray a lot and often spoke at our informal Sunday night 'Lost Sheep' gatherings at Cornhill for the under-thirties. We were concerned for our own youth, some of whom were strongly attracted by the world. Some feared we might lose our second generation. Steve, for one, felt that unreality amongst us was to blame and he became increasingly burdened for the church.

Within two years our rather Hutteritish church-community had been transformed into an army of would-be evangelists. But, though we had almost reached our 200 target, many of us were jaded, drained and spiritually thirsty.

20

Fire! Fire! Fire!

1985

'What's got into Steve, Rufus?' Nathan scratched his head. 'He used to be one of the lads. Now he comes in from the yard and disappears up the attic. We never see him.'

'Yeah. He was an honest slob!' said Steve 'Zealous'. 'He's gone thoughtful like.'

'Yeah,' said Dave 'Forthright'. 'I found him in the orchard — just staring into the sunset.'

'In this weather?' growled 'Zealous'. 'He's losing his marbles!'

'He was in tears,' whispered 'Forthright'.

Nathan whistled. 'Man! He's sure got a serious dose of somethin'.'

'Bros! Don't you see?' said Rufus. 'He's in love.'

'What, again?' sighed 'Zealous', clutching his forehead.

'With God, with God!' Rufus beamed.

'Wow!' said Nathan.

'...You what?' said 'Forthright'.

Steve 'Genuine' had been keen to get married quickly.

'Bro,' said Rufus, 'you're becoming dynamic, and the teenagers respect you. Zion is in need right now. Why not put this off for six months? Let God really use you.'

'No way!' said Steve. But he was uneasy. His tough guy image was crumbling and he longed for God. Lukewarmness was around, and it was true – Zion was in need.

He spent hours sitting before God, and it wasn't long before his thoughts about marriage evaporated. God became his passion. God's presence was captivating, awesome, holy. 'Sometimes,' he said, 'a stillness came on me. The brothers called me for dinner but I couldn't move. I'd read how Evan Roberts would spend hours lost in God. That was how I felt. Then a burden for holiness came upon me.'

One evening the household went round claiming the power of the Blood of Jesus over the rooms at the Farm.

'Bro,' Steve said to Noel, 'what we really need is to get low before God. The church needs to regain its first love.'

'I knew this was God's word for us,' Steve said later. 'It burned in me day and night and I cried out amongst the cattle, "Lord restore your Zion!" I was jealous for God, and tired of our flippant ways.'

The flame spread and one of the farm teenagers burst into action. Steve 'Strengthener' and Steve 'Genuine' would pray together and were fearless in speaking out.

One night Rufus was leading the house meeting.

'Rufus, bro, you haven't got the word!' said Steve 'Genuine', as he stood up.

'Look, brethren, we've gotta stop grieving God. Where is his fear? Can't you see his judgements amongst us? Brethren, our God is a consuming fire. Look how Ezra felt: "O my God, I am too ashamed and disgraced to lift up my face to you" (Ezra 9:6). We ought to cry for mercy! We gotta let him plough us up! O God remove our reproach! God will make Zion beautiful again if we stop our arrogance and get low before him.'

FIRE! FIRE! FIRE!

Everyone went quiet as an awe settled on the room for what seemed like hours. All was still, apart from a few whispered prayers. Some fidgeted and couldn't handle the silence. Outside the cold wind blew up clouds of snow.

'Right!' said Steve. 'I'm going outside. I'm walking once round the lawn out front to show God I mean business. It's got to be everything, brethren! If you want to follow me, then you come – but make it real!'

One by one, they walked out into the snow. That night was a turning point. Rufus got fired up – praying, and fasting and going for long walks. He felt like he was married to God. 'It was like heaven!' said Rufus, 'But I couldn't convey the bliss I felt.'

Jess and the kids soon brought him down to earth!

In February we started Friday night revival gatherings in chapel. There was no formal leadership. We came in silently and prayed, and it was obvious who carried a real burden. Often it was sisters crying to God for their houses, and that meant a lot of pride-swallowing for leaders. Our eyes were opened to backsliding – rebellious kids, prayerlessness, shallow conversions, complainings, worldliness and lack of zeal. We confessed sins and pleaded for our households and businesses.

Rufus and the two Steves visited other houses, bringing the message of repentance. Sparks flew when a few elders resisted this input, but the revivalists were undeterred. Zion was going to be cleansed.

The tide began to turn. Some brothers were praying at Cornhill when, around two in the morning, Steve 'Genuine' broke into a chuckle. Then he laughed and laughed. The joy of the Lord came on them; the other Steve trembled and shook, and Rufus was prostrated and overcome.

Cornhill caught the fire, and when one of their sisters attended her disciple band at Vineyard the flame spread. It was electric. They prayed, wept and sang in tongues. Mike 'Rockfast' had found a breakthrough too and late that night came home to Vineyard with a sense of expectancy. He found the disciple band leader aglow, and, as others joined them they began to pray. When one sister entered the room she cried out because of the presence of God.

'Mike came up,' wrote one brother, 'and said, "Come down quick! The Lord's doing something." We rose and dressed, and found the sisters calling on God. I felt a flood of the Spirit and fell on my face. "Lord!" I cried, "I feel like Jonah who must be thrown overboard!" It felt like white light. Sin was instantly exposed and you either broke down or hardened up. My sins were so many I thought they would bring judgement on the house. We continued praying for hours, and one sister all night.'

The next evening after Agape, a sister wrote in her diary: 'We gathered as soon as possible. Even the children confessed their sins. The elders knelt in the middle and the children prayed over them...I feel different now and the joy of my salvation is returning.' She put down her diary and continued praying – in her sleep!

'That night,' wrote another, 'the Spirit kept rising within me. Tears came to my eyes and I got up to tell someone what was happening. Such gratitude was in my heart.'

Amazed, Mike surveyed his new household and wept for joy. 'Everything was topsy-turvy,' he wrote. 'Sisters carried the anointing and leaders were humbled. The issues of blessing and judgement became so real. Everything was transparent – it was marvellous! As we knelt, praying and weeping, and singing and rejoicing, I wished it would never end.'

There were similar stories in other houses. We virtually forgot evangelism, and people prayed in the morning, at work, after lunch, and at night – they prayed any time, any place. We duplicated accounts of past revival movements and circulated them around the houses. We saw a pattern in revivals, as hunger for God, repentance and brokenness were followed by the cleansing blood and the power of the Spirit.

An old revival song was popular at this time:

FIRE! FIRE! FIRE!

> Now the cleansing blood has reached me.
> Glory Glory to the Lamb!

We saw the power of the blood as never before. Revival was blood and fire! *Holy Fire* was the title of a book by Colin Urquhart,[80] whose community at The Hyde had also experienced God's awesome holiness. Fire was our watchword too.

By April many households were revived and love for Zion rekindled. Children responded well, as one mum from Eagles Wings recounted: 'Peter (8) felt water moving inside him and knew he was being filled with the Spirit. He prayed with James (6) and during Agape, Peter, James, and Rachel (11) were confessing their faults. Later I looked into the bedroom and they were on their knees, hymn book open. So I left them.'

During Easter week forty hours were given to prayer, and each house aimed for a corporate pentecost. 'Then Zion shall be holy ground,' wrote Noel, 'and the presence of God will convict sinners.' We daren't resume mission work till we had received the 'power from on high'. But not everyone had. There was still pride around and elders were amongst the worst offenders.

Noel spoke to the leaders from 1 Kings 13 on the man of God and the prophet of Bethel. The altar there had been given over to the worship of Baal, but the old prophet had said nothing. God sent a young man to prophesy against the altar, but out of jealousy the old prophet deceived him and he was killed. So, too, would pride in leadership destroy the anointed ones of God. When the ministry had finished many were prostrate or knelt and wept. That night God humbled us.

May Bank Holiday was scheduled for 'praise and pentecost' on the Hall lawn. When the day came, it rained and rained and rained. We sang 'Rain from heaven, fall', and laughed. God had done great things among us. We leapt and shouted and sang. Many testified at the microphone and one brother reminded us of how Elijah drenched the sacrifices before the fire of God fell.

Noel suggested we sing 'The Lord reigns'! We booed and clapped. Revival had done little for his corny humour. Verna played the organ under a wet towel and we sang, 'When I survey the wondrous cross'. Many knelt in the puddles as the tears mingled with the rain. That day everyone was soaked and the brothers went off with half the Hall's spare jeans!

Noel was ready for action. 'Faith works with God!' he wrote on the notice sheet. 'Faith carries the gospel of grace and sinks it in the souls of men. Faith is active courage, a flame of holy fire! Faith yearns, prays, receives. Faith blazes, glows, burns! Faith dares, fights, wins! It embraces every trial as a friend. Faith is visionary. It heals the sick, casts out demons, raises the dead! Faith sees the kingdom and will not rest until "Jerusalem is a praise in all the earth!"'

It was now June and all systems were go. Among us *Jesus 85* had been forecast as a year of Pentecost, Pioneering and Peoplehood. In *Jesus 84* we had been in large meetings most of the time. *Jesus 85* was to be grass-roots again. This meant pioneering evangelism from small teams and 'Spirit-anointed initiatives' which would operate on five levels.

First there were servant groups. We had 150 of them (not yet 200!) and the target was for one new member in each. 'Do you have the explosive power of Pentecost?' wrote Noel. 'Are you soul-winners?'

Second, Jesus Pilgrims would travel around for up to a week using a Jesus People caravan.

Third, Fire Teams would live in an area for two or three months to evangelise, gather or plant.

Fourth, Beachfire Teams would go out to the holiday resorts. 'The crowded beaches are fields white to harvest,' wrote Noel. 'Revival will see multitudes of young people saved. The need is immense and we want to get where they are.'

FIRE! FIRE! FIRE!

The fifth level of evangelism involved Jesus Marquee Missions in each of the areas where we were working. 'We are buying a marquee and we want it filled with sinners; a place of revival with many conversions and signs following.'

The Marquee Missions would be led by four special JET or Jesus Evangelism Teams which included healers, singers, and intercessors. Marquee meetings would run all week (apart from Agape night) with Noel leading on Saturdays and Wednesdays, and the other meetings taken by the JET teams. The preachers were Mick 'Temperate', Kelly, Pete Matt and Mark 'Strong', another main leader.

The Golden Marquee looked fit for a jousting tournament. It was in Jesus People colours: yellow and white stripes, with blue panels and red crosses. A large banner with ENGLAND FOR JESUS! rode the crest. At the entrance was WELCOME! GOD LOVES YOU POWERFULLY! while THERE IS POWER IN THE NAME OF JESUS! hung in red letters over the platform. The brother in charge had some experience with big tops and tent evangelism. John 'Fortitude' was huge, soft-spoken, and built like a tank. You didn't argue with him!

In Northampton, where the mission lasted three weeks, we began with a march. For old-timers, it was uncanny to be marching once again from Midsummer Meadow to All Saints. The early seventies freaks had become the Jesus People of the eighties. One hundred had become eight hundred, the boys were men, and the men were veterans. Kneeling at All Saints, we marvelled at God's mercy. There had been heartbreaks, but God had given us a second generation.

Our interest in revivals gave us a shot of old-time religion. We were a blood, fire, and hallelujah church and introduced kneeling benches at the front for the 'altar call'. The counselling room was abandoned and the action remained in the meeting. We painted a tea chest black, placed it up front and wrote SIN BIN in white letters. Night after night we emptied it of drugs, lighters, cigarettes, syringes, charms, studded jackets, records and earrings. John 'Fortitude' had a regular bonfire.

What with the brightly coloured Marquee, the march, daily street work, large badges, and three editions of *Lifenews*, we had well and truly hit town! Handouts invited folk to lunch and a team of catering sisters arose with endless supplies of filled rolls, teas and soup.

The late night spot attracted bikers, punks and drunks. While John 'Fortitude' kept a fatherly eye on things, time was spent making friendships and gaining trust. Then Kelly or Rufus might share at the microphone. Sisters sang moving solos or gave their testimonies. One brother touched many hearts with his folksy songs. 'Seek the mercy of God, my friend,' he sang gently, 'he has opened a door in Jesus.'

Visitors increased. There were conversions, healings and deliverances, and stories abounded in the daily *Marquee News*. Touches of God were many but often claims were too high and too soon. Testimonies were encouraging but miracles were few. And where was spontaneous revival?

The firebrands were disappointed and Steve was heartbroken. He had expected something more. But as he cried to God he took heart. This was but a beginning. The reviving work had begun 'at home' and was a preparation for something greater. A new wave would hit Britain, and the Jesus People would be amongst the front line.

Meanwhile, our burden was how to touch the heart of this generation, how to stem the flood of darkness in the land. 'As I marched through Northampton,' wrote one brother, 'I thought, "Imagine if all the Christians in this land stood for the Lord and marched on their town. What a revival of faith and holiness would follow!"'

In 1985 many Christians in the UK were stressing the urgent need for national repentance and there was a growing hunger for revival. But what were we looking for? Shouldn't the trumpet first sound in Zion? Indeed, one article in *Buzz* magazine spoke of the church 'spiralling into an abyss of worldliness,' and being 'guilty of a massive accom-

FIRE! FIRE! FIRE!

modation to the world'.[81] God was wanting to refine his people, and restore the purity of the church.

David Pawson was one among many who warned against the inadequacy of ventures like Billy Graham's Mission England. He insisted that the charismatic movement had come to prepare for greater things – the establishing of New Testament radicalism. The purpose of renewal was restoration of the church, holiness and national awakening.

Our July Church Week was in Northampton and once again we focused on Zion, the people of God. After that it was back to the mission field. The marquee moved to Milton Keynes. What a potential harvest amongst the aimless youth! But we needed 'on fire' youth to reach them. Our lads wanted something adventurous, and some were already on Beachfire in Yarmouth and Hastings. We sought to channel their youthful aggression against the devil. A meeting was held for under-thirties (plus a bit over) and Operation Mark was born. (Mark had been a zealous young disciple of Jesus.)

We printed leaflets:

OPERATION MARK!
A RESISTANCE MOVEMENT OF HOLY REBELS!
WANTED: 500 young men and women:

* committed to Jesus Christ
* alive with the enthusiasm of the Spirit
* ready to be Jesus commandos and fight the sins that are degrading the youth of England!

Our weapons were the love of Jesus and the word of God, and during marches the 'rebels' carried crosses and Bibles. REBEL FOR JESUS stickers appeared and the logo showed a figure with raised Bible and cross. Operation Mark 'rebels' promised to live for Jesus and be loyal disciples and inspired personalities. They were to accept trials and never give in, gain others for Christ, and actively witness to their faith.

Songs appeared: 'We are at war!' and, 'I'm revolting!'

Nathan put, 'I'm a rebel for Jesus, from head to toe!' to a rock tune! Some made waistcoats with a red cross and REBEL FOR JESUS on the back. Ian, the solicitor, was like Superman. When he got home from the office, he threw off his pinstripes, donned his 'rebel' waistcoat, and went out evangelising. One night, as he was talking to people in a pub, he began to feel very warm. Someone had set his waistcoat alight!

One young man turned up at New Creation Hall who fitted the bill exactly. He'd even been a soldier. Mark 'Warrior' was twenty-three, a muscle man and a rebel. He'd seen the world in the merchant navy and his arms were tattooed and scarred. As a biker he'd smashed a lot of shop windows in Huddersfield, fled the law and crashed his bike. He'd lived with the Hare Krishnas, and ended up in the Spanish Foreign Legion. He deserted, escaping in a yacht, but it ran aground, and he was caught, flogged, imprisoned, and put to hard labour under the scorching sun.

One day, in preparation for a ceremony at the Spanish prison, Mark climbed a roof to fix a statue of Christ on to the cross. Alone up there, the eyes of Jesus seemed to pierce his soul. 'I forgive you, Mark,' they were saying. He broke down and wept. On his prison bed, reading his Bible, the power of God came upon him and he was baptised in the Spirit. The Spanish officers were so shocked by the change that they offered him promotion! He declined, and was released from the Legion.

Mark arrived back in Huddersfield to find his family already converted. The parish church was good, but Mark felt like a caged lion. He wanted a twenty-four hour a day commitment. He considered Bible college or a monastery, but the church sent him down to us! Mark wasn't disappointed. He wrote later:

I walked into the Hall and the Spirit came on me again. I was on cloud nine for three weeks. They had a church gathering in a theatre and all I heard was Zion, Zion, Zion! But it was the brotherhood that really amazed me.

Simon came up and met my folks. We walked on the moors. He enthused about Operation Mark and offered me a place in the Banbury household. It was like a family to me. I was very excited with the kingdom of God and keen to learn, but I was hot-headed, too.

At one Banbury meeting, I prophesied.

'What did you think of that?' I asked.

'Not a lot,' Simon grunted.

I was so frustrated with him when I got home that I smashed the bedroom door down! But we had to laugh – lying there on the door was a convicting text: 'I can do all things through Christ who strengthens me!'

We were inspired by the New Testament image of the army of God. The apostle Paul expected his men to endure hardship and be fully committed. 'No-one serving as a soldier gets involved in civilian affairs,' he wrote to Timothy (2 Tim 2:4). The New Testament unveiled a spiritual war – on one side the kingdom of God – on the other, the world, the flesh and the devil.

'We are the Jesus Army' was splashed on *Marquee News*, and Operation Mark took the lead. At their 'War Council' they read the Salvation Army *Articles of War* and spoke of city invasions and dawn raids. We wanted a strong image and felt the church in Britain needed vigorous men on the front line.

More flak came our way as we took our Marquee over the Midlands. But, flak or not, the army of Jesus People marched on into 1986 with increasing determination.

21

When They Exclude You
1986

JESUS CULT – REV STANTON'S KINGDOM. That was us – according to a pamphlet that started to have a wide private circulation! This virulent little job carried allegations of heavy shepherding, deprived kids, infallible authority, legalism, empire building, world-hatred, recruitment and even forced labour. The authors twisted the truth until it was barely recognisable, and Noel in particular came under vicious personal attack.

Sadly, there was a ready market for sensational rumours, half-truths, and lies. What gave this pamphlet more credibility was that it was written by two ex-members, supposedly with 'inside knowledge'. But as Stanley Jebb had pointed out in *Renewal*, few churches would want to be judged by those who left them. The views of these brothers were particularly distorted. One elder who had left us received a copy and tore it up in disgust. Then he pieced it together and passed it on to us!

A group was formed to 'pray' against us, and they motivated a smear campaign. The 'Jesus Cult' pamphlet was distributed to ministers, relatives, new converts and the press. The Jesus Fellowship was discussed in churches, on radio, and even in *Woman* magazine! Letters flew around, and the media were fed with titbits.

The effect was poisonous, and suspicion spread like cancer. A Christian church had been reviled, and the name of Jesus dishonoured. New friends and converts stumbled as critics sought to turn away those whom we had led to Christ. We expected opposition, but this was shameful.

On December 24th the *Daily Star* accused us of denying our children the innocent joys of Christmas. Innocent joys! In fact, we had already scheduled December 26th as a special Children's Day. (The Hall kids enjoyed an outing to a wildlife park.) Many laughed at the press, and relatives and friends were often supportive of the Fellowship. In the school where I worked they respected us. (They said I had a 'calming influence' on the staff room!) However, many Christians seemed gullible.

Dave 'Resolute', our PR man, had a busy time. In 1986 we were embarking on a two year programme of 'explosive pioneering' all over England, evangelising and planting 'church households'. Noel had his hands full and Dave had the unenviable task of heading up a PR battle, answering the press and shuttling between leaders. Eventually we asked the Evangelical Alliance to stand with us publicly.

The Jesus Fellowship had joined the EA after Gilbert Kirby's visit in 1982. They regarded us as a controversial but doctrinally orthodox church. Not everyone agreed with us and some regarded 'community' as near heretical. Nonetheless they knew we were true evangelicals and the Alliance had welcomed us.

The EA suggested a meeting with our attackers, but we felt that unless they desired reconciliation, a meeting would achieve nothing. We were keen, though, to meet with responsible leaders and answer their questions. Dave corresponded with Clive Calver, the General Secretary of the Evangelical Alliance. In January 1986 Clive proposed a meeting of three of our leaders with some of the EA executive, and with leaders representing our opponents, to investigate 'the accusations made against the Fellowship...that these matters might be properly resolved'.

We arrived in London eager to clear our name, but the EA had been receiving complaining letters and phone calls and feelings were running high. Churches, it was rumoured, had even threatened to leave the Alliance if we remained. The EA were under pressure.

We had innocently expected the accusations to be dealt with, the vendetta exposed and our integrity upheld, but the matter of the accusations was dealt with quite briefly. However, a different issue of poor relationships with local churches was raised. The EA felt compelled to suggest that we resign on this issue.

We felt totally let down. As Noel wrote to the chairman: 'It was an unusual experience. It was like being condemned without trial.' Relating to other churches was scarcely the issue on which we had approached the EA. On that basis, we felt, many others could be disqualified from membership. Anyway, enforced resignation was an unusual way to strengthen relationships!

However, the EA prided itself on being an alliance of member churches at a local as well as a national level. In their view, the word 'alliance' hardly described our position. The Council sent Noel a letter assuring him that the question was not one of orthodoxy but of whether continued membership of the EA was desirable. On other matters they 'had no wish to sit in judgement'. It seemed as if they were washing their hands of us. A saddened Noel wrote back:

Is it not surprising that a saga, which began with our advis-

WHEN THEY EXCLUDE YOU

ing EA of a defamatory pamphlet and requesting their support, should end with the EA virtually dismissing us?...

The EA has found this church an embarrassment because of opposition we are attracting in our stand for scriptural holiness...The issues were:

1 Are the critics using lies, distortions, and unbalanced comment, and should they be reproved?
2 Is this smear campaign in the Spirit of Christ?

Our appeal for support had been rejected. It felt like being handed over to our 'crucifiers'. Once again we experienced pain and humiliation. But the path of suffering would lead on to fruitfulness.

And so, in 1986, the Jesus Fellowship Church resigned from the Evangelical Alliance. When *Buzz* magazine interviewed Clive Calver, he was conciliatory: 'We have encouraged the Jesus Fellowship to develop links with other Christians. There were no doctrinal grounds for the EA's decision.'[82] The EA recognised us officially as a 'genuine Christian church'.

In April *Buzz* produced an article: 'Bugbrooke: Cultic or Christlike?' which in places was quite positive and included testimonies from our own people:

> The Bugbrooke community have faced accusations of breaking up families...and aggressive authoritarianism...No evidence has been put forward to substantiate these claims...Theologically they appear as sound as a bell...No other group of Christians has been at the blunt end of so much criticism, lies, scandal, accusations, and suspicion as the Jesus Fellowship. On the other hand there are numerous Christians from house fellowships and other denominations who have visited and gained a very favourable impression of the Jesus People.[83]

Buzz quoted a local vicar: 'I see nothing less than God's love among them flowing from a radical discipleship which is a reproach to most of us.'

'They are a Christ-centred group,' added one elder from

the Bethany Fellowship, whilst the local Baptist youth leader, Harry Whittaker, felt: 'We ought to be glad about Bugbrooke when so many churches are dead.'

But the Baptist Union officials were also becoming keen to lose us. There were complaints, letters and gossip, apart from which, we appeared to have gone national. The Jesus Fellowship had spread out in its church-planting activity and, in some ministers' eyes, we appeared to be stomping over 'their patch'. Also our links with the local Baptist Association had been somewhat tenuous for a number of years. It seemed we didn't fit the mould. Our church was one of the biggest on the Baptist Union list. It was also their biggest embarrassment! Eventually the BU council threw us out, after refusing to allow Noel to address them. It was all a lesson in loving our Christian brethren even when they rejected us and wanted little to do with us.

However, the constant exchanges with press, critics, advisers and umpires were wearing down our PR man. Dave 'Resolute' was a senior leader in the Warwickshire area and a good evangelist. As editor of our *Newness* magazine he'd written profound articles on the radical church and celibacy. In his PR role he'd both sat down with Christian leaders, and fended off the tabloids. But it seemed that his visionary sword was being hammered into a diplomatic shield.

Dave came to feel that some of the critics were right – we should tone down and accommodate. Gradually other serious reservations became apparent. Some of us urged him to regain a radical vision, but he was adamant. Unless we changed our whole approach he could see no future for himself in the Jesus Fellowship. We stood firm but were sad to see him go.

Had diplomacy gone too far? It was great to have good relationships, but if other Christians chose to exclude us, that was their problem. The Anglicans all but kicked Wesley out; the Methodists kicked Booth out; and everyone kicked the Pentecostals out! We were in good company.

WHEN THEY EXCLUDE YOU

God had given us a task and we were going to get on with it!

That year *The Fight Of Your Life* by Clive Calver and Derek Copley appeared. In it they wrote: 'Your heart is beginning to cry out for a positive, militant, Christian lifestyle. Such sentiments are not terribly popular today...Fear of accusations of fanaticism and eccentricity prevail.'[84]

'I once heard a neat definition of a fanatic,' Clive wrote later, '...someone who loves Jesus more than I do! Yet today anything which seems to disturb our middle-class, middle-of-the-road existence is treated with a combination of caution and contempt.'[85]

Good stuff! We agreed! Of course the cult smear was inevitable. Any pioneering movement is likely to be called a sect or a cult. The early church was no exception. Paul the apostle was regarded as 'a troublemaker' and 'a ringleader of the Nazarene sect' (Acts 24:5). He couldn't deny it! 'I admit,' said Paul, 'that I worship the God of our fathers as a follower of the Way, which they call a sect' (Acts 24:14).

Sociologically, Jesus and his followers bore many of the marks of a cult! Our church was distinctive, as were the Jerusalem church, the Quakers, the Methodists and many other churches throughout the centuries. We were pioneers.

David Matthew, writing of radical movements, warned that, 'It is important not to ridicule those moves of God that the official church tends to frown upon as fringe groups, for the outside runner, the breakaway has always played an important role in God's plan.'[86]

In *Church Adrift* he explained how a ridiculed Joseph and a hounded David were raised up by God to bring blessing to Israel. Such was our long term hope.

Ironically, when the Baptist Union was throwing us out, a Baptist minister was staying with us on a sabbatical. In his report he remarked how he felt there was great power to be released through Christians, like us, who were deeply committed to one another in love.

'Their existence,' he wrote, 'is a prophetic witness to the church which has, by and large, rejected radical obedience to God's word. Therefore the Christian establishment find them a thorn in the flesh.'[87]

We would not be ashamed of our cutting edge. Breakthroughs are made by breakaways! As we realised this we found renewed vigour and vision. The beauty of Zion blazed up afresh in our hearts and the courage of a Gideon's army inspired us. The religious had rejected Jesus, but 'the common people heard him gladly' (Mark 12:37). We addressed ourselves to the need. The poor in spirit would welcome God's message of love, equality and justice.

'Rough is the sea that we're sailing, and the storm clouds burst overhead! Rebels, we are rebels. We're the outcasts, the outcasts of hell!' So growled Steve 'Zealous' in his song.

The concept of being 'Jesus rebels' against the powers of evil flourished amongst us. We issued a regular leaflet, *Join Us!* We were so fed up with the taunt of 'recruiting' that we took the idea aboard. Yes, we would recruit an 'army' of zealous disciples. Like David on the run, we received 'all those who were in distress or in debt or discontented' who were gathering to us (1 Sam 22:2).

Booth had encouraged his soldiers to go for the worst. We looked for vagabonds and hoped to turn them into a force for God. As Jesus had remarked, it was the tax-collectors and prostitutes who made it into the kingdom before the religious.

1986 was a hectic year with Operation Mark, Fire Teams, Beachfire, Jesus Street Teams, Marquee Missions, Jesus Church Planters and Elisha Leadership Training. No rest for the righteous!

Share Our Bread was our 1986 outreach slogan, taken from Isaiah. This was what God required of us: 'to share your bread with the hungry' and to 'bring the homeless poor into your house' (Is 58:7, RSV). There would soon be room for 250 new people in our houses, our businesses prospered and resources had grown. Everything was the Lord's and we wanted to share it with others.

We set targets for 50 church-households, with 250 leaders, 250 servant groups, 250 celibates, 250 new members, 250 new residents. 250 was the number! There were now 250 on the Prayer Watch, too. The work was expanding and we all wanted to hear from the front line and give prayer support. Evangelists sent in their reports to *Jesus Happenings*, a monthly news-sheet. They were getting bolder in following their spiritual intuitions. John Wimber's book *Power Evangelism*[88] had inspired us and we expected 'power confrontations' of the supernatural.

Jesus Happenings reported that in Leicester a broken wrist was visibly healed, and in Tunstall they prayed with a woman, rebuking demonic powers. Shrieking and shaking followed and evil spirits were cast out. They left a New Testament and soon she was born again and healed of a ten-year back complaint.

Jesus Happenings also told how a Christian in Loughborough asked our young evangelists to pray with a friend with leukaemia. That week she saw her consultant.

'What pain killers are you taking?' he asked.

'None,' she said. 'There is no pain.'

'I'll soon trace those pills with a blood test!' he said.

The test revealed no trace of pills – or leukaemia!

One story was of a sister who had to be at hospital for 11.15 am. It was 11.00 am and raining. It was a forty minute walk, so she prayed and set out. The Lord seemed close and she felt unusually light. When she reached the hospital, she looked at her watch and gasped; it was 11.15 am! Then she noticed her clothes – they were dry!

Healings, deliverance and the supernatural were increasing along with our faith!

We were now enamoured with the Army image. *Join Us!* carried a photo of an Irish lad: 'Sign Up! Mark has joined the Jesus Army!' The next one read: 'Urgent! Join the Jesus Rebellion' and showed a grinning street lad with a cross around his neck, badges, army jumper, and a broken nose!

That summer Operation Mark ran a small 'Jesus Army Camp' for our teenagers in the Peak District. Badges and car stickers also appeared inviting people to 'Join the Jesus Army!'

We wanted to plant twenty church-households at short distances from the thirty we already had. LEAP teams (Location Evangelism And Planting) would evangelise and hold meetings in these areas. Supported by Marquee Missions and church evangelism, they would form a core and build others in. So we would 'leap' from one location to another close by. However, a survey showed new activities as far afield as Newcastle, Liverpool, Chester, North Wales, Sheffield, London and Margate. We also sent historian Trevor with our Dutch brethren to Holland.

In June we were campaigning in Birmingham, where faith was running high, and visitors often outnumbered members.

'I was snorting coke and heroin, smoking pot, and eating hash cakes,' one lad told us, '...it was getting me nowhere but high! I believed in God and called him Jah, but hated him when things got heavy. I dabbled in witchcraft, travelled around, and ended up in prison. The first time I heard about Jesus, I thought it was crazy, but I was moved by seeing these Jesus People really cared.'

He went to the Marquee and cried for the first time in two years. 'I knew my sins were washed away and my guilt was gone. The Jesus People are the sort of friends I've always been looking for.'[89]

Teams visited the beaches at Hastings, Weymouth, Blackpool and Brighton. We were loaned a farmhouse in Luton and bought more houses: Standfast in Birmingham,

Trumpet in Northampton, and New Wave in Yarmouth. In Birmingham we made friends with Muslims and Sikhs and now established a terraced house in the heart of the Asian population.

In Nottingham, a local paper reported:

> A fanatical Christian group has set up a tent mission on Nottingham Forest's site. And its extreme stand against 'today's sick society' has seen petrol bomb attacks on the marquee and guy ropes slashed. The Jesus Fellowship campaigns against crime, unemployment, drugs, the occult, sexual permissiveness, marriage breakdown, abortion, child abuse and other social ills. The members, who share their possessions, intend to march through the city centre.[90]

The media hadn't finished with us. That August a journalist came to our Bank Holiday Conference at Cornhill, and stayed at the Hall masquerading as a Christian from another church. She was welcomed, and Ken, an amiable five-footer, looked after her. Within weeks we were splashed over the *Sunday Mirror*.

> The man with the manic eyes moved closer. Lips pursed in fury, he prodded me with his finger and demanded, 'Where have you been?' I froze and he raged on. I had slipped away from a marathon all-day prayer session. Now I faced the wrath of Noel Stanton's henchmen. It was brother Ken, previously a kind, friendly, father figure. 'We had you watched. You sneaked out of the meeting to go to the pub.' His piercing stare unnerved me...[91]

It was gripping stuff! But it bore only the faintest resemblance to reality.

> They wail and go into a trance-like state. Their chants reach a crescendo as 'Svengali' Stanton murmurs Bible passages and whips them up to a frenzy. He brings them down again, saying, 'Beloved, can ya hear me?' ...and quotes more of the Bible with a slow drawl.[92]

Noel was a 'power crazed lunatic'! It was the usual stuff. C. T. Studd once remarked that 'a lost reputation is the best degree for Christ's service.' We were well qualified!

In September we issued our first *Jesus Army* magazine. ALL OUT WAR! was the front-page headline, and Noel had this to say:

> Britain is sinking into moral chaos! Only a moral and spiritual revolution in the power of the living Lord Jesus Christ will change that! That revolution must shake the nation and change its heart! And God is forming an army of Christians who are ready to pay the price!
>
> *Blow the trumpet! Church of Jesus!*
> *Rise up and fight!*[93]

22

A Sound of Marching

1987

'I saw our Zion as a woman, her clothes tattered and torn from battle. She sat alone, looking weary, the lines of travail etched upon her face. She bore the marks of age — yet was agelesss. In her quiet strength, she carried a simple beauty.

'Her Lord approached. "My beloved daughter," he said kindly, "has the battle proved too much for you?"

'The woman looked up into his face. The sight of him brought strength and his voice cheered her heart.

'"I have much yet for you to accomplish in this land. Come, my daughter, and follow me."

'He led her to a high mountain and she looked upon the land where she lived and worked for her Lord. There, a light radiated from his face, but below, all was darkness save for a few patches of light that shone like stars in the night.

'"Listen," he said. She heard the piercing cries of an imprisoned multitude and began to weep.

'"It is good to weep, but not enough."

'"But, Lord!" she cried. "I am weary and the task is great."

'"It is I who call you and I shall strengthen you."

'They went down the mountain and he led her to a solitary place, where they were alone, Zion and her Lord.

'"My daughter," he said tenderly, "I need to gain the fulness of your heart. Love for yourself has crept in. I called you as light to this land, but how dimly you shine. Remember when you loved me more – when the cross filled you with sweetness?"

'She slipped to her knees. He was right. The darkness had rubbed off on her and she was grieved.

'"Remember when I first called you Zion. The thrill of it filled your heart and your delight was to be mine."

'She remembered and was ashamed. Then the Lord stretched forth his hands. In one was a sword, in the other – a tiny golden cross.'

The wisdom was prophetic. It was now December 1986 and campaigning was over. We had broken through to the 'forgotten people': street kids, addicts, the poor, the homeless. We were learning to be patient with our new friends and 'lay down our lives' for them. Over a thousand had passed through the Marquee. Conversions and healings abounded and demons were removed.

Operation Mark had targeted for seventy young men and sixty-four were baptised in 1986. Although the majority of them were still around at the end of the year almost a quarter had gone. In Birmingham, four campaigns had left our people drained. With two new houses there, leadership was thinned out and overstretched. The work required sacrifice of time, energy and personal feelings. The battle was fierce and some began to fall. The team was shaken and by the new year three of the Birmingham leaders had left the work. For a while our hopes there seemed shattered.

Then God brought us wisdom in the Spirit. Where was the secret of a love powerful enough to reach the masses? The answer was in the heart of Jesus. It was the cross.

'"Let me plant this cross in your heart again," he said.

'"It will hurt, but it will be healing for yourself – and for your nation."

'She flinched, then nodded quietly. He took the sword and cut through till her heart lay exposed and there he buried the golden treasure. From the cross came a sweet, healing oil, and soon, with new strength surging within her, she arose, her face shining. He smiled.

'"With this sword of your suffering you will cut into the darkness and release the captives...Now take this also..."

'A tiny jewel lay in the scar of his hand.

'"This jewel of Covenant is worth more than all riches. Guard it with your life! When temptation is near, look upon it, for I have promised to be your God and you are my people."

'She bound it to her and now Zion was ready. With the sword of suffering going ahead and the light blazing from her heart, she descended into the darkness. The light penetrated and exposed, and many fought against her. They snatched at the jewel, but as she held it fast and advanced, a glorious thing happened. For following her was a path of light. Stepping out of the darkness, many caught hold of her robes and danced like children in the radiance she brought. And so Mother Zion was joined by the multitudes who longed for her coming, as she travelled on heralding the dawn in a darkened land.'

Samson used a jawbone. So would we. JAWBONE was conceived as the Jesus Army War Battle Operations Network. Inspired by the early Salvation Army, we continued to think in military terms. A 'War Fund' was set aside, community houses were seen as battle stations, the Marquee as a battlefield and inner city houses as 'Battlefronts'.

JAWBONE co-ordinated leadership. We had brought system and management to our businesses, but church administration had been fairly loose, with households running their own affairs and 'covered' only informally by senior brothers. Now was the time for efficiency. The group of Covering Authority brothers had expanded to ten and began to meet monthly. There was more delegation. Pastoral administration shifted towards Mark 'Strong', more of the community management came under Mike 'Rockfast' and evangelism was headed by Mick 'Temperate'.

More brothers came into JAWBONE to motivate and administer special areas such as discipleship, literature, new converts, backsliders, LEAP teams, distant households and campaigns. PR fell mainly on Noel's secretary, Liz, who became, for the press, the no-nonsense spokeswoman of the Jesus Fellowship.

JAWBONE toured the church, motivating the household leaders. The drop-out rate of our converts was disappointing, and we needed to nurture them more effectively. Administration improved, although no amount of organisation could take the place of the life of the Spirit.

As the Jesus Army began to take shape, some of us hoped we wouldn't go overboard on this military thing. After all, Jesus Army was only our campaigning arm, the church on the streets. As for the Salvation Army, they had been brilliant at soul-winning, but had neglected baptism, communion, charismatic gifts, and much that makes for a full-orbed New Testament church. Their outdoor, go-for-the-worst approach was superb, their holiness stance admirable, and their concept of the battle, marvellous – but their captains, peak caps and uniforms were a bit over the top. 'At least there'll be no uniforms for us!' we thought.

Meanwhile, Noel had been noticing the combat jacket that the leader of Operation Mark was wearing.

'Ummm,' he thought, 'there's a manly image. They're easily available and cheap...Let me see now – 300 men's jackets...Sisters can have green skirts...We need to be an identifiable people on the streets.'

'Yes. The Jesus Army! Now what about the logo? The cross must be central to it. Ah yes! A blood red cross between JESUS and ARMY, and below LOVE, POWER AND SACRIFICE! That's it – a people who live sacrificially.'

'"The Army with a heart to fight for you!" can be the motto. Booth was right! An army of the blood of Jesus and the fire of the Holy Spirit – but also of covenant with God and with our brethren. Yes, BLOOD! FIRE! AND COVENANT! That must be our battle cry.'

He could see the Army in action – banners waving, colours flying, guitars strumming, shouts ringing, and the name of Jesus echoing through the streets. The Jesus Army! It would be a beacon to the masses and a cause for the radical. It meant commitment, compassion, loyalty and self-sacrifice.

We quoted C. T. Studd in our magazine:

> I would sooner have a few dare-devil, care-for-nothing-and-nobody soldiers aflame with love for Christ than a million workers just ten per cent below the standard...Christ's call is to raise living churches of souls amongst the destitute, to capture men from the very jaws of hell, to enlist and train them for Jesus and to make them into an almighty Army for God. This can only be accomplished by a red-hot unconventional, unfettered Holy Ghost religion. Soldiers of Jesus! Nail the colours to the mast![94]

Jackets would be purchased. Colours would be displayed – army green, red for the blood of Jesus, white for purity, black for the darkness and gold for God's glory. We would buy a double decker and paint it up in Jesus Army colours — and the coaches, Crusader 1 and 2. Patches would be ordered — and badges, arm bands, khaki shirts, flags and banners! We would march in London! There in Trafalgar Square we would read the Jesus Army Manifesto. But first there would be a commissioning in Northampton Town Hall, and this time we would invite the press!

On April 18th, 1987, the Jesus Army was born.

A long column, something under a thousand strong, moved through the busy shoppers. Combat jackets, banners and excited faces broke into the Saturday scene. Jesus shouts split the air. Green, gold, red, white and black — the flags waved defiantly in the spring breeze. A few skinheads marched with us and others tagged on the end!

We arrived at the Guildhall and streamed inside. Still singing, we squeezed through the stone corridors. Somehow we all got in and from the platform I enjoyed the sight of my friends.

Mick 'Temperate' tapped my shoulder from behind. 'All right, "Overcomer"?' he asked. 'Good to see you wearing your combat jacket!'

That irritated me (slightly). I was a pacifist at heart and might have felt more at home in a friar's habit!

My eyes scanned the portraits on the wall. What would those dignitaries make of the Jesus Army? 'These men who have caused trouble all over the world have now come here!' I quoted to myself, and smiled. They didn't look very amused. We had gone off the rails — again! The Jesus Army were 'rebels', soldiers of the Lamb. Our heart had opened to the needy and our community houses would be places of healing that welcomed the downtrodden and attracted the strong.

Up on the platform stood a map of England. BRITISH CAMPAIGN! (Noel loved exclamation marks!) Every community house now had this wall map with places of Jesus Army activity marked by plastic pins. A brother pointed out our projects with a cane – all good Montgomery stuff. We planned campaigns in London and the larger cities. Marching through them, and pitching our Golden Marquee, we would witness to thousands. In pubs, night clubs, red-light areas, squares and back streets, the Jesus Army would befriend people and bring them the love of God.

Noel spoke of how the harvest was plentiful and a hunger for God was growing in the nation. The church as an army was becoming a visionary concept throughout the radical churches. We, and others, were to go on the offensive, challenging the devil, storming his strongholds, and proclaiming release to the captives. Mark 'Strong' read out the *Jesus Army Manifesto* in his clear preacher tones:

'The Jesus Army is the campaigning arm of the Jesus Fellowship Church. It is created in response to God's call for his church to be an army of his kingdom conquering the spiritual powers of darkness...

'The Jesus Army campaigns aggressively against the social evils so common in our ungodly British society, and also against religious hypocrisy...

'The Jesus Army will go where others will not go. It will take the gospel to the "forgotten people", the crowds outside the influence of Christian religion. It will bring healing to the sick and deliverance to the oppressed...

'The Jesus Army respects all Christians and churches, and will not deliberately compete. It will not however allow the necessary all-out offensive to be slowed down, nor the prophetic word silenced, because churches are defensive.

'Jesus Army soldiers pledge full loyalty. They will receive any training to make victory possible and are committed to sacrifice and hardship...

'The Jesus Army unites believers into holy and loving

church-communities, which show the end of all divisions and demonstrate a sharing lifestyle, true brotherhood, and a light to this world...'

In fifteen clauses we promised to be a one hundred per cent, red-hot, Christian army. Then the Revd Ken Thomason, a faithful friend from the early days, stepped forward.

'My brothers and sisters,' he said quietly, 'acknowledging the supreme authority of our Lord and Saviour Jesus Christ who has commissioned his church to "make disciples of all nations", do you receive his commission as members of the Jesus Army? Do you promise to obey his commands?'

A loud, 'We do!' shook the air.

'Do you promise to be faithful in prayer, in reading of the Scriptures, to be loyal to your brothers, to build the church in truth and peace, to live a life worthy of this calling as members of the Jesus Army?'

'We do! The Lord being our helper.' We bowed in reverence.

'Eternal God, our Father, strengthen with thy Spirit, these thy servants in the Jesus Army, as now, with prayer we set them apart as ambassadors of the gospel.'

I looked up and saw that many were moved. After this, we sang 'Onward Christian Soldiers!' and a stirring Salvation Army song: 'Wanted hearts baptised with fire!':

> Wanted, hearts to love the masses,
>   Hearts to help him seek the lost,
> Hearts to help him save all classes,
>   Hearts to help him save the worst.

A time of loud praise followed, then Noel asked us to look up. High on the wall, encircling the hall in huge golden letters, was engraved a verse from Psalm 115. We read it out together: *'Not Unto Us, O Lord, But Unto Thy Name Give Glory!'*

I found myself loving God. His faithfulness was superb! What God had begun with some humbled failures in a tiny chapel with a funny name was now a challenge to the nation. *Buzz* magazine had called us 'one of the most controversial Christian groups in the country'.[95] As we joined under those banners, I felt the thrill of God's call.

The commissioning finished and we filed out. I glanced up at a friendly portrait. *William Carey, Missionary Pioneer.* Carey once spoke of the power of 'loving brotherhood', and out in India had set up a multiracial household with 'all things in common'. The school where I worked was yards from where he once laboured as a shoemaker, and every day, for years, I had read on Carey's plaque:

> Expect great things from God!
> Attempt great things for God!

That was our heart, too.

'The Jesus Army will go where others will not go.' As I pondered the words from the Manifesto, my spirit rose to the challenge. I smiled at my combat jacket with its colourful badges – *We Fight For You!*

'Lord,' I thought, 'how did you get me into this?'

I looked up. 'Power Coach leaving in three minutes!' someone shouted.

And then a familiar voice in my ear. 'Don't miss it again!' said Malcolm, the music teacher.

The Jesus Army marched into the press and on to radio and television. We now courted publicity, and certainly couldn't avoid it. With jackets, banners, marches, city action days, marquee missions and convoys, we were unmistakable. We even had a four-man, Jesus Army quadricycle!

Soon we were in London and pitching the Marquee in

Battersea Park. Mounted police flanked our 'march for Jesus' from Hyde Park to Trafalgar Square. It was an unforgettable day. There in the square we had a rally and a national commissioning. Then Mick 'Temperate' took a small group and carried the flag to 10 Downing Street. The letter they handed in to the Prime Minister (one also went to the Queen) was printed in shortened form in *Heartcry*, our magazine of 'social concern and action':

> Dear Mrs Thatcher,
> We urge you to call the nation back to faith in God. Christians are praying for a revival that will change society. The members of this church have become a Jesus Army to fight the evils in society and bring the gospel to the victims of vice. We pray that God will give you wisdom, compassion and strength for your responsibilities.
> Yours respectfully,
>
> *The Jesus Fellowship.*

Heartcry focused on areas of need: homelessness, alcoholism, racism, abortion, AIDS, drug addiction, violence, prostitution and crime. It was great to tell the stories of those who had broken free. We issued a 'blood and fire' edition of *Jesus Army* magazine. 'We declare WAR!' it read, 'on behalf of every man, woman and child in need of God's life-changing love.'

Two brothers were arrested in Soho for obstruction. The pimps had got annoyed – the gospel wasn't too good for business! The case was dismissed and we were awarded costs. All this appeared in the press. Our courage grew. We prayed on the street and often people felt a touch of God.

'I met a Jewish man in London,' wrote Bill 'Truthful'. 'We talked and I prayed with him to receive the Spirit. As I laid hands on him and spoke in tongues, he reeled backwards under the power of God. "Where did you learn Hebrew?" he asked as he got up!'

We became well-known as people recognised our jackets. Street kids found us unusually down to earth and friendly for Christians. 'Anyone in the Jesus Army is a friend of mine!' said one skinhead. At London's Cardboard City, Victor's wife, Sheila, was treated with reverence – like a nun. They even called her Sister. With her Army headscarf she looked like one!

Channel 4 filmed us at the Glastonbury Festival when we took our Crusader 2 bus there in July. Several came back from the new age hippy scene and joined us in community. Two of them had their wedding in chapel. The local newspaper showed them in uniform with an archway of flags behind them. The sister's kit included a green skirt, blue body warmer, khaki blouse and headscarf. Brothers, as ever, wore jeans.

Of course, the image provided a field day for critics. Northampton's Archdeacon compared us to paramilitary rebels and one local MP described us as a 'Rambo' cult. Others found the association with war a little disturbing. We understood, and ensured that the jackets were well adorned with badges and a large golden JESUS ARMY patch on the back. Red epaulettes were added to distinguish us further from any other 'street people' with combat jackets!

But many greeted the army image enthusiastically. It was strong and dynamic. God was in this latest initiative. Men and women were attracted and a fresh batch of zealous Christians joined us.

The press was full of headlines like 'Onward Christian Soldiers!' and 'Jesus Army Marches In!' 'Bugbrooke' still carried some shrouds of mystery but 'Jesus Army' belonged to the public. It crystallised our vision of commitment and compassion. As the months went by we learned more and more to lay down our lives and love the needy ones. As this was seen, our acceptance with church and people increased. We 'did a good job' – there was room for us in Britain.

But what of Zion? A hunger grew amongst the veterans. What about our standards, our depth, our holiness? The eighties had doubled the church and now many knew little of the way we'd come. The glory of the early days burned in our memory. Then we had thrilled to be a people for God. Jesus Army was exciting, but did we really have the depth and anointing to take the nineties for Christ?

23

The Anointing

1987–88

Church Week 1987 came round in July and Jesus Army banners spanned the Golden Marquee in Coventry. Below, a thousand people praised God, hands raised and scarves waving. There in the crowd stood Zion's veterans: Dave Lants, Kelly and Norma, Val, Rufus and Jess, Ralph, Victor and Sheila, and many others. Verna was still going strong, her fingers now skimming over a synthesiser. Miss Campion had passed away peacefully at the Hall at the age of ninety-three. Some had left us; those who remained were weather-worn and wiser.

From the first charismatic discoveries in the manse to the vision of community at Malhamdale, from the hilarious hippy days of Argyle Street, through to the rubble and chaos of the Hall and the first wintry days at the Farm, God had urged us on. Almost hallowed now were memories of the summer days at Ashburnham when we learned to meditate on God, open up our hearts and disciple one another.

There the vision of Zion had exploded on us. We were never to be the same.

God's word had inspired us and revealed the narrowness of Christ's path. As we sought to reach out to others with the gospel of the kingdom, we found humiliation in the press and suspicion from churches. At times the battle had been intense, but we had pressed on regardless. When friends deserted, more came to join us. Slowly we had forged a culture that was godly, deep and precious. How could veterans forget?

Now years of campaigning had gone by and the church had expanded. A new generation of Jesus People had arisen who didn't fully understand a beauty born of tears.

We had put everything into launching the Jesus Army. On one hand there was an aggressive evangelistic endeavour, on the other, an almost mystical heritage of community. Campaigning had stirred Zion to pour out her life, but many of us longed after purer brotherhood and the deeps of God.

As the sun filtered through the marquee, Noel stood up in his Jesus Army jacket and began to speak of the 'treasures of Zion'. Once more the preciousness of brotherhood passed before us – its loyalty, simplicity and sacrificial love. We sang a new hymn that expressed this longing for Zion:

> Treasures of Zion here we seek;
> > Wisdom of all these God-filled years,
> In which were formed the wise, the meek,
> > Mature in warmth and love and tears.
>
> A generation new arise!
> > To stand on ground that we have trod;
> Live for the sight that thrills our eyes,
> > The sight of kingdom brotherhood!

THE ANOINTING

This touched a deep nerve among us and some wept. As Noel ministered, pride in our heritage sprang up again. Treasures were unearthed and the simplicity and beauty of God's kingdom shone out. As I looked around, I thanked God for the many younger ones ready to launch us into the future. Some were already in leadership, for now we had a hundred elders and many trainee 'Leading Serving Brothers'.

Most of the leaders needed to move in greater confidence, so we arranged monthly 'Elisha' training sessions where leaders could be encouraged and put through their paces. The leaders' meeting at Cornhill now started in the mid-afternoon. Noel would speak informally and then we would split into groups to pray and share together. The serious old guys (even the young ones) looked as though they needed loosening up.

'Right, sit back,' said Noel one afternoon. 'I'm going to play you part of a Wimber tape.' We looked surprised and smiled, winked or frowned at one another. This was a new departure. We were aware of a 'third wave' in the Christian church, but hadn't seen it all as quite our scene. We listened to the tape of John Wimber chatting to a large gathering of leaders about the need for emotional healing and release. Then he asked the Spirit to take over.

'Let it come!' Wimber said quietly.

'Let the fire fall!' he said more loudly.

Slowly we heard the sobbing start, then outbreaks of crying and laughter until the auditorium sounded like a farmyard! Most of us enjoyed the tape and felt it was probably what we needed. We went home saying, 'Let it come! Let it come!' in an American accent and wondered what was in store!

In 1987 the Jesus Army had burst on the scene, and was here to stay. We had pushed outwards in our church-household planting and now had additional houses in Northampton, Kettering, Hastings, Hinckley and Leicester. Battlecentre in Acton, London, was also a significant new development. We had seen two years of 'explosive pioneering'. By the end of December there were 49 households with 900 adults in covenant and 200 children.

Mike 'Rockfast' wrote to Noel of the need for a sabbath, a year of rest. The church had to regather strength. Expansion in business and community had stretched us to the limit. We lacked extra finance and leadership and many needed refreshing. 1988 must be a year of waiting on God, of inspiration and rediscovery of Zion. Noel (ever dynamic) agreed, but saw it as a stepping stone to even greater activity. 1988 and 1989 must be vital years of preparation for a massive launch into the nineties. We had only just begun!

In the early spring, prophetic wisdom indicated that a fresh wave of spiritual power lay ahead for us. We were shown that as we moved into a new level of worship, God would bring to us a new and powerful anointing. This would be as holy fire, infectious and unstoppable and would bring upon us a mantle of love-power that would reach the hearts of men. Zion would yet be a 'city sought out', a clear trumpet sounding in the nation.

We were reaching into our destiny. Yet still we were lacking. What of deeper purity and sanctification? And what of greater power? We continued to hear interesting things of the ministry of John Wimber and Reinhard Bonnke, but were reserved about the spectacular: what some called 'being slain in the Spirit', and so on. It was intriguing, 'But,' we asked, 'does it build the church?'

Nonetheless, some of us, like Bill 'Truthful', were keen to see God's power demonstrated in such ways. When Bill prayed over a drug-dealer at the end of *March For Jesus* in London, the guy was floored by the Holy Spirit!

March for Jesus, held in April 1988, and organised by national Christian leaders, was a new departure for us. We frantically learned Graham Kendrick's songs and sent 400 'soldiers' down to London to join in the March. Enthusiastic, combat-jacketed, original and noisy, we marched past Gerald Coates, Roger Forster and the other charismatic leaders. A few eyebrows were raised, but they had known we were coming and we felt accepted. The response from fellow Christians was heartening.

'Hey! You look great! Who are the Jesus Army then?'

'You heard of the Jesus People...or Bugbrooke?'

'Bugbrooke?... Bugbrooke!! (You could see wheels turning rapidly in their minds.) The smiles faded and returned: 'Well, good on you! Praise God! Times are changing!'

They were. It was time to bury differences. The harvest was great and we needed to join hands for revival. Our warm (if cautious) reception encouraged Noel. His seat in the office was taken over by the farm cat as he went off round the country visiting Christian leaders. The day of communication had arrived.

Another spin-off from the March was the birth of our music group. The songs we learned opened us up to other Christian music and we caught up on the praise songs of recent years.

Praise took us back into liberty. At the Easter Jesus Army Festival we leapt, danced, stood on chairs, waved scarves and sang 'Jesus is Risen!' We shocked even ourselves as we threw off our inhibitions. But worse was to follow!

Reinhard Bonnke was partly to blame. In July Noel, with others, called in on the Eurofire Conference at Birmingham and there people were 'falling under the power'. Noel was impressed but still a little sceptical.

'Well, God likes this, even if I don't,' he thought. The Spirit urged him to 'go for it' so he wasted no time and introduced it at the young leaders' meeting the next day. Two days after that was the beginning of our annual church week. Seven newly-baptised members lined up to make their covenant pledge and receive the right hand of fellowship.

'Right! If brethren could stand behind them,' said Noel (as if it was always done like this!). As he moved along the row laying hands on each of them, they went down like nine-pins!

'Anybody who wants prayer for the anointing, just come to the front,' Noel offered.

'Bill "Truthful", come and give me a hand!'

From then on, all heaven was let loose. It was chaos! There were people on the floor everywhere, heaped up on the platform, or sprawled all over the auditorium. The musicians tried to strike up some worship songs, but it had gone beyond that. One leader rolled under his seat in a daze, laughing uncontrollably. He was the first of many to be carried home.

A whirlwind swept over the church. Some responded like concrete blocks but others were as leaves in a gale. The fire spread and households flared up with spiritual activity. The new anointing immediately exposed the powers of darkness and a number of us were delivered from long-standing problems. Demons were expelled and the supernatural was almost commonplace.

Many, like Janice, found emotional healing. 'A real joy hit my being and worship rose powerfully,' she wrote. 'All the strength went from my knees and I fell to the ground. I found amazing joy and love for my Lord as I'd never experienced before. I was aware of the meeting but unable to move till laughter in great waves rolled over me. It was so healing, as hurts and discouragements just melted away.'[96]

As the days went by we saw the funniest sights. Janice slipped under her desk at Skaino – incapable. In the same office, Ian 'Willing', one of our leaders at New Creation

Hall, was too weak to leave his seat. Henry, his fellow elder, took him home in a Goodness Foods lorry. But Henry soon came under the anointing and they had to pull into a lay-by!

When the Tuesday Agape came round, Henry went to bless the wine and burst out laughing.

'Lord,' he said recovering himself, 'how good and pleasant it is for brothers to dwell in unity.'

'Oooh!' exclaimed Ian. 'Say that again!'

'How good and pleasant it is for brothers to dwell in unity.'

Ian reeled backwards, went bright red and began to tremble on the floor, overcome by God's power. Then Chris, a larger elder, crashed down and began to breathe heavily and twitch, as if he'd been connected to the mains! Others fell and lay on the floor laughing, weeping or looking quietly beatified. I surveyed the scene amazed, amused, and annoyed at my calmness. I'd read lots about revivals, mystics and pentecostals. Raptures, visions and crisis experiences were marvellous in my eyes – but they never happened to me. Oh well.

Linda went down with her hands clasped gracefully like a praying madonna. She lay there all night. About one in the morning someone threw a quilt over her.

'The word "covenant" was burned into my heart,' she said. 'Something happened inside, and I've never really been the same.'

The Birmingham campaign followed a few days later and Linda was there as an evangelist. One night she saw lights in the darkness of her room and sensed the angels. She wrote: 'In the mornings the team prayed for the anointing before going out. We were getting bold and God touched people when we prayed with them. One or two even landed on the pavement, and some of our own evangelists had to be carried back to the bus!'

'What will happen at the leaders' meeting?' we

thought. When it came, Noel spoke from Scripture about falling and trembling under the power of God. He expected a time of weeping away past sins, and emotional hurts, but soon the King's Room at Cornhill was in an uproar. Laughter was everywhere – great guffaws and belly laughs! One brother swayed on his feet groaning and bellowing as Noel tried to minister. He gave up! Respected elders were rolling on the floor clutching their stomachs. Others were in varying degrees of consciousness.

'A sense of awe descended on us,' wrote one young leader. 'I heard the words "Lord anoint this one..." then the floor gave way, and I felt myself caught up into the heavenlies. I lay there for hours, trembling and talking in tongues. Time appeared unimportant as I bathed in God's presence. Later they dragged me into the minibus, got me home, and put me to bed. I stayed there for hours but not asleep, and came to about five in the morning with praises on my lips and peace in my soul.'[97]

An evangelists' gathering ended up the same way. Cornhill Manor had never seen such days. One brother was delivered of a spirit of rejection as he lay under the power of God. It wasn't long before his 'mouth was filled with laughter, and his tongue with singing'. Even I got a little 'inebriated'! But as Peter had said at Pentecost, 'These men are not drunk, as you suppose' (Acts 2:15). They were filled with God.

Linda saw the room on fire! A flaming sword hurtled towards her and she went over. Gripped by God, her senses were paralysed. An awesome presence pervaded her soul and she felt as if she were held in the very sanctuary of God.

'I read St Teresa shortly afterwards,' she told me casually and I thought, "That's it! That's how I felt."'

'Man!' I thought and realised the truth afresh: 'In the

last days, God says, I will pout out my Spirit on all people. Your sons and daughters will prophesy, your young men will see visions, your old men will dream dreams' (Acts 2:17). In the Bible, ecstasies, trances and fallings under the power were well-known and happened to men like Peter, John, and Paul.[98]

There were later pioneers: mystics, Quakers, Methodists and the like, but since the awakening at the turn of the twentieth century, these experiences had become widespread. Now we lived in days of pentecostal spirituality. Singing in tongues, miracles, visions and raptures – all were New Testament phenomena. And they happened now!

And so we approached the end of a memorable year. The new wave of power had landed us on higher ground. Twenty years had passed since the Holy Spirit had first fallen on the manse in Bugbrooke. One of our stewards was then a village teenager laughing under the manse chairs. He was now doing it in our Celebrate Jesus gatherings – along with his son!

1988 had been, to quote our new generation of hippies, 'Amazing!' But, amidst all the supernatural activities of that summer, the word of God had emerged, giving us clear prophetic direction. With a fresh anointing, and a renewed sense of destiny, we were to take our place in the mainstream of God's purposes in Britain.

The years ahead seemed full of hope for all who could hear the 'sound of marching'. It appeared to many that revival was drawing near and a new dawn was breaking in British Christianity. Noel's vision now was of a 'fire movement' in Britain – a million people ablaze for Christ's kingdom:

Twenty years ago we were caught up in the charismatic movement. Christians everywhere received the bubbling, liberating baptism of the Spirit. Hundreds of churches found new vitality. Now there is a new beginning. New fires are being lit! Another movement of God has begun! And the power of a throbbing holiness is going to drive back the forces of moral decadence in this nation.[99]

Communicate!
1989–1993

24

Flowing with the Mainstream
1989

I saw a beam of light that was slowly emerging out of a dark mist. As it came into focus I could now see it was a city whose light was of many beautiful colours. This was so striking that many, who'd paid little attention to it while it was in the mist, now looked on with great interest.

Of all the colours of this city, gold was the most powerful and represented the kingship of Christ among his people. Deep red symbolised the blood of Jesus proclaimed in power. A penetrating white stood for the purity of lives laid down and shared in community. Weaving through them all was a fresh green light: a fearless army who were reaching out to those who were lost in the blackness all around.

The Holy Spirit brought this vivid picture to Pete 'Just' shortly before the Jesus Army was launched. We adopted these colours for our banners. By 1989, after the impact of the anointings, many were seeing us in a new light as we entered a major phase of communication. After pondering on the 'wisdom picture' he'd seen, Pete explained:

> For many years God kept us in a mist of quietness, misunderstanding and rural isolation. In this way he caused our colours to develop undisturbed and uninfluenced by others. Through much patient endurance God has established our foundations and given us some radical distinctives. We can be confident as we arise and shine as the Jesus Army.

God had been urging Christians in Britain to tear down barriers, to forgive and to support one another. We had responded and were now building bonds of trust with others. The outcome was dramatic. As we flowed with the mainstream we found ourselves being swept along by a new wave of the Spirit. Heaven alone knew where it would lead us!

The second half of 1988 had run its chaotic course as the new wine stretched, burst, and overflowed the wineskins of our hearts. God was healing our emotions, bringing a deeper sense of his love and rekindling the fires of worship. None but the cynical could fail to realise that we were entering a new era.

The Jesus Army was carried along into 1989 with an unparalleled freshness and creativity. This expressed itself in music and dance. We threw ourselves into wild praise and invited others to 'Celebrate Jesus and Catch Fire' with us. Praise brought tremendous spiritual release and the upbeat style of music communicated the strength of the gospel.

It was fun too, and the celebrations we held throughout the country ended with streamers, balloons, party-poppers and air-horns. Our liberty had grown once more to 'worrying' proportions and I got a lot of exercise dancing in these meetings (writers need it!)

The music group led us into unexplored regions of worship, and some of us (brought up on Bach) were amazed to hear sanctified disco-sounds, as guitars and drums, keyboard, fiddle and flute joined in praise to God. Together we found jubilation and joy, as adoration songs from the Vineyard Fellowship, the melodies of Graham Kendrick, and prophetic songs from the People of Destiny blended with our own to convey the energy and anointing of the Spirit.

Many responded to the powerful atmosphere of these celebrations and streamed forward to meet with God, or were filled (and felled) by the Spirit where they stood. It was when God's temple was filled with music and praise that the cloud of glory came down[100]. Music was high on God's agenda.

The anointing that inspired celebration was still urging us to communicate, to take risks in this area, and to be vulnerable. Noel had already enjoyed renewed friendships with men like Gerald Coates and Roger Forster. Now, he reached out further, visiting many other leaders and sharing with them.

Interviews with these 'men of vision' soon appeared in *Jesus Lifestyle* which had quickly changed from a small magazine on community lifestyle into a 32-page quarterly of wide prophetic thrust.

We had our own contribution to make to the Christian scene: special treasures like covenant love, celibate commitment, community life and compassionate street work. Other streams like Ichthus and Pioneer had developed their own distinctives and we were beginning to enrich one another.

Flowing with the mainstream was a whole new chapter in our story. What was now happening amongst us was precious. I wept to see our church becoming young again. At times we had been proud and pushy. The sword we wielded had wounded people unnecessarily. But God had applied it to us. We had tasted humiliation, rejection, failure; God's woundings had caused us to need others, to recognise our mistakes and weaknesses, to forgive and be forgiven. And through that open door sprang a new anointing.

Noel's new vulnerability touched me, his painstaking efforts at reconciliation and the genuineness of his vision for

Britain. But some Christians elsewhere doubted his motives. Was it all a cosmetic job? Another ruse to sign people up, promote ourselves? Cynicism came our way and it hurt – tremendously.

We held a big Celebration that April in Westminster Central Hall, London. There we presented our first Jesus Army video, *Fighting For You,* along with Reinhard Bonnke's *A Blood Washed Africa.* Also a well known worship leader joined us for the evening. The next day in Basingstoke, he sported a sweatshirt with these words:

> Dave Bilbrough appeared with the Jesus Army
> And survived!

Dave's warm-hearted support provoked a fresh burst of controversy in the magazine *21st Century Christian.* The editor had to call a halt to the avalanche of letters with a final word from John Noble pointing out: 'All the criticisms of Noel Stanton and the Jesus Army were also made of William Booth and the Salvation Army.'[101]

John stepped forward at a crucial time for us. As a pioneer in the house churches himself, he was convinced that God's agenda was far wider than restorationism, renewalism, or any other 'ism'. We were grateful for his support, for this was no time to be isolated and ostracised.

Criticisms continued to come our way but it was the heart to heart exchanges, the integrity of *Jesus Lifestyle,* our compassionate outreach and the genuine efforts to 'pursue peace with all men' that helped soften suspicions about the Jesus Army. It might take a few years and we wouldn't please everybody (sharp swords aren't meant to!) but, as Roger Forster assured us, many now admired what we were doing.

The Spirit brought a surge of creativity in the whole area of communication. Photographers, writers and editors; art, design and graphics bods; technicians, musicians and songwriters all put their talents to work. Rufus came into his own in prophetic drama and a host of prop-makers arose in his train. John 'Good', the part-time cattleman, played stage manager for the Celebrate Jesus events. (When the smoke-machine went wrong, John was to blame!)

We developed our own Jesus Fellowship Resources. An old outhouse at Sheepfold Grange was converted into a sound studio where Andy, the lead-guitarist, edited some live worship tapes. At Festal Grange John 'Perceptive', our communications man, took over the attic as a video studio, adding it to his poky office and darkroom.

The circulation of *Jesus Lifestyle* mushroomed and was now reaching many countries. Literature that originated from a little village in England was being read in Spain and Russia. One magazine was picked up from a dusty African road on the way to market! In fact, an overwhelming number of letters began to flood in from Africa with requests for help, money and Jesus Army jackets!

Our influence was far wider than we'd imagined. Some looked to us as pioneers. Others waited in the wings to see how things would turn out. A few groups wanted a closer link with us, so we arranged occasional gatherings at Battlecentre in London where leaders of other churches could meet with us over a meal for friendship and encouragement.

As well as offering encouragement, we also had a lot to receive. From the fiery zeal of Bonnke to the relaxed humour of Wimber there was so much by way of example. Noel would return from his Christian travels with more than just new friendships: anointed songs, ideas, advice and sheer examples of skill.

One example was the New Zealander, Bill Subritzsky. We had often cast out demons, but Bill had something to teach us. The accuracy of his words of knowledge, his sensitivity and the success with which he ministered, all impressed us. At our July conference we watched him on video. Then, as we challenged the demons ourselves, the place erupted with the sounds of screaming, coughing and vomiting. God's temple was being cleansed and some nasty squatters removed!

But even more inspiring that summer were the delicate experiences some had of smelling beautiful perfume, feeling a gentle breeze or sensing the presence of angels.

God had created a culture-shock amongst us. Fresh sight blew away narrow-heartedness, opened up new horizons and baptised us into an awareness of God's movement world-wide. We felt his heart-throb for the nation and his urge to reach the unreached. It permeated the songs we sang; 'I have a destiny', 'We'll walk this land', and 'Heal this nation'.

'Rise up you champions of God!' we cried – 'we'll reach this generation'. But how? How could we touch a generation so desperate for reality? Only by being approachable and relevant. To reach and win people was the fire in our hearts that demanded constant change, ever-fresh initiatives.

Before the melting experiences of 1988 there was a degree of stiffness in our bones, of awkwardness in our style and of narrowness in our approach. God coloured us in. We became warm and attractive again.

Symbolically the now rather drab and tatty combat jackets were laid aside in preference for bright tee-shirts and sweatshirts. New 'space-age' jackets were also on their way. Mottled in red, green, blue, black, brown and khaki, with yellow patches – the Jesus Army would be about as camouflaged as a parakeet in Trafalgar Square!

That summer we scattered 75,000 highly coloured *Jesus Revolution Streetpapers* around cities, towns, beaches and festivals. (At least one road sweeper came to the Lord!)

We felt the time was ripe for a new Jesus movement – for Christians to swarm the streets, promoting Jesus as the hero of the 90s. It was now twenty years since Britain had seen such an upsurge of excitement amongst the youth with all their 'Give us a J!' shouts and 'One Way' signals.

Noel (who aims to initiate something every day) came up with a greeting for the 90s Jesus Movement. When you meet a Christian, whether in the street or a crowded supermarket, you lift your right hand and with five fingers spread out (representing the five letters of Jesus) you shout 'JESUS!' to him. Hopefully he returns the greeting. The 'Say Jesus' campaign was launched, complete with tee-shirts, badges and stickers, at our summer festival.

These bank-holiday festivals, now held three times a year in the Giant Marquee at Cornhill, were becoming major landmarks in our calendar. Many stayed in our community houses. With so many guests around, this generated a very lively and brotherly atmosphere.

The programme began with baptisms on Friday evening and finished on Monday with a queue of people telling how God had met them over the festival. Some of the stories were hilarious, others deeply moving. Sandwiched in between was a lot of vigorous preaching, the occasional video, much personal ministry, music, praise and rolling in the aisles (for some). As a leader of King's Church, Chatham, remarked at the microphone, 'If I'd known the meetings were going to be this long I'd have brought my flask and sleeping bag!'

The Spirit that urged us to celebrate and communicate inspired us into greater evangelism. Our frontiers opened out. Mick 'Temperate' was church-planting in Liverpool using a rented house as a base. His team travelled up from Birmingham gathering new friends and developing links with local leaders, but not without some opposition.

Kelly was on the go in Glasgow and others were pioneering in Sheffield, Norwich and Oxford. We held 'Beachfire' missions in coastal resorts and Pete, our Dutch medic, took a team to Amsterdam. The English double-decker had to have its tyres deflated to get under the bridges! Proud thing.

At Glastonbury Festival we joined with groups like

YWAM and British Youth For Christ as part of Vic Jackopson's 'Hope Now' team. The evangelists provided a real Christian presence there and more than one searcher was baptised in a barrel of water!

Once a month we ran four-day missions in London known as EDP (Eat, Drink and Pray!) Brothers and sisters would walk the streets well into the small hours befriending night-clubbers and the homeless. At intervals they would return to the warm bus at Trafalgar Square, sit their friends down with a cup of tea and fix them a hot meal. They shared God's love and often prayed with them.

Dave Wilkerson once prophesied that God would 'adopt the lost generation'. We found the young homeless very open to God. Spiritual experience and brotherly love made a big impact on them. Quite a few came back to community, and the Farm, especially, began to burst at the seams with young men finding life in Jesus, a family and a cause to fight for.

On our part, we needed to be gracious and tolerant. Without the soul-healing dynamite of the Spirit some of us fuddy-duddies would never have got there! As it was, it seemed like things were hotting up. Revival was in the air.

At our August Festival we staged some drama which brought home this sense of a spiritual awakening. Lights went out in the Golden Marquee as the keyboards built up some intriguing sounds. The narrator (a heavily-bearded Rufus) was reading from Ezekiel 37:

'So I prophesied as I was commanded. And as I was prophesying there was a noise and the bones came together, bone to bone.'

A puff of smoke, a play of coloured beams, and three skeletons jerked upwards from the stage! Gasps arose from the thousand-strong crowd. But before they could recover there was a quick light change and the skeletons were replaced by a host of farm brothers standing perfectly still, dressed as the fierce warriors of Israel.

Some of our friends from Chatham looked mildly surprised. Mind you, they'd seen us doing 'prophetic drama'[102] down in London. Rufus was in his element.

'Come O breath! Breathe into these slain that they may live!'

The music grew stronger as it portrayed the swirling winds of God's power. At its climax Rufus thundered:

'They came to life and stood up on their feet, a vast army!'

As the motley bunch of ex-homeless, converted new-agers, travellers and old stagers threw themselves into a wild dance, we all sang 'Mighty warrior, dressed for battle!' 'Dry bones' were springing to life in this land and taking their place in God's army.

On the eve of the nineties we all met together for a bumper Celebration in Northampton. Noel spoke of what lay ahead: 'Beloved, the nineties will be a time of great victories in the midst of great pain. You see, it's warfare! Praise God we're fighting, and not drifting! It's a wonderful thing – all that God has brought us into. Thank God we responded!

'Now the hours of an old decade are dwindling away. For us, nothing is negative, either now or in the future. As I read Acts 2 and 4, I'm twice as enthusiastic about Pentecost and community lifestyle as I've ever been. Nothing I've found in my travels has persuaded me there is anything better. There isn't!

'So let us stand with our brethren and sound the trumpet more clearly than ever before. And in this nation where sin and desolation have reigned, there will arise the glorious sound of the triumphs of the gospel!'

The Spirit's wind was blowing stronger now – not only through obscure little chapels, but over peoples and nations. As the last day of a decade rolled by, who could not feel that this was an hour of destiny? So we sang:

For the glory of the Lord, we advance united!
    Following Christ's blazing sword, his dominion
        sighted.
All that has been taken, it shall be restored!
    This eternal anthem: 'For the glory of the Lord!'[103]

Before the midnight chimes of Big Ben were relayed to us from London, many flocked onto the stage to rededicate their lives to God. Others moved around praying and counselling.

Then the floor was cleared for a dramatic sketch based on the message of Luke 14 and Matthew 21: a king sent out messengers to call his people to a feast but these despised his invitation and beat the messengers. So he sent them out a second time to bring in the homeless, the needy and the poor. And these feasted at his table.

There was a buoyant spirit around and some of us, seeing our friends putting on a superb act, were reduced to tears of laughter. But at one point the action paused. As the lights dimmed and the laughter faded away, Rufus walked on in rags, sat on the table and spoke gently to the audience:

'You know, it's all for real.

'It seems to me that the call of God starts with the religious. And he had a pretty good go at getting through to the likes of me and you! But there comes a time when the Lord says: "Look, there are people out there who are hungry and thirsty and desperate." And then he needs messengers who are willing to go. And that's me and you.

'And that's serious. Because Britain is hard and people are cold, spiritually. We've got to relate to where people really are. We've got to get down on their level. We've got to weep if we're going to heal the weeping. We've got to feel rejection if we're going to get to the rejected. You see what I'm saying? And that's God's call to us as Christians – to be his messengers for the nineties.

'And let's face it! We may never see a sudden explosion. We're going to know a lot of hard work. A lot of tears. A lot of rejection. Probably receive a little bit of violence as well. Are you ready for that?

'Because the reward is beautiful. The palace of the King is going to be filled – not just in the eternal kingdom – but here on earth. That is, people can be brought in to the banquet feast here and now.

'But we've got to do it and take the beatings. We've got to do it and take the rejections. We've got to do it and take the critical looks. And most of all, we've got to do it together – as servants of the King.'

25

Refiner's Fire

1989–1990

During the summer of 1989 disaster had suddenly struck New Creation Farm. Driving up to the Farm office one afternoon I noticed that smoke was pouring into the sky above the hill on which the Farmhouse stood. I guessed that a haystack had caught fire.

But when I reached the top of the drive the stark reality hit me. Flames were leaping high into the air. The pigyard was a raging inferno. Haystacks, sheds and poplar trees were all alight. Women and children looked on in horror. The Farm brothers ran around desperately carrying squealing piglets to safety as the smoke and smell of the roaring fire increased.

Worse was to follow, it seemed, for the wind was steadily blowing a wall of fire towards the house. Soon New Creation Farm would be engulfed. Noel and the others in the office started praying and commanding the flames to retreat. The wind dropped, the firemen arrived and the advancing flames began to falter.

Thus far and no further would they come. Some of the poplar trees, the proud protectors of our large orchard, had already been destroyed. But the tree nearest the house remained unburnt, a silent witness to God's intervention.

These natural events now seemed highly symbolic. A spiritual fire was raging through the church and some of her trusted 'protectors' were going through the flames.

A prophecy, written just before the new anointing, had warned that God would 'search our motives, chase out deadness and awaken the very soil in which Zion was planted'. So it proved to be. The Spirit we had first experienced as sweet wine and healing oil now came as gales of upheaval and fires of cleansing. At the height of the anointings God had spoken about this very dramatically to two brothers.

The leaders' meeting was going wild. Many were shaking, laughing, crying and falling under the power of God. As Rufus was quietly praying he saw a field of wheat. At its centre a swirling storm was brewing up. Rufus opened his eyes to view the present chaos.

'Wow! Is this really happening?'

Steve 'Capable' was spinning like a top, swirling round and round, his arms going up and down, his body swaying and bending. Lower and lower he swept, faster and faster.

We looked aghast.

'Amazing!' said some.

'Demonic!' muttered others.

'Prophetic!' whispered Rufus.

'Impossible!' thought Steve as an unseen hand lowered him onto the floor. He landed, his legs shaking violently and his head banging from side to side on the wooden floor of the King's Room at Cornhill. Steve felt an incredible peace, a mental clarity and a beautiful closeness to God. Physically, it was impossible – the angle and speed. Spinning of any kind made Steve feel sick. But he felt wonderful.

'What's going on, Lord?' he asked.

God spoke in his heart: 'This is a sign. I'm doing a new thing and there will be upheaval. I'm shaking up the whole mindset of your church.'

Steve remembered how God told Peter, in a trance, to eat what was unclean and then sent him to the non-Jews.[104]

'What I am doing will be equally shocking,' the Lord said. 'This new direction will take you forward into my purposes. I hate your nice British culture. Mine is a new creation. I will bring upheaval and there will be division.'

Steve sensed a group of leaders who were standing outside the circle, detached and cynical. He knew they wouldn't last in that condition. The Spirit continued to speak:

'Some looking on think this is demonic, counterfeit. The reverse is true. People in this nation have been seeing the counterfeit for too long. Now is the time for the real thing, a demonstration of a supernatural Christian counterculture. The counterfeit, the cults, the New Age – all these are but imitations. This will be my culture, my Zion.'

Now, a year later, there was a divine insecurity around. God was disturbing us, bringing back the freshness, buzz, and sense of adventure we'd known at the start. But as we entered the new era some clung to the past. Others held onto wrong attitudes: self-righteousness, hypocrisy, lukewarmness and legalism. As God shook us up everything came to the surface. Hearts came out for good or ill. And in the midst of the shaking some of us were caught out.

Over the years some had been unable to cope with our pioneering and had left. Any army on the advance has its losses. But now there was a double reaction. Some welcomed our new direction as offering them a broader path and the opportunity to embrace the world. Others were too narrow and resisted the innovations, whether boisterous praise, drama, videos, flashing lights or flowing with the mainstream.

As for Noel, he seemed an annoying blend of stubbornness and flexibility. Though resistant to criticism, he was full of surprises and ready for change. When sufficiently convinced, he could enthusiastically preach what he had once had little time for. Some couldn't take that. They saw the way we were now going as a sell-out, the end of what we'd fought and sacrificed for. They lost confidence in the prophetic direction and became cynical.

Amongst those caught up in this was the senior man at Cornhill. Mark had been with us almost from the beginning and typified all we were in terms of 'Zion'. A leading celibate, his emphasis was on purity, unworldliness and brotherhood. Mark was highly regarded and influential.

Over recent years he'd developed reservations about the direction we were taking and, despite being one of Noel's closest advisors, was unable to resolve them. Mark wasn't keen on the Jesus Army image, nor was he impressed with all the changes that had come from hob-knobbing with other charismatics. Shoutings and shakings, dancing and drama were, in his eyes, so many fireworks that distracted us from our true calling.

Most of us were happy with the new direction, but those who resisted it increasingly lost their bearings. Some of them gravitated towards Mark, who became more and more bogged down with their problems. The new anointings came as a divide. The cloud moved on, and those who did not move with it found themselves struggling.

The whole Fellowship was going through a time of sifting and refining. The central ground was under attack and enthusiasm for our special distinctives was being eroded in the minds of some of our members.

Families who'd found it hard to keep up with the pace in the Jesus Army were tempted to compare our rigorous standards with the less demanding lifestyles enjoyed in other Christian scenes. Maybe community, or even covenant commitment, wasn't such an important issue after all, they thought.

Some celibates began to question their lifelong vows; a

few brothers were losing their way by getting too involved with sisters. The London household was badly hit when their main celibate brother and a leading sister whom he pastored suddenly left together.

September 1989 was declared a month of cleansing. The outward move into the mainstream had partly strengthened, partly weakened our central vision. It was sorting people out. The focus now shifted to the internal strength of the church: her holiness, distinctives and prophetic call.

Victor, myself and Justin, a bright-eyed hippie, met privately to encourage one another in the pursuit of holiness. Wesley was a major inspiration to us at the time:

> Refiner's fire go though my heart,
>   Illuminate my soul.
> Scatter Thy life through every part
>   And sanctify the whole.

The experience of 'entire sanctification' had been at the heart of the Methodist revival and the Salvation Army and we wondered if it was a treasure to be recovered in our day.

A much broader group of brothers and sisters, led by Steve 'Capable', rose once a week before dawn and converged on New Creation Hall to pray. There, above the foodstore, inspiration flowed as the 'watchmen' prayed, lay prostrate, listened to God and gained fresh vision. Prophetic wisdom came thick and fast; judgement had begun at the house of God. God was humbling and purifying his people.

That autumn we reprinted an article by John Wimber, whose Vineyard churches had received some corrective input from Paul Cain. God was pruning many vineyards, exposing sin, humbling the proud and creating holiness. John wrote:

> The true call of the church is to the cross. We are called to die

to ourselves and the world. This might mean lowering standards of living and giving up a significant amount of recreational and entertainment time for higher purposes.[105]

John Wimber felt that Western Christianity was lukewarm and needed to repent of its materialism. God was after servants not self-helpers. With the people crying out for reality, God was intent on blasting away the blockages in the church and getting us into shape for the harvest.

1990 opened with tremendous vision for Christians in Britain. Life and colour was invading the churches and everybody was talking (and writing) about revival. We too were expectant. Men Alive for God, our own leaders meetings and the first Wembley Praise-Day all carried a 'buzz'.

Noisy, colourful and powerful, Wembley was for us a landmark, a prophetic pointer to the wide and warm-hearted friendship that was beginning to characterise Christian leadership in Britain. As John Noble shared, he admired the fiery spirit of Peter, but we also needed the heart of John to mend the nets. Philip Mohabir from the Afro-Caribbean Evangelical Alliance moved some of us to tears as he pleaded for a 'passionate passion' and for the healing of divisions.

We realised there was a need for us to forgive. This was emphasised by some wisdom that a sister had received.

> I saw a beautiful city. It stood on a hill whose warm red glow was drawing the people like a magnet. The hill was made up of thousands of interlocking tiles. Each tile represented a single act of forgiveness. 'Because there has been so much forgiveness,' the Lord said, 'I have been able to raise my city high. But should you not forgive, then it will sink and none shall see her beauty.'

We determined to forgive one another and to forgive all who'd written or spoken against us. We also took what steps we could to be reunited in heart with the Baptist Union and the Evangelical Alliance. We prepared a Declaration for Wembley in which we resolved 'to love, forgive and encourage one another and enthusiastically believe that fires of revival are breaking out in church and nation.'

At Wembley, Lynn Green from YWAM challenged us to catch some of the fire now blazing in much of the third world and to plant churches throughout Britain. We had already set targets for church-planting but resources were low and some problems still unresolved. We opened a new house in Oxford but it was our only purchase. 1990 was a year for mending nets.

The tearing and repairing went on. Church membership was growing but more were moving out of community than in. These included a handful of committed celibates who now wanted to marry. Such breakdowns in celibacy showed the need for pure motives, caution and wisdom in dealing with a gift as vulnerable as it was precious. We urged a trial year before making a celibate vow.

Happily many who struggled with temptations found a deeper reality, not in repressing their emotions, but in rekindling their passion for Jesus. First love was really what all this upheaval was about.

At the Easter Festival the theme was full surrender. Many came forward for 'sanctification' but I found it hard to believe that all who shot their hand up afterwards had really entered the sunlit regions of perfect love. Especially those who then lit up outside!

By this time I was between the millstones. I'd moved to Oxford full of vision and expected God's glory to follow my ministry. I wanted to call the new place 'Shekinah House'. 'Crucifixion House would be more like it,' retorted Noel. He was right, of course. God's agenda of humbling proud leaders graciously took me in. Desolation and inadequacy clipped my wings. I forsook my crumbling celibate commitment, relinquished all my apostolic aspirations and came home with a broken heart.

More serious was the situation with the critics. The boil

of cynicism seemed to be growing. Noel's interest in the 'prophetic movement' did little to please them. During the May Festival we listened to a tape about the 'Kansas City prophets' with their uncanny words of knowledge and predictions of fireballs of revival falling on London.

When Roger Forster went to see Paul Cain, Paul prophesied over him: 'There's a breakthrough like you've never dreamed of. God's new thing is coming to England, and he's going to call it his strange act. It is going to be revolutionary.'

Though we couldn't approve of everything we heard about them, these men did bring a timely emphasis on the prophetic dimension – especially as it related to purity in the church.

Amongst us things came to a head. During the festival some of the community stalwarts stood at the back of the marquee or disappeared into the grounds. It was all too much; all this bopping to the beat and falling around!

'What's Zion coming to?' they murmured. 'Spirituality means holiness and discipleship, not a load of circus dramatics.'

As the July convocation came round, Mark and others abandoned ship. At Cornhill disillusionment threatened to set in. Some there felt that God was judging their household. They prayed fervently and repented. Amidst a tottering scene, a banner of loyalty was raised and the humble stepped forward to fill the gap. Their young musician sang this lament to the church:

> For those who once walked in your light,
> > For those who once fought with us in the fight,
> For those who have wandered away,
> > For those ones we pray.

Rob walked off stage unable to finish and many wept.

The rest of the summer revealed the sad effect of compromise and human cleverness throughout the church. Well-established families were shaken and a few made a sad exit from community. Most remained in membership, but others left us completely with all the pain of breaking covenant.

Pete, my buddy from the Hall days, was on the way out with his family. It gutted us to see 'princes in Zion' and old friends leaving. Breaking covenant wasn't some kind of legalistic crime. It was more like divorce. We had stood side by side, had fought, loved, laughed and cried together. How could we forget that? These guys were precious. They were Zion's heart.

The senior men now closed ranks and trod gently in a situation which could have been very serious. The quality of relationships amongst its leaders determines the fate of any church. We had to get this right for the future.

At our leaders meeting we sang 'For the glory of the Lord we advance united' with a new determination. But it was a chastened people who were entering the 90s. Building the church and bringing the gospel was nothing if not heartbreak. We felt, deep down, that an amazing spiritual revolution would sweep Britain. But, as our songs reminded us, this meant 'sowing in tears', and 'bleeding with Jesus'.

A new wave of prophetic leadership emerged. Steve 'Capable' said goodbye to his sheep (woolly variety) at Plough Farm to rebuild the damaged household in London. Pete Valiant left Shalom farmhouse to take the helm at Cornhill. He arrived like Nehemiah; sat, listened and grieved. Then he rolled up his sleeves and got down to work. God gave Pete one word for Cornhill: 'Behold I make all things new.'

Huw, an Oxford man and old friend of mine, came to the fore combining school-teaching with magazine editing, church-planting and writing the occasional hymn. Huw oozed warmth and friendship and was a brilliant advert for celibacy. He wanted to see its cutting edge sharpened. 'Go for it if you dare!' he wrote in *Jesus Lifestyle*:

The spirit of the world has invaded the church in this whole area. But God is raising up a band of spiritually undiluted men and women whose sacrificial offering and prophetic sharpness will be the strength of the future.[106]

Huw, Pete and Steve (and a married Rufus) were a part of God's move to establish the church in the new anointing.

At the August Festival Noel referred to *The Gravedigger File* by Os Guinness.[107] This book spoke of the devil's strategy to subvert Western Christianity. Doubts and discouragement sown in the mind would produce cynicism causing the church to abandon its radical call. Only constant pursuit of the prophetic vision could stop the church digging its grave.

It was time to tackle cynicism head on. We launched a campaign to strengthen the heart of community and to sharpen up our distinctives. The previous year we'd used in our weekly Agape a basic Bible study by Bob Gordon. We now focused on our own accumulated wisdom about 'Zion', setting out the biblical basis of our radical teachings and lifestyle.

Opening ourselves to the mainstream had threatened to blunt our prophetic edge. Easier paths were on offer. That was why we had once stood apart. The city needed to stay firmly on the hill, undiluted, undiminished and uncompromised if ever she was to meet the desperate need for God's alternative.

It was the Zion vision that had captured Steve 'Capable's' heart back in 1975. As a searcher and psychedelic hippie, Steve was looking for a spiritual counterculture. His instinct for holiness found a home in Jesus and amongst us.

Now Steve was a sensitive leader and the anointing that had swallowed up his negativity began to work wonders in London. The family at Battlecentre rallied to Steve's warmth and inspiration as he spoke of the city of God from Isaiah: 'Your sons come from afar and your daughters are carried on the arm. Then you will look and be radiant, your heart will throb and swell with joy' (Is 60:4, 5).

Things began to happen. Ian 'Courageous', desperate to break with the cynicism in and around him, went down to join Steve. Another young leader who'd left us in frustration returned.

Steve correctly prophesied that the phone and the doorbell would be constantly ringing as people sought them out. Christians with real kingdom sight began to turn up – one arriving after the wind had wrapped a streetpaper round his feet! During one mealtime Steve suddenly had a conviction that God would knit a black brother to them. He said so. The next day YWAM rang about a young man from Zimbabwe looking for a church. Edwin took to this vigorous brotherhood and made a lively addition to the London scene.

Glastonbury brought another 'son from afar'. Aussie Tim was on a world tour. He knew about Jesus but couldn't relate to the middle of the road Christianity he had encountered. For him it was all or nothing. So he continued his pursuit of pleasure. Then a bad LSD trip at Glastonbury shook him. He stumbled his way to the Christian tent and gave his life to God. Back at London Tim seized the radical vision with both hands and soon took his stand for celibacy. Steve was delighted. Tim grinned. His girlfriend burst into tears.

So it went on. Other prophetic words were fulfilled. A strong core developed. Battlecentre became a 'city sought out.' Community, covenant brotherhood, consecration, celibacy; wherever the anointing flowed the four 'C's flourished. God showed us the reality of this in some very significant wisdom.

> In the centre of Zion stood an old leather chest which contained the many treasures God had given us. A crowd of demons were trying to drag the chest away and were meeting with some success. As I watched them, I grew anxious. Then suddenly a magnificent young lion sprang in and scattered the demons. He sat majestically on the box and guarded the treasure. To my horror, some were ordering him to go.

Ironically those who had feared for 'old Zion' fought most against her. They wanted a tame lion. But the anointing had come in wild and was renewing her. Only pride and legalism were blown out. The heart of it all, brotherhood love and radical New Testament faith, remained and was made young.

1990 had been a painful turning point. A second Wembley Praise-Day later that year was a resounding success and received support from a very wide spectrum of church leaders. Dave Fellingham from New Frontiers helped to lead the worship and spoke of many streams flowing together as one great river. Then the American, Larry Alberts, spoke with a prophetic clarity that said it all:

'God is shaking us. A sword is passing low over the body of Christ. The proud are being taken out.'

In the world, the nations too were being shaken, and in the climate of failed materialism people were turning to God. But only from a humbled church would God's river truly flow.

26

Jesus Revolution
1991

The rock group explodes into action and 600 worshippers jump to their feet in an eruption of happiness. Arms stretched heavenwards, feet tapping, they sway together, exuberant in their song of praise. They belt out 'I believe in Jesus. I believe he is the Son of God.'

Many are in their late teens or early twenties. All are casually dressed. Disillusioned by the selfish, grabbing philosophy of the 80s, these new young Christian soldiers, many of whom come from broken homes or have been in trouble with the law, are seeking happiness and fulfilment. For more than an hour they sing their heart out until the atmosphere among the Jesus Fellowship becomes electric. Then, standing in front of a huge banner proclaiming *Love, Power and Sacrifice*, their leader, Noel Stanton, tells them; 'We are part of a revolution that is taking place in the land. A revolution of love, of joy, of justice.'[108]

So ran a colourful centre-page spread in the *Daily Mirror*. As 1991 broke upon us, national papers focused on the startling results of a UK church census that had just been released in the book *'Christian' England*.[109]

As the *Mirror* informed us, 'Figures show that the evangelical movement is booming – fuelled by the more extreme charismatics.' The report continued:

> Half a million people have stopped going to church in the past 10 years, yet each Sunday 130 Christian soldiers swell the ranks of a new church army. While the pews are continuing to empty, a huge religious revival is underway.[110]

The *Daily Mirror* reported that 'house-churches have gathered more than 120,000 followers in an explosion of commitment.' It concluded: 'Though more traditional forms of religion are in decline, the new churches – noisy, informal passionate – go from strength to strength.'[111]

The *Independent On Sunday* was also hot on the trail of these Christian enthusiasts and sent a journalist out to investigate. She arrived at our second Wembley Praise-Day:

> At the sound of the very first note, hundreds leapt to their feet with hope in their eyes and hunger in their hearts. There followed 12 hours of exhausting bouts of singing, excited preaching by a succession of speakers from around the world, and a circus of 'signs and wonders' as faith healers, exorcists, tongue talkers and prophets performed ... And, on cue, hundreds poured forward to be saved.[112]

The 'highly charged' atmosphere at Wembley was not unique. The reporter noted that, 'hundreds of such gatherings took place last year'. Her research ranged from John Wimber, ex jazz-player, to George Carey, the new Archbishop of Canterbury; from the Evangelical Alliance and March for Jesus to new churches like Ichthus and Jesus Fellowship.

She judged that 'the continuing ascent of the evangelicals can only be accelerated this year'. The press had been alerted to an 'extraordinary charismatic renewal worldwide' – and it was transforming church life in the UK.

There was now a strong sense of destiny for Britain. The

empty materialism of the 80s had produced a huge reaction and spiritual hunger was taking millions into drugs, mysticism and the occult. It was also drawing them to Jesus. As the media travelled from New Age sites like Findhorn, Glastonbury and Stonehenge, to the Jesus marches, Christian festivals and celebrations, they noted a major spiritual uprising in the UK. We were in for an interesting decade as New Church and New Age movements both gathered momentum.

Fresh winds were also blowing into the more traditional Church of England. But whatever form church life took, it needed to be sufficiently anointed and relevant to reach people.

The *Daily Mirror* had told the story of Frankie, one of a group of warm hearted and quick-witted young men whom the Farm brothers first met as homeless rogues in London:

> Frankie McGaughey, 19, had already served 11 months for burglary and was on the run with an 18-month suspended sentence hanging over him, when he met two members of the Jesus Army. 'The world was doing my head in. I was a tearaway, a thug. Prison didn't change me, it only made me worse. I changed when I decided to follow Jesus,' he said. 'I gave up crime and drinking. It's beautiful what Jesus can do. My mum can't believe the change in me.'[113]

When this issue reached his home town in Northern Ireland, all copies quickly sold out as people read the amazing news that 'bad' Frankie had been converted. Thousands heard Frankie tell of his conversion on Irish radio.

Ronnie, a young Anglo-Indian, soon joined Frankie in his pilgrimage from the streets of London to the home-fires of the Farm. As Ronnie 'Zealous' told me: 'We got a lot of racial abuse in the East End. My dad got stabbed on his own doorstep. We had to board the windows up at night. For two years I was living on the streets doing crime and dope. I knew about God and my conscience plagued me. Then three of us were invited up to the Farm for a weekend. As soon as I stepped into the house I knew I belonged. I could be myself. The next day there was a wedding in chapel. We skinned up and went for a smoke outside. Rufus was brilliant. He came out and prayed with us. I found the Lord in a big way.'

Roger Ellis, leader of Revelation, a new youth church in Chichester, made this observation to the *Daily Mirror*:

> 'Young people among us find a Christianity that is relevant to their everyday needs. Sometimes youngsters with nose rings and spiky hair aren't welcome in traditional churches. They don't feel comfortable. We welcome anyone. We don't say, "Get your hair cut, take your earrings out, get a Cliff Richard smile." We say it's the heart that's important.'[114]

Charismatic worship had made some amazing inroads into the churches yet the mood was too often white, western, middle-class and selfish. So many were good with the comfortable, but not so bright with the outsiders and rebels.

During the 60s Jesus Movement in America many in the counterculture found in Jesus their model revolutionary – the Messiah who kicked the old system and established the new. Sadly few evangelicals were big enough to accommodate their unconventional zeal. Some of the hippies became cult fanatics. Others fizzled out. Those who stood were often isolated in a youth-culture which lacked the breadth of God's real alternative.

The searchers of the 60s found the establishment a turn-off. But things were changing. God's Spirit was breaking the chains of culture and freeing his people emotionally.

At our first Marquee campaign in Liverpool, Noel spoke of three breakthroughs – in the heavens, on the streets and in the church. The angelic war had been engaged and God's power was breaking through. Hearts were hungry as never before. The 60s Jesus Movement had barely touched this country but now a new wave was on its way. Thousands would find God at festivals, on the beaches and in the streets. This was God's hour for the church as one favourite hymn declared:

> The time has come to favour Zion,
>   The King of glory is marching in this land!
> Oh, a mighty Jesus revolution
>   Is advancing! The kingdom is at hand!

One person was guaranteed to be ecstatic about all this, as my journal showed:

> Yesterday Huw and I bumped into an inspired Rufus on the blackcurrant field. He'd had a brilliant prayer walk with his new 'son' Ronnie 'Zealous' and they'd prophesied together. He was full of this Jesus uprising; the hunger, teachability and readiness for sacrifice among the youth.
>
> 'Ah bro', he said, 'people are desperate for Jesus. They've tried everything. They know its all a rip off. It never produced the goods. Now's the time for Jesus. They're talking about him. They're singing about him. They're writing about him. The very earth is crying out for him. Can't you feel it? It's had enough of new-agers and priests and pagans. The very soil of Britain is thirsty for God!'

That summer we concentrated our faith and resources on the Jesus Revolution. Image and dress were progressively updated. Exuberance, festivity and buzz characterised a church that was beginning to put on its festal garments and dance through the streets. A drab nation needed a colourful church and all over Christendom God was waking his sleeping beauty.

Under a hot August sun we staged a Jesus Demonstration in Trafalgar Square. With the foot of Nelson's column adorned by a Revolution Flame banner and the band belting it out between two bronze lions, we sang and danced the afternoon away in a fast moving programme of power, testimony and sheer exultation. Airbrushed tee-shirts, painted faces and break dancing emphasised its informality.

A new Jesus movement was taking off and we wanted to

be in at the start. We were limbering up, getting God's new society out into the open. Fortunately we had a crop of new disciples like Frankie and Ronnie 'Zealous' who were better on the streets than us oldies. They'd been there.

Personally I liked the vision but took some time getting my head round it. Surely, God's revolution overturned the world's values. So what about this upbeat, like-unto-the-world stuff? It was to communicate with the youth-culture. Hence the beat, the colour and the drama. The shock did us good, but it was really for those we were trying to reach.

Jesus called his people to be in the world but not of it. Gerald Coates reckoned that most Christians were better at being 'of the world but not in it'! We were finding the balance of being different, yet relevant.

Youngsters were hungry for warmth and experience. They found God 'mind-blowing', community 'amazing' and the music 'cool'. But it was love that kept them. Houses where love was weak stood half-empty. But houses where warm, inspired leaders devoted themselves to their 'sons' both grew and prospered. Battlecentre and the Farm were outstanding examples – as I noted in my journal:

> At a Farm prayer time, someone saw a pair of shoes. The next day Paul Raj, John Noble's friend from India, walked in, took off his shoes and worshipped. 'I've never felt God's presence like this in Britain,' he said. Then Paul, who's in revival back home, prophesied how God would use us. Already the homeless, addicts and rent boys are finding God. They're coming home with extremist hearts. But they need fathers.

Most books I'd read on revival majored on prayer, spiritual warfare, and the like. But the father-heart was also vital. Much of the anointings had been to this end, not just to bring power, but to release us in love. It was one thing to minister from the platform, quite another to get deeply involved with people.

Leaders who experienced hearty friendships were very attractive. Our group in Leicester was one example.

Springfield House had been having a bad year. Clive, the cutting celibate, couldn't gel with Victor, the mystical married. But when Victor went off to Africa, Clive soon rang him up to tell him how much he was missing him. That day they became friends and when Victor got home things started to happen.

Jez had been deeply affected by a visit to our community a long time ago but had blanked God and devoted himself to his guitar. For ten years he'd fought his conscience, plunging deeper into the music scene – drink, drugs, and the like. At last, with his friend Craig playing drums, he began to make it big in Spain. Then, with success in his grasp, Jez flew back to England, climbed a hill and gave his life to God. He laid down his guitar, cut off his long ginger dreadlocks, burned his designer clothes and embraced celibacy. Amazed, Victor and Clive welcomed him in. Craig soon followed.

Springfield's sisterhood also thrived as two girls, friends of Jez and Craig, came to the Lord and moved in. Lesley, a leading celibate, was already looking after a pair of sisters who'd come out of the New Age scene. She was now surrounded by a growing flock – motherhood!

Africa was one of God's surprises. A student from Ghana had met us on our Oxford campaign, stayed at Vineyard for a while, and returned to Kumasi as a covenant member. Before long Steve 'Ambassador' had gathered 80 people around him. Mike 'Rockfast' (prophetic administrator), Victor (inspirational teacher) and Bill 'Truthful' (the power man) went out to nurture the young church and meet others from Ghana and Nigeria. The team found new power in healing and deliverance and baptised 34 members of Jesus Fellowship Kumasi in the river – once a thirsty camel had moved out of the way!

Shepton Mallet was another surprise. We'd targeted 28 new households in cities ranging from Brighton to Manchester and from Norwich to Bristol. Shepton wasn't among them. But a cell group mushroomed there through prayer, faith and a lot of travelling. Mature Christians were joining them.

Shepton attracted one seeker who'd taught Krishna consciousness in India. Graham's search for purity had been frustrated till he found Jesus back in England. When he visited a friend who was also newly converted, Graham heard our latest tape, *Blazing Sword*, and was very challenged.

Days later his friend was throwing some things from his past onto the fire when the music-centre switched itself on. The song came through, 'Not for nothing are we leaving all behind'. They were stunned. That night they met with the Shepton group and Graham was baptised in the Holy Spirit. All thanks to an invisible finger on the ON switch!

Angelic activity seemed to be increasing. Some often saw angels – especially women and young children. It was not unusual for a little girl to tell me that two angels were dancing at my side or that a huge warrior was guarding the Golden Marquee with a drawn sword. One blind sister informed me that the angels got excited when we sang 'Servant King' and our own song, 'One touch of God'. Well of course.

Late one night Wilf and another brother from Living Stones were up late making a recording of 'Servant King'. When they played the song back they heard a high, sweet voice joining in. The hair on Wilf's neck stood on end.

Another incident at Living Stones was also remarkable. A Spanish sister had gone to her room to pray before dinner. She received a powerful anointing of the Spirit. This spread to the other sisters and soon the shrieking and laughter alerted the rest of the house. When two brothers reached the foot of the staircase they were overwhelmed by a wave of power. It was swiftly followed by a pair of intoxicated sisters who tumbled down the stairs. They all crawled into the lounge where the household had gathered to 'say grace'.

There was more grace than bargained for! As the worship

became awesome many saw or sensed angels; some in the room joining in the praise, others dancing on the lawn or sitting in the trees. One striking figure Norma saw was so tall that his belt buckle was level with the ceiling.

The worship time lasted all evening. Wilf, one of the least affected, spent most of his time getting dinners out of the oven, looking on in dismay and putting them back again! At 1.00 am Kelly, the practical mystic, suggested they call it a day. After all, they did have work in the morning.

Another story came from our Sheffield evangelism; a brother was trying to rescue someone from being beaten up by a gang when one of them flew at him with both fists. Suddenly a smart young man leapt in and shielded him from the blows.

'Thanks!' said the brother afterwards.

Noticing he was carrying our *Streetpaper*, he added: 'I'm from the Jesus Army.'

The stranger smiled warmly. 'Oh, I know all about you!' And he wandered off.

The evangelist turned to the sisters opposite. 'Did you see that?'

'Yes. Amazing. His fists kept stopping in mid-air.'

'I mean the guy in the suit.'

'What guy?' they asked.

Angels, anointings, adventures! The summer began to crackle as the disappointments of 1990 turned into to a fresh exhilaration. The first edition of *Fire in our Hearts* was well received and many, on hearing the story 'from the horse's mouth', became firm friends and supporters. Not all were convinced, but new church leaders like Gerald Coates were very appreciative, and Bryn Jones described God's work among us as 'a miracle in our time'.[115]

New members glimpsed the treasures of our heritage and veterans sniffled and laughed their way through a story they knew so well. It was all part of a rediscovery – of our call to be a people for God and of our mission to the 'poor'.

JESUS REVOLUTION

After the book was launched I locked horns with Mike and Huw over my intention to marry. Sometimes authors disagree and Mike lived up to his name – 'Rockfast'! I decided to go for a walkabout. It was a chance to see how green the grass was outside.

Visiting new churches broadened my outlook, but I missed the 'gutsy' types I'd grown to love in the Jesus Army. The absence of tattoos, weird haircuts, nose-rings, lace-less squaddy boots and friendship bands made me a little homesick amongst the well-mannered, the groomed and the beautiful. There were exceptions, but it struck me how hard the average Christian finds it to relate to people 'on the level'. Hence so few of the liberated, the outrageous and the different. I missed the raw energy of the sons of thunder.

And where on earth was the church on Monday? Seriously. I tried the Yellow Pages. The City Christian Fellowship or the Lord's Community Church sounded tasty, but all I got was a recorded invite to the Sunday meeting. I could be dead by then! In the early days at Bugbrooke we met six nights a week and God led us into a kingdom culture. I knew that without such an ever-present alternative many of our guys would never make it. Nor would I. The church was in my blood. 'Zion' was my life, my dream, the fabric of my soul.

Fortunately, the brethren at home proved more accommodating than first appeared. After meeting some good people and tasting a little of the sweetness elsewhere, I found myself back at Wembley. Back to excitement and colour; to flashing lights and videos, to fast-moving programmes and to wild and tattooed youngsters. To loud music and to noise. To noise!

'Oh God', I groaned, 'do we really need all this?'

My mind turned to pleasant house-groups, to quiet early nights in my own room, to undisturbed morning meditations, (Ah!) and to the sweet freedom of sunny October days.

Then the lights went on. Noel had asked three lads onto the stage and was telling their stories:

'This is Pete "Noble". Pete's mum was 15 when he was born and he was adopted by a middle class family. In his early teens he left home a rebel. Living on the streets and in squats he got into drugs; speed, coke, crack, anything. Pete had a faith in God but didn't know where to find him. He became a registered heroin addict and a dealer. At 18 he jumped off a 30-foot bridge on acid and broke both his legs. After he came out of hospital things got worse. When a sister met him in Bristol he weighed 5½ stone and had been given less than a year to live. Pete came back to one of our houses, found the love of Jesus and was baptised in the Holy Spirit.'

The tears began to fall. I was overwhelmed by God's kindness, amazed that these were my brothers. Here was conversion, raw, radical, powerful. Soon all who'd been homeless, abused or in prison were climbing onto the stage. And they just kept coming. This was it. This was Jesus. Then the Cornhill family came on doing a dance routine. Rob was rapping:

> A new revolution's happening in town,
>   We're the Jesus People, come on down!
> There's revolution talk right out there –
>   There's revolution power right in here!
> You see, this revolution is one of love,
>   And this revolution is one of joy,
> And this revolution is one of peace,
>   And this revolution is one of justice;
> Where people of all class and race
>   Get saved and healed in Jesus' grace;
> The lame, the sick, the dirty, the drunks,
>   The posh, the poor, the bad, the punks,
> The tall, the short, the fat, the thin;
>   Anyone who wants can all join in.

And in they came: dear old John 'Venerable' dressed as a vicar; Lionel wearing a dinner jacket and Marion in a gown,

Janie as a hippie, a sister on a stretcher, a traffic warden, a lollipop lady, street kids tumbling in, a beggar and a bishop – even the BBC – all joined in, till the stage was all life, energy and colour. The audience was taken by storm. The young lion had sprung into Cornhill. The revolution had begun.

The author of *'Christian' England* predicted that 'leaders, pioneers and visionaries will be of the essence in the 90s'.[116] *Alpha* magazine too was urging us all in the new churches to 'break the mould'.[117] By 1991 people in Britain were beginning to realise that a giant had awoken in their midst – if an article in *Elle* magazine was anything to go by:

> Evangelicals are successfully tapping into a collective mood that crosses all boundaries and satisfies the desire for spiritual absolutes. Their campaign to win the nation for Jesus will be long and arduous, and not without its casualties. But know this; in the battle for souls, tomorrow belongs to them.[118]

27

New Horizons
1992

The Wembley gatherings expanded our vision way beyond our own work. Reports of growth in South America, India and Korea were staggering. We saw Chinese believers on video, tearstained and passionate. Africans in their thousands looked like fields of ripe wheat waving under God's power. In so many nations there was fervour, spirit, life.

In the light of this, Europe was a darkened continent, a secular jungle. If Britain looked a little brighter, the flight from the churches continued here unabated. And if North America had its display of power, it lacked the purity of the people's movement that was sweeping the third world.

The West was in trouble. Whilst poor Christians were spiritually rich, rich Christians were poor. In the global church, pale faces now stood in the minority. Interest in church growth soared as white westerners stooped to learn from their coloured brothers.

Peter Wagner wrote of the pentecostal churches in Latin

America.[119] Here were red-blooded enthusiasts who took the good news to the people. Pastors were poor, often illiterate, and bore more resemblance to the disciples of Jesus than the bible students of the West. Poverty kept them in touch with the common man. Their college was the street, their success measured by the number of churches they'd planted.

In the third world poverty and hardship had produced good soil for the gospel. By contrast so many westerners were weighed down with wealth and stunted by comforts. What hope was there for us? In 1989 Rob White of British Youth for Christ told us in an interview for *Jesus Lifestyle* how he'd seen Jesus with his back on Europe.

> 'You've waved me goodbye in Europe', the Lord said.
> 'Do you really need me?' And this he asked three times.
> 'Yes Lord, we really need you!' I cried in earnest.
> 'But do you realise that will mean holiness?'
> And it was like hanging on his coat tails saying, 'Turn round Lord. Please turn round!'
> And he began to turn round.[120]

Within a year communism had collapsed in Europe and people were dancing on the ruins of the Berlin Wall.

Economic recession, family breakdown and moral decay had opened people up spiritually in Europe, especially Britain. The massive response to March for Jesus revealed a grassroots movement hungry for spiritual life. When 50,000 Christians crammed the streets of London some had felt that a major awakening in the UK was at last a possibility.

Many Christians now carried a vision to see a vibrant church operating in every local community in the UK by the year 2,000. Lynn Green of YWAM, who was closely involved with this Challenge 2,000 vision, explained:

> In some cities church leaders were already working together in a shared strategy. Against this background a consultation on

church planting was held at the invitation of March for Jesus, the Evangelical Alliance and the Bible Society.[121]

They agreed on a method which had met with success in the third world. DAWN (Discipling A Whole Nation) was a strategy to mobilise all the Christian groupings into widespread church-planting throughout their nation. Planting new churches, according to church-growth experts, had proved the most effective method of evangelism in the third world. It was clearly the way forward for the UK.

The DAWN Congress gathered leaders from 32 denominations in the UK. These agreed on a target of 20 per cent of the population attending church by the year 2,000. To achieve this goal, Christians in the UK would have to plant 20,000 new churches in the space of eight years – a staggering number.

Some of our own men attended this Congress and submitted the Jesus Army targets for those eight years. Shortly after, a DAWN representative spoke to our gathered leadership. From then on it was all targets, goals, reports and endless reams of paper! Our plan was to divide up the UK into 24 regions and apportion them to regional leadership teams. New style Jesus Army maps were soon hanging boldly in our houses displaying these 24 regions and their pioneering activities.

We had now converted a two-storey outbuilding at the Farm to house our enquiries, communications, accounts, resources and graphics departments. Alongside Noel's crowded Farm office these Central Offices formed a well defined 'HQ' that shouldered much of the administrative burden for the newly-formed regions. Under its watchful eye, regional leaders developed their own genius as pastors of the Jesus Army congregations in their area. The main regional men met together regularly with Noel as the senior leaders of the whole church.

Steve 'Capable's' region included London and the South East and he was responsible for Brighton, Hastings and the two households at Battlecentre. His new 'sons' were doing well and Steve had targeted for a third London household in 1992.

They'd been looking for property for months but weren't sure where God wanted them. Eventually Steve found a large detached house in Ealing, a bit upmarket for the Jesus Army, but OK. The purchase was about to go through when Steve went for his usual prayer walk up his street. He suddenly noticed a FOR SALE notice at Number 13. NO CALLERS, it read. He knocked anyway.

'I see your house is up for sale,' said Steve.

'What!' the man exclaimed. He rushed out and uprooted the sign. 'I told them not to put one up!'

'Oh well, you might as well have a look around.'

The house was tempting, but too small. If only they had the one next door – but that would take a miracle. Steve went home and mused. The sign had only been up for half an hour – funny. That evening there was a knock at the door.

'Hello, I'm the lady from Number 11. I hear you're looking for a house and wondered if you would like to buy mine.'

Two houses in one day! Next to each other – and four doors up from Battlecentre! Steve was stunned.

That was how we got 'Spreading Flame'. Evidently God wanted their community to stay together – as one big fire. My diary captured the general excitement in Emanuel Avenue, Acton:

> They're pretty wild down there – lots of praise and presence and laughter. Steve says: 'If revival is just round the corner it's time we went round the corner.' At one mealtime someone had a picture of a man carrying a flaming torch. Another saw a spark setting the whole land alight. Fire is the image time and again.

That summer we held a marquee mission near Acton. A young New Zealander with a backpack met us at Trafalgar Square. She was soon unpacking it at Spreading Flame.

We had a word in one prayer meeting about someone crying out to God on the Embankment. At about the same time a young man was praying desperately for God to help him.

Paul's girlfriend had left him, he'd hit the bottle, lost his job and was now homeless on the Embankment. We brought him back to the Marquee where he found Jesus and joined the team.

That year the London congregation gained 32 people, a colourful mix originating from Trinidad, Tobago, Fiji, Zimbabwe, Ireland, Cornwall and 'Sarf' London.

With our continued expansion I noticed many new faces at the leaders meeting. The southern brothers I knew pretty well, so I assumed these hailed from up north; from Manchester, Burnley, Newcastle or Preston (not to mention Scotland).

Ian 'Greatheart' was an old worthy now operating up north. Twenty years ago Ian and his wife had moved to a quiet village called Bugbrooke. Discovering a little chapel down the road the stalwart evangelicals had walked straight into a bunch of charismatic, communitarian fanatics. Normal life soon came to an end as the young family began the journey of a lifetime. Now Ian was a Senior Leader, manager of Skaino Services, and church planter in Sheffield.

Though we were famous for reaching 'street-people', this was hardly the whole picture. Up in Sheffield a notorious criminal soon joined hands with a university boff. A young Polish doctor, Andrzej and his wife Sharron (who'd once planned to be a nun) also provided the strength for a second household there. Likewise in Manchester; it was a university lecturer and his wife who opened their large house to provide a good base in the city.

The shape of things was changing. The previous year had seen record growth among those who did not, as yet, live in community. This type of membership we called Style 1. Style 2 embraced a greater degree of accountability and financial giving whilst Style 3 was our classic all-things-in-common community membership. Growth in this style was disappointing.

However there were encouraging signs. In areas where new groups had no community house, people just wanted to be together. Church households were springing up in places like Glasgow and Manchester which produced their own home-grown leaders. All this encouraged initiative.

Then there was the 'Multiply Network'. Multiply was launched as a new stream uniting Jesus Fellowship churches with other groups with a similar vision. King's Church, Chatham, was one of our first open supporters and 'friends' who eventually joined us in Multiply. They also released a few of their people to us who were eager for community. One young family lived at Battlecentre for a while before heading up our work in Brighton.

Many still came to us from far and wide hungering for a Christian alternative. Cornhill Manor, (led by Pete the Dutchman), had a European flavour and a daughter household in Sweden. The Farm had members in Spain who were interested in community. We were also friendly with a number of community groups in Europe and one dynamic youth-church in Germany, led by Walter Heidenreich, joined us in the Multiply Network.

Relating to others was very healthy. Some of our senior men spent more than one enjoyable afternoon with Tony Morton and team from Southampton. We found Tony down to earth, humorous and very brotherly. But he didn't lack punch: 'God uses zealous, idealistic, sacrificial people who are outspoken, possibly obnoxious' was one of his comments in *Jesus Lifestyle*.[122]

We probably fitted that description! But we didn't relish isolation. It was encouraging to be invited to talk about our work at London Bible College. We also spoke at Spurgeon's College where Steve 'Capable' and I bumped into Nigel Wright, lover of Anabaptists, author of *The Radical Kingdom*,[123] and wise observer of the New Church movement.

Reviewing the first edition of *Fire in our Hearts* in *Renewal*, Nigel wrote: 'Whatever the Jesus Fellowship has done has its parallels in Christian history. Those like the Hutterites or Booth who took such stands in the past are now treated with honour and respect.'[124] He wondered if he could cope with our 'intense lifestyle' (It's not that bad!) and added, 'But there again it takes a movement that breaks the mould to reach those who are unreachable.'

I had managed to reach at least one unreachable during my abortive church-planting session in Oxford. The miracle of unlikely friendship happened around the kitchen table whilst singing 'One touch of God' to a very brewed up, growling skinhead. Ben was larger than life, extremely funny and wept easily. What hadn't he done? Which 'nick' hadn't he been in? But the character loved Jesus (after a fashion) and followed me back to Palm Tree Cottage next door to Cornhill. My diary showed community life in a less than romantic light:

> I came back to find a wife. Instead, I'm helping to look after six assorted, so-called disciples who are up and down like yo-yos. The need is to build, build, build and it's hard work. Our house meetings are good, sometimes powerful, but their day to day battles with the flesh and all their instabilities, bickerings and temptations to smoke, drink and split are quite something. A few days ago one of them tried to strangle Alasdair. In the midst of this I'm supposed to be doing another book!

I was writing about church as a counterculture and asked some of the Palm Tree crew why they'd joined us. One sister with a degree in philosophy explained: 'The churches I knew catered for middle class couples and were a bit boring. I was looking for something more unworldly. The group at Oxford attracted me. There were so many different types; skinheads, hippies, a doctor, a zany housewife, an ex-actress. They were getting to grips with the need.'

The ex-actress, Mary, and her friend from theatre were both single mums who enjoyed the everyday drama at Palm Tree Cottage. Mary was finding some deep healing in community:

> When I arrived five years ago with my two-year-old boy, my husband had just left me. I'd known a lot of heartbreak. At 17 I was assaulted and had numbed the pain in a succession of fantasies: Teddy boys, Gothics, New Age and theatre.

Marriage gave me some happiness till that was shattered. But then I found Jesus. The day I walked into this little haven in Northamptonshire I felt God's presence and a real peace. There are some right characters here, but among them, and with prayer, I've begun to find the real me.

A gracious addition to this eccentric bunch was a family who had fled from war-torn Uganda. Ketty was a tall young woman whose father was an African pastor. She'd lost her home and her husband but had found refuge with her two children in this English oakbeamed cottage.

Ketty was a prayer-warrior (we needed her!), loved holiness and often praised God. We must have tried her patience, but as Ketty remarked, with a very wide smile: 'I feel I've found a family.' That said it all. Sadly this noble African refugee was seriously ill and the first to grace our new burial ground at Cornhill. Zion was truly a home for the widow, the orphan and the stranger.

At Palm Tree I delved into the writings of former radical Christians and noted the frequent use of the word 'Zion'. Inspirationally it described the church. But it wasn't that simple. In scripture, 'Zion' could mean natural Israel, the church or the heavenly city. I felt it was a touch of heaven when 'brothers dwell together in unity' – but I'm a poet.

One evening I sat down with Andrzej and asked what 'Zion' meant to him. He responded with total enthusiasm: 'It was like when I first met Sharron. Something leapt inside.'

Andrzej gesticulated, flinging his arms around wildly.

'I was Catholic, you see ... charismatic. But I longed to see evangelism, community. You know ... the zeal of the early church. So did Sharron. Well, we met the Jesus Army singing in Sheffield. Ian 'Greatheart' was playing a banjo in the square. I can see his face now. God spoke to us and we started coming around. It was all so exciting – the vision – everything. It was like ... like falling in love again. Zion! You know! It was just like coming home ... coming home.'

He sank back exhausted with inspiration. I laughed. But

his heart fire had touched me. The next morning I grabbed a pen:

> We have found the best all,
>   Zion, joy of every soul;
> Drinking of one spirit now,
>   Jesus takes the royal crown,
> World and sin are trampled down!
>   Zion is our home!

Inspired by the new bloods at the Farm, Noel added a verse:

> Satisfy your deep desire
>   In this church of love and fire!
> Here the friends for whom you cried
>   Always loyal at your side,
> Arms of welcome opened wide:
>   Zion is our home!

Such was the beauty of covenant love. Celibacy too was advancing. The 200-strong meeting of vowed and probationary celibates excelled in worship as one sister recorded:

> It was incredible! When we started to worship I sensed fire racing through our hearts. I was weeping to God to so cleanse me that the fire would stay and never go away. I heard instrumental music and angels with really high voices. An amazing spiritual song swept around the hall in ever increasing waves. After that we all broke out in thunderous Jesus claps and cheers.[125]

A celibate power-switch was thrown and the whole spirit of celibacy became futuristic. Frankly I was amazed to see young people with everything going for them in terms of marriage cast it all aside for the sake of the kingdom. The day of sacrifice wasn't over. We were limbering up. There were signs of a golden age to come.

Our strategy in 1992 was not only to regionalise but also to release the dynamic of the converted. Regular leadership training sessions were held at Cornhill and included many potential 'Timothies'. The apostle Paul had 'fathered' and apprenticed young Timothy. This kind of spiritual mentoring was growing amongst us and was really the hope of the future.

All around we sensed the mood of a new generation looking for challenge. The need for adventure, to take life on and to explore the limits was raw material for the Spirit of God. MEN WHO DARE! was a bold headline that summer in our *Jesus Revolution Streetpaper:*

> Rugged, lively, new Christians! High profile, outfront! They belong to the revolutionary dynamic of the early church. They take up the torch of those who 'turned the world upside down'. New Christians are courageous, daring! Dangerous to demons! They live to promote the gospel of Jesus Christ. Ready to give up jobs, sports, wealth, marriage. Sold out to the new Christian cause. These are men and women who dare![126]

But the future of our own youth caused concern. Many Fellowship sons and daughters had been brought up in our most sober, disciplined era. Though we were more flexible nowadays, our children still faced a major crisis when they became teenagers. Many rebelled as they fought for their personal identity. Some left the church outright but a number returned after tasting what the world had to offer. But whether they stayed or not, all needed their own experience of Jesus.

Twenty years had flown by since Noel and his friends had patiently won the hearts of people like Rufus and Jess, sitting where they sat – on orange boxes, drinking herbal tea and just listening. Noel and Rufus now found themselves in a similar situation with two of our teenage 'rebels'.

Nathan and Phil were both sons of Fellowship leaders. Nathan's parents had joined our Oxford group in the early 70s. They were gripped with the vision of Christian community and had left everything to follow it. Now, as a large family, they all lived at King's House in the Warwickshire countryside.

Nathan was 16 and making friends at sixth form college in

Rugby. A group of them had a good scene together and would often meet up, chatting late into the night, playing reggae and smoking dope. The brotherhood appealed to Nathan. There he could relax, be himself and do his own thing.

Phil, who lived in our Nottingham house and attended drama school, was on a similar journey, experimenting and 'finding himself' – often at all-night raves and parties, sleeping on floors and returning home as little as possible.

Nathan and Phil compared notes and smoked hash together. Nathan was the more emotional and keenly felt the conflict that was raging within. 'What's happening to me?' he asked himself. 'I love God and the church, so why am I going off the rails like this? Why do I want this scene?'

After one meeting Noel encouraged him:

'Nathan, you're going to be a real man of God.'

'How?' was the curt reply. Nathan badly needed some answers.

One night he was feeling so desperate that he turned up at the Farm. He found Noel and Rufus very helpful. Over a period of months they talked things through; Nathan, rash, confused, defensive, trying to understand himself; Noel and Rufus quietly listening and giving help where they could. Often Nathan rang up in the middle of the night, stoned. They understood.

At one Jesus Revolution meeting in Coventry Nathan brought his girlfriend along. But when she started to mock, he lost his cool. 'I would die for these people,' he shouted. Realising what he'd said, he rushed backstage and wept.

The next evening he appeared with the band in Northampton (to the delight or dismay of many). Noel invited Nathan, Phil and two others to the parents meeting at Cornhill the following night. He intended to focus on our community teenagers and wanted the 'rebels' to speak for themselves.

Nathan's frank sharings had alerted Noel to the acute needs of our youth. Growing up within the 'straight and narrow', some had struggled with feelings of frustration and rejection. As they now entered maturity they needed to be trusted and given space. Many had made friendships with older brothers and this helped enormously to work things through outside the family circle. Parents could often do little more than step back and cling to God's promises.

At the packed meeting in the King's Room Noel spoke of his vision for our somewhat neglected teenagers. We'd given much to evangelism but these young men and women were destined to be the springboard for greater things amongst us. Isaiah had once mourned that Jerusalem had 'none to guide her' among 'all the sons she bore' (Is 51:18). Zion's sons were meant to cherish her, 'take her by the hand' and lead her on. Ours first needed winning, healing, and giving opportunity to express their creative energy.

Nathan and Phil soon had the gathering in stitches with their memories, candour and funny remarks. During that memorable evening mums and dads faced their failures and triumphs as forgiveness, humour and hope flowed between the generations. When Nathan and Phil sat down they were clearly rebels. But, strangely and movingly, the impression that lingered was of their love for the church – and her Lord.

Nathan continued to struggle. His ambitions were set on music and he'd started to play for a local band. At this point Jez came into the story. Jez had heard about one of 'Zion's kids' who had a talent for keyboard, was on the way out, and wanted advice on the music scene.

Rufus set up a meeting for them at Sheepfold where they could make some sounds together. The two musicians gelled from the word go. Soon Rufus had an inspiration. He'd been wondering how to capture the energy and mysticism of creation in music. Maybe... Yes. He shot off and came back with a copy of *The Magician's Nephew* by C.S. Lewis.

Nathan and Jez were still jamming as the December sun sank low over the hills and the little studio began to fill with atmosphere. Rufus began to read aloud and Nathan's keyboard followed with moody, mysterious sounds. The guitar sang and soared. Caught up in the imagery of the moment, Rufus began to weep. They'd hit on something deep.

28

Spiritual Searchers
1993

'Hush!' said the Cabby. They all listened.

In the darkness something was happening at last. A voice had begun to sing. Its lower notes were deep enough to be the voice of the earth herself.

Mary and her six year old son, Faolan, sat entranced as the low music throbbed and rumbled through their seats at the Derngate Theatre in Northampton. Then...

Two wonders happened at the same moment. One was that the voice was suddenly joined by other voices. They were far higher up the scale: cold, tingling, silvery voices. The second wonder was that the blackness overhead, all at once, was blazing with stars.

The high ceiling was lit by a thousand points of light as the deep throb was joined by delicate silvery cadences. Rufus continued the drama, as he read, by pencil light, from *The Magician's Nephew*.[127]

> 'Glory be!' said the Cabby. 'I'd ha' been a better man all my life if I'd known there were things like this.'

The music grew stronger and, as the lights came on slowly...

> The sky grew paler, then changed from white to pink and from pink to gold. The Voice rose and rose, till all the air was shaking with it. And just as it swelled to the mightiest and most glorious sound it had yet produced, the sun arose. As its beams shot across the land the travellers saw the mountains. The earth was of many colours, fresh and vivid. They made you feel excited; until you saw the Singer himself, and then you forgot everything else.

The theme was creation, and this was the founding of Narnia. It was Faolan's favourite story. But to see it now with real scenery, coloured lights and mist. Ah!

> The Lion breathed out a long, warm breath. Then came a swift flash and every drop of blood tingled in the children's bodies, and the deepest, wildest voice they ever heard was saying, 'Narnia, Narnia, Narnia, awake. Love. Think. Speak.'

As the drama reached its climax the ambient music glided upwards from a song about creation to heavenly worship. Voice and flute, guitar and keyboard harmonised and danced with the colours as we joined in the spiritual song.
As the anointing of the Spirit fell, the atmosphere became thick, golden, heavenly. On and on went the sounds, weaving, blending, soaring. What was programmed for 15 minutes had run wild in the Spirit. Then people began to

come forward, deeply moved. For Mary, the ecstasy of that moment on New Year's day re-awakened her waning love for God. For guitarist Jez it swallowed up ten years of wilderness.

A.W. Tozer complained that the evangelicals of his day lacked awe in God and wonder at his creation. Not so the searchers. As a teenager, I found that sunset, stream and star awakened in me a deep desire, but the Christians I knew seemed cosmically numb. Their attitude to the planet was to abandon it as soon as possible! With such a negative outlook in the church it was small wonder that all the nature mystics, earth crusaders and pagans were on the increase.

Our view of creation was positive. We recognised that man was made in God's image, and though fallen, he was hardly Satan's friend. He desired goodness. This was easier to see in the spiritual climate now developing. All around were confused, longing people sick of material values and hungry for love, warmth and reality. Our task was to identify, show a brotherly alternative and gently guide them to Jesus.

In the light of this, any aggressive overtones in the army image were played down. *We Fight For You!* and *Love, Power and Sacrifice* were mellowed to *Jesus People – Loving People.* We were a JESUS army with the emphasis on Jesus. Recently God had changed the face of our church. We now needed a new image, a new approach. So at the 1993 Easter Festival we launched the 'modern JESUS army' in all its rainbow colours: its commission – to flow with the people.

The following months found us at raves, in pubs and night-clubs, at parties, on the beaches and at festivals. We baptised people in rivers, the sea, even the fountains at Trafalgar Square. A fast-moving video, *We're Jesus Revolutionaries,* captured some of the excitement. But the heart of this revolution was Jesus, friend of sinners. Loving people was the key.

The creation sketch from Narnia was repeated in Manchester and Sheffield and the marked anointing on it suggested that God could use technology as a servant of the Spirit.

SPIRITUAL SEARCHERS

At clubs and festivals we noted the tremendous influence of music. If music communicated so powerfully, then maybe God was calling us to speak in its language. Everywhere we saw the instinct to worship. Whether dancing before a totem pole or raving the night away on ecstasy, people wanted to abandon themselves in a group experience akin to worship.

The present culture was also highly visual. Pictures speak more than words and even books were becoming outdated in a world of videos and high tech computers. God communicated visually; through creation, and in water baptism, oil and wine. Christianity was full of visual symbols.

So we began to develop our media technology using film, sound and lighting. Techno took us down two lines: videographics and computerised music. John 'Perceptive' and his boffs could handle the first. For the second we drew on Jez who gingerly introduced Noel to a world of modern dance; of jungle, rave, ambient and house music; of drum machines, sequencers and samplers. Noel was interested, for he had something (in the Spirit) up his sleeve.

We'd done prophetic drama many times now since we filled Westminster Central Hall with smoke in 1989. The risk of using drama was that a serious message could degenerate into mere entertainment. It also took a lot of time in prop making, organisation and rehearsal.

Our dramatic presentations needed refocusing to communicate the gospel effectively. We'd gained new skills and better equipment. We also wanted to harness the creative energy of the youth. Was it time for a big project? A presentation that would speak into the current mood?

The idea evolved of a multimedia event using videographics, film, sound, light displays – the lot; powerful images showing the beauty of creation and its devastation; sights that captured the desperate need of humanity; songs that spoke of God's love; colourful celebrations of a new brotherhood. All from the gut, raw and in tune with the cries of the people. The vision caught on.

Rufus asked Nathan and Phil to get involved but Nathan was blowing hot and cold, afraid of being drawn in. A meeting was arranged at the Farm but they turned up four hours late, stoned out of their heads. They put a downer on the whole thing. It was far too square and, besides, Nathan had his musical career to consider. Rufus felt like strangling him but swallowed a further dose of patience and humility. He remembered a difficult young actor from the past.

Soon Noel was ringing up Phil with questions about the latest music and fashions. 'What exactly is Grunge?' Noel asked.

He saw Phil as a link with the youth culture. Saved or not, Nathan and Phil were our men on the ground and in touch. Phil gladly sent down tapes and articles. He even spent an occasional night at the Farm, beating a hasty retreat back to Nottingham in the morning.

One night Nathan was celebrating his seventeenth birthday when Rufus and another Farm brother turned up. They piled into the car and drove out to the Derbyshire hills. There was a mad climb in the dark and, on the top of Black Rocks, swept by a wild, chilling wind, Phil unburdened his guilt to Rufus. As they prayed Phil broke down, found forgiveness and was freed from a spirit of rejection.

This was his first touch of God and he ran down the hill feeling like air. From then on his spirit began to come alive. But there was no sudden clean-up. That summer Phil abandoned himself to loose-living, wild parties and raves. God was there too, waiting.

Nathan was equally wild and had left King's House to live with friends near Rugby. Noel stayed true to him through a few explosions and gave him an occasional lyric which he put to music. One evening Rufus found him in his gran's summerhouse, stoned (as usual). They worked on a song that Rufus and Ronnie were going to introduce at Spinney; 'Do you wanna have a father's heart, brother?' It was apt. Rufus's own father's heart was working overtime.

Recently we had focused on soul healing. Many came to us with deep emotional scars and there were some heart-rending tales. A survey showed that one out of five girls had suffered sexual abuse by the age of 18. Many youngsters in fact left home in their early teens fleeing from some kind of abuse.

> So many wounds, so many wounds,
> Heal me now with your powerful love.

Many sang this with tears. It seemed that the erosion of real family life had devastated the youth of Britain.

Paul had walked out of a broken home when a young teenager and was roughing it on the Strand in London when Steve 'Capable' met him. Steve gave him his card and Paul thought no more of it. But soon the rejection that had dogged his life became unbearable. He decided to throw himself off Waterloo Bridge. As Paul stood looking down at the murky waters of the Thames he felt something in his pocket. It was Battlecentre's phone number. He rang it up and Steve came out and brought him home. With a powerful combination of healing prayer, family life and some good fathering, Paul soon became a young man of God and a valuable worship leader. He doubled in weight too!

Darren also left home in unhappy circumstances at 13. After four years living on the streets in Ireland and in London, Darren staggered onto our Jesus coach at Trafalgar Square, drunk and abusive. He wept his way to God. His friend Trev, who'd slept in shop doorways and squats, begging and mugging for a living, saw the change in 'Daz' and joined him up at New Creation Farm.

These strong characterful men responded to fathers in God. But many of us old-timers needed healing too. A true leader was warm-hearted, patient and loving. Rigidity and legalism was a curse. We'd learned that. Relaxed flow was where it was at. When we allowed God to love us and heal us, we gladly shed our hard 'Christian' skins and began to win hearts.

So many were searching. Not just new-agers but ordinary people who through hurt, heartache and distress longed for what was good. We wanted to accommodate ourselves to them, use any means, make a bridge, help them reach out to God.

We aimed at being more user-friendly and informal in our gospel presentation. Sunday nights at Spinney Hall, Northampton, now included a snack and coffee bar in the foyer. With smiling welcomers, colourful resources, background music and lots of friends, a good scene was well on the go before the main programme started.

When it did, our new friends were encouraged to relax and enjoy the atmosphere without feeling obliged to join in. The non-threatening approach attracted many who might avoid religious meetings. Invitations were to a:

Sunday Evening At Spinney (SEAS)
A Jesus Revolution evening of music, friendship,
faith, life and worship with the Jesus Praise Band

SEAS soon employed UV lamps, strobes and 'intelligent' lighting. The London congregation's version involved a brother switching coloured light bulbs on and off – fast!

That summer 100,000 festival-goers converged on Glastonbury pouring into the campsites, marquees and field-markets. The Glastonbury Festival was a showcase for the many ways folk in the 90s were searching for spiritual reality. Drugs, occult, New Age, eastern religion, music, they were all there. Centuries old druidism rubbed shoulders with high-tech attractions like virtual reality; as did rich yuppies with hippie travellers.

One of our teams was in the thick of it all seeking to bring the Jesus experience, as our *Streetpaper* reported:

> 'I guess you Christians are going to tell me I need to be filled with something like your Holy Spirit because I have a gap in my life.'

Sam and Fabian were down by the main stage talking to a young man when his friend burst in with these words. They liked his comment and asked if they could pray for him. The Spirit came upon him and he fell over right in the middle of the crowd. When he got up he was so excited he started to hassle his friends to get prayer too![128]

Many felt a touch of God's love. Not all were immediately converted, but God responded to their openness. From the hills that overlooked the festival one could see thousands of searchers. So many were on a spiritual journey.

New Age seemed to mimic the charismatic movement. Here were prophets, healers and counsellors; here too we could find prayer and music, conferences and festivals; and, for the radical element, simple lifestyle and community.

So many had a thirst for wisdom, a hunger for experience, and a desire for a better world. We weren't interested in simply faultfinding. True, much was deception and seduction. But among it all were kingdom seekers and God's men of tomorrow.

Our place was to respect, listen and look for common ground. They counted creation as sacred. The world-denying image that Christianity portrayed was not only sad but false. Scripture placed earth on centre-stage as man's first paradise and, when renewed, his final destiny. It was this ache for a lost Eden that motivated them, as I wrote in our revamped *Jesus Life* magazine:

> The vision of a Golden Age! How it captures the romantic, the idealist and the radical. In its purest form it embodies the aspirations of a man awakened to his fall; the quest for a lost innocence, for social transformation, for an age of peace, for New Jerusalem.[129]

We had what so many longed for; the hope, the promise and the certainty of a golden age. We, if any, were the 'people of the rainbow', the keepers of the keys. Where we stood on the Rock, they sailed on dangerous seas. How important then to communicate our vision with humility.

Here were echoes from the 60s of quiet protests and hippie alternatives. 'Gurus came to these shores by the boatload,' Rufus remarked, 'but where were the Jesus radicals? Where were the spiritual masters with the true enlightenment?'

Timothy Leary, a leading psychedelic, had accused the Christians of his time of being 'emotionally constipated' and unspiritual. Hopefully, in the 90s, the charge was no longer accurate. God was making his people attractive to spiritual seekers.

One night Nathan and Phil were out in the fields all night tripping on acid. Looking up at the stars through rustling leaves and waving branches the semi-Christian searchers were spellbound. Lying on the cool earth they talked about God.

Eventually the charm of the night gave way to a stunning sunrise. As they revelled in the song of birds, the pure morning light, the cool breeze and the million diamond dewdrops scattered on the grass, they worshipped. Then wild, free and loudly singing the praises of God (though still tripping), they danced through the dawn-streaked streets of Rugby.

By July Noel had persuaded Nathan to get involved with Jez in the multimedia project and threw a massive wad of lyrics their way. They worked non-stop in a little studio at the Farm turning out sounds for 'Jesus Live'.

Phil worked with Rufus on the drama side and relished friendships at the Farm. His heroes had always been the raw converted street lads like Daz and Ronnie. He was now fed up with his hippy-trippy image and the rather 'poncy' scene at drama school. The time had come to open a new chapter in his life. But what? And where? Rufus encouraged Phil to get baptised at Jesus Live. 'No way!' said Phil the cool. But in secret he was very encouraged that Rufus believed in him.

The flurry of creativity ran straight into the August Festival and by now Nathan was softening up. As the new band set their kit up amongst the regular musicians, Jez was nervous. 'Techno, a stoned keyboard player and a computer? Will this be acceptable? Will God really be in it?'

At the opening bars of the song 'Jesus is Live' the whole audience rose to its feet in excitement. Jez breathed a sigh of relief. Then as they launched into 'So fed up with myself' and reached the second line, 'Longing for love that is real', the Holy Spirit touched Nathan and he wept. That day the Beta band was born.

Immediately after the Festival Nathan went up to the Lake District and immersed himself in the beauty of the mountains and lakes. As he sat on a hill in the moonlight, absorbing the stillness, he turned things over in his mind. He was young. Life was before him. Should he pursue his own wild path – or flow with the Jesus Army? Noel and Rufus were good friends and the Beta band was taking off. A door had opened and it seemed easy now to just walk through. In the solitude of the moment Nathan felt the kiss of heaven.

As summer rolled on a colossal amount of work went into the preparations for the premiere of Jesus Live in November. Apart from all the prop-making, band practice and stage rehearsals, there was the sheer complexity of the programme. The 40-page script included graphics, background music, film sequences and hundreds of slides, statistics and newsreel items. All had to be orchestrated through a relay of headsets. As the deadline loomed, the autumn stress levels gave ample opportunity for abiding in Christ. Talk about team effort!

One inspiration was to use a group of 'searchers' dressed in brown hessian clothes that represented their various backgrounds. A young couple who'd lived as new-agers in Cornwall spent their spare evenings making hippie gear out of sackcloth. Others created suits, African dress, even a bowler hat and brolly, all out of sacking material!

When the big day eventually arrived, we all hit the ground running. Wembley opened with a leaders' breakfast and continued through two long sessions of guest speakers, music and sketches. After refuelling at teatime we fastened our safety belts for four hours of non-stop, multimedia action.

Jesus Live was nothing if not a sensory experience. If the theme was creation, the audience had to see, taste and smell it as stewards passed round grapes and sprayed us all with strawberry mist! If our worship was as 'fragrant incense rising', they were there again, swinging some smoking objects that looked decidedly Catholic. Boring it was not.

During the praise there was a mass distribution of fluorescent yellow cloths and red crosses. Ultraviolet in the dark not only highlighted an impressive praise wave and 2,000 glowing crosses but did amazing things for my white shirt!

But this was no mere extravaganza. There was tenderness. Through deeply moving songs and images we felt, with the searchers, the pain, the outrage and the shame. Rob sang gently:

> Dear broken-hearted ones, your face is full of hurt,
>   Feelings of agony; we long to share your pain.
> Let our eyes run with tears,
>   Let our hearts flow with love;
> Our arms stretched out to you our friends,
>   Like his who wept and died.

At one point Daz and Trev were dragged on stage, put into stocks and pelted with words like 'hatred', 'rejection' and 'injustice'. The searchers, who could no longer endure all the abuse they'd already witnessed, rushed onto the stage shouting 'Enough!' It was powerfully symbolic. As the section 'Jesus, Radical and Redeemer' unfolded, the searchers were found at last kneeling at the cross.

> A garden and a cup, a cup of suffering,
> A cup filled to the brim, a cup only for him.

A moment of quiet followed the song. Suddenly Daz jumped up shouting: 'He is risen! He is risen!' The searchers went wild. With 'angelic' music filling the air, they threw off their sackcloth, revealing the brilliant clothes of resurrection and hope. Soon, during the 'Church' sequence, all who'd been homeless or in prison gathered on stage. As they sang and swayed together, the video-camera zoomed in on Paul from London. We could see him on screen as he smiled, arm in arm with his friends. For those who knew, it was a moment of tears. It was his song:

> I've been crying in my soul; I've found the brotherhood,
>   With a love not known before, now I know I belong;
> This love I've been shown is really so strong;
>   And I'm crying with my brethren, tears of joy and love.

After a brief message hundreds came forward to receive prayer. Then the baptistry was opened. Phil collared hold of Rufus backstage. 'Bro, if I'm to get baptised, I need to know the Spirit is with me.' As Rufus laid hands on him and prayed, Phil spoke in tongues for the first time. Then swiftly crossing the stage, he jumped in and was baptised.

The Spirit came so powerfully that Phil could hardly stand. During the final celebrations many went through the water, but Phil's parents only learned about their 'newly-washed' son when, in the midst of wild rave, stage-diving and flashing lights, someone grabbed the mike and shouted, 'Phil's been baptised!'

He seemed to carry the torch of a new generation.

We had called 1993 'The Year of the Spirit'. It had not disappointed us. Inspiration and creativity had been powerfully released. God had given us 450 new people and some of our own teenagers were coming through.

We were flowing with the Christian mainstream, tapping into the culture and communicating with ever increasing skill. But community had barely grown. Jesus, friend of sinners, was ever more popular. His passion for sacrifice was not so easy to inspire. Maybe we'd lost it ourselves.

New Generation
1994 onwards

29

Passing the Torch
1994

We'd just come back from a community tour and Jason was staring at a picture on the oak-panelled wall of Cornhill Manor where I now lived. The tapestry showed a golden city out of whose gates a river flowed down a hill into the chequered fields below.

Jason looked spaced out. After a while he turned to me.

'Babylon's the world, isn't it?'

'That's right.' I nodded, rather surprised.

'And that city? It's Zion isn't it? The bride.'

I smiled. (This was music to my ears).

'Yes, Jason.'

'That's well sound.'

I agreed.

The house meeting was about to start so we sat down on the carpet. This was the first time I'd met Jason. I wasn't sure how he was getting on. He was a funny bloke, now dreaming at the picture again. I'd met his friend a week back on a

Bristol coach campaign. There had been a word of knowledge that we'd meet a young man who was going through a marriage breakdown. We had. He was now paying us a visit and had brought Jason down as a bonus.

Soon we were sharing and praying together. Jason, now out of his coma, explained, in a Bristol tongue, how his head had been 'done right in' by what he had seen of our community. Apparently this was a favourable response. Jason reckoned we were 'well dodgy'. Not 'dodgy', meaning suspect, but 'well dodgy', which meant radical, distinctive and dangerous to the devil. I marvelled at the English language.

Moments later it was my turn to be gob-smacked as the one-time glue sniffer, burglar and car thief went on to reveal a depth of biblical knowledge and spiritual insight that shook me. God, and no one else, had opened this young man's eyes.

We discussed the kingdom of God and he bubbled on about 'the holy bride' from Isaiah and Revelation, elated to find someone who understood. We made friends. I laid hands on him; the Spirit of God came and he started to shake.

So began an episode which, repeated with many other people, was prophetic of a new phase amongst us – the dawning of a new generation, the passing of the torch.

1993 had been an inspiring year with record growth. Jesus Live had been a definite hit and was scheduled for a six city tour of the UK. Searchers were everywhere, with people queuing up for baptism. My diary for 1994 began on an unusually positive note (maybe coloured by the fact that Mary from Palm Tree had just agreed to marry me!):

Jan 4: The year of the people. Away with spiritual snobbery! In with Jesus, the One who walks with the crowd. This is all about release – of heart and spirit – of colour and creativity. Nowadays we are vulnerable and accessible. The flag that flies from our turrets is stained with blood; and the more colourful, the more attractive for that. It is the warm blood of compassion.

PASSING THE TORCH

> Zion may have walls. She is holy to the Lord. But her gates are
> open. The drawbridge is down. The dancing is in the streets.

Poetry apart, the times were good and a lot was 'cracking off'. At the Easter Weekend we received over 100 new members on stage amongst a happy chaos. The Festival theme song, 'Now the strong wind is blowing', was backed by hail and fierce winds that shook the tent and threatened to rip it open. To us, it symbolised a spiritual wind that was blowing ever stronger in Britain.

A major encouragement was the way fellowship sons like Nathan and Phil were beginning not only to come through with God but also to find a burning vision for community. Phil, now mentored by Rufus, gave up his place in drama school for discipleship at New Creation Farm. Phil had already cleaned up his life; now he decided to get rid of his possessions and follow the call of Jesus to full commitment. Nathan was to follow.

This was the break we were hoping for: a second generation not just sticking around, but radically taking up the torch. There was also a growing number of visionary new people, whether zealous Christian couples or streetwise Jasons who came, like Jesus Live, 'raw, deep and from the heart'. Here was our future.

Since 1989 the focus had been on communication with fellow Christians and with the youth culture. Whilst retaining this, God's spotlight now turned on the heart of the church. We realised that it was only apostolic character that could produce apostolic fruit. Mellowness was good but the future lay in courageous mission, passion and self-denial.

The Jesus Army had become a national movement. Noel's ministry maintained a strong, united vision. But now we'd spread throughout the UK the need was for key men to bring that kind of apostolic spirit to their own regions. Noel was nearly 70 and his mantle must eventually fall on a new generation.

The Jesus Fellowship was now undergoing a major transformation. Only apostolic power would ensure that the new version would be better than the old. The torch must be passed on. Inspired leaders and their spiritual 'sons' must reinforce the simplicity, sharing and sacrifice that was the heart of our 'Zion' vision.

This was what searchers were crying out for; something solid and undiluted. 'Looking for a cause to fight for' was a popular song in Jesus Live. Youth were drawn to the bold, the wild and the strong; definitely not middle-class boredom, but risky adventure, challenge and exploring the limits. Red-hot Christian brotherhood fitted the bill. We had become culturally relevant. That was a good step. But it was our holy vision that really brought in the radicals.

Jason went back starry-eyed to work things out in Bristol. His church was shy of charismatic gifts, let alone community. He enthused, inspired, and even raged about 'Zion'. They understood. He was young. But in the end he was unable to cope with a tamed life. Jason pined away and began to stumble. I found him in Bristol and brought him back to our Men Alive For God day. *Jesus Life* captured the mood:

> Bright banners and swirling patterns; the name of Jesus in colours spinning on the wall. Smoke, lights and wild dancing. The strength and sound of 600 men worshipping together, holding high the torch. Masculinity and friendship. Informal seminars. Energy, buzz and anointing. Flowing with the river or climbing the spiritual mountain. Exuberant youth abseiling from the ceiling and challenging us to be daring. Adoration and rave culminating in a spine-tingling finale, 'All hail the power of Jesus name'.[130]

But it wasn't the amazing technicolour that touched Jason. It was the prophetic clarity and the common cause. Jason wept his heart out. The following morning, as we all worshipped together, he seemed to see just one man, one body. 'This is it,' he said. 'This is the bride.' And the tears flowed. We called him Jason Tenderheart.

A few days later, he said goodbye to his old council estate in Bristol and moved to Cornhill Manor. Jason was a hungry disciple who wanted the works and milked me for wisdom. We would go off adventuring, sometimes following 'words' from the Lord. 'Fox and Hounds' was one of his. But there were so many inns with that name in the county that our would-be evangelism turned into a non-alcoholic pub-crawl!

I had a word too while praying one morning: 'Go to Bath and you will find a group of young people who meet regularly in a pub seeking spiritual things.' Then: 'The White Dog'. I looked up this name in the Yellow Pages but it didn't exist!

Undeterred we set off: destination – Bath; mission – locate hippies and evangelise. The friends we stayed with knew of two off-beats, Dave and Steve, who had a kind of Jesus pub scene going. So the next day we headed out with our guitars, hot on the scent. A guy with a twelve-string caught us up in the park.

'Hi! Who do you play for then?' he chirped.

'The Lord.' I said.

'Good. I'm off to a prayer meeting. Do you want to come?'

'Definitely,' said Jason. 'Let's go for it.'

Next thing, we were in a pentecostal church, singing and praying. Then two hippie characters walked in. I nudged Jason, 'I bet these are the ones, Jase.' When the meeting ended we walked over to them:

'I'm Dave,' said one with a grin.

'I thought so,' I said. Turning to the other, I added:

'And you're Steve and you meet in a pub every week seeking spiritual things.' They were wide eyed.

'How do you know?'

'God told us about you in Northampton.'

'Wow!'

We made friends, laughed about 'The White Dog', and spent the afternoon singing in the streets. Mission accomplished, we met the rest of the group the following week. Half way through the evening, Dave blurted out. 'Hey look! Amazing!' In trotted a white dog. Jason was well impressed.

We used to drive up to Bristol every Wednesday night for housegroup and evangelise at weekends. At one Jesus Revolution meeting in Bristol I spotted a colourful character waving a big flag with his long hair wrapped in a red bandanna. He looked like a pirate. 'Looks a pretty normal Jesus Army recruit,' I thought and smiled.

The following Wednesday he turned up at our housegroup. Stroppy, streetwise and loveable, Andy took to us right away and joined the gang. He was himself, praised God with swear words and regarded discipleship like medicine, nasty but needful. But he loved us to bits.

Andy had been brought up in care. Jason had rarely seen his dad. This was the pattern; family break up, adoption and even abuse. When these young guys sang 'This is home' or 'This is my family' it meant so much.

The fathering we gave them was not just passing on some kind of spiritual mantle but really getting involved. This was the task of us golden oldies, now well into our 40s. Rejuvenated veterans brought solidity and security to the lads and shared from their treasure store with the buzz of a new era. Young dynamos, for their part, jostled, goaded and wheeled us out onto the streets. So two generations took their place for the harvest and the church regained her youth.

Cornhill, a community flagship, was in the throes of such a renewal and was gaining new people. Jason, with his passion for God and prophetic artlessness reminded me of an early Franciscan. Andy came as a rougher version! A young couple who'd been new-agers in Germany also rolled up with a travellers' bus and a restlessness for a new society. Cornhill, struggling out of her institutionalism, was given a helping hand and a raw taste of the future.

Youth was in upsurge. 'A rising star, that's what I am!' was a hit when *Crossrhythms* reviewed our tape *The Greatest Cause*. New bloods wanted to win their spurs and this could mean releasing treasured sons to pioneer new scenes.

From Ian 'Greatheart's' base in Sheffield, the north was wide open. Ian was keen to give his 'young turks' their head. We now had a bus, kitted out with bunks, that Ian's men took over the Pennines in search of adventure. The mould-breaking team, without established leaders or community members, descended on Barnsley, Wakefield, Bradford, Halifax and Huddersfield ending up in Leeds where a church plant was now under way. Their success pointed the way ahead.

Ian was emerging as a pioneer with an apostolic spirit. Steve 'Capable' was another folk hero with church-building skills. Charismatic personalities like these foreshadowed the future which must lie in gifted people birthing church and community at a distance.

Our Northampton community had come into being through apostolic ministry but daughter churches in Warwickshire, Birmingham or even London were transplanted from mother stock. Locals swelled the numbers, but the core group always came from 'home'. This wasn't on. We couldn't be forever dividing up the clump.

Ian's base was 100 miles away. He felt their situation was similar to Antioch's in the early church. The Jerusalem community had spread through Judea and Samaria and up to Antioch by migration. But from Antioch onwards the thrust outwards was mainly from small apostolic teams. Ian believed this missionary model was the way ahead for his region.

When we'd first commissioned Ian to lead the new house God's word to him was to 'multiply'. Ian envisaged Sheffield not just as a satellite of 'Jerusalem' but as a new centre of missionary activity. He'd experienced church-building on the Bugbrooke estate and in Warwickshire. Now Sheffield was prospering and Andrzej was all set to lead a second house there. Ian had set his sights on the regions beyond.

At the present rate, planting in new territory was taking at least three years. At that rate Ian might plant six households before he was 70. But that was using the community house model. We had already begun to shift the focus away from community houses to congregations. The old mindset was hard to change, but the shape of the future was going to be a church with a minority of community members.

Ian realised that the dynamic of church planting was not in shipping in ready made communities but in the outworking of the kingdom word. God's messengers weren't called to transplant; but to sow seed which would spring up, 'first the stalk, then the ear, then the full grain in the ear' (Mk 4:28).

At Bugbrooke the steps into community had been slow and steady. Noel had steered the Northampton base through a long and, at times, turbulent history. Ian could hardly do that in each new location. Sheffield would have to function as a mother church sending out small church-planting teams. These would produce a body of people whose future would be mainly in the hands of local leaders.

By 1994 things were taking shape. In Preston five single brothers made an attempt at community living. The experiment failed. Ian balanced their zeal with wisdom and by August the Preston group, which included three families, was in good fettle and recognised as a new church household.

Mick 'Temperate' shared Ian's vision. His Birmingham-based team had established a group in Manchester and was now working on a small church in Stockport. At Tyneside too, in the north-east, Pete 'Just's' 'baby' was showing some promise. These groups were all led by northern 'natives'.

Each new work would develop its own flavour. Central Office could give strong input with resources, directives and leadership days, but the pressing need was for holy sowers; brothers with apostolic vision. Given that, new fires of community would spring up elsewhere. The UK might yet see a multiplied repeat of the 'Bugbrooke Miracle'.

Church plants had their own special genius. Whilst the brothers up north were seeking to plant small churches in many towns, the Shepton team in the rural west was drawing Christians into community. On the south coast our huge new house in Seaford, near Brighton, was led by a young couple who'd never been to Ashburnham or lived through our 'golden days'. But with the help of three Farm 'missionaries' the Abundant Grace enthusiasts were gathering a very Farm-looking bunch.

In London Steve had his head down building up his Acton base which was becoming very multiracial. In cosmopolitan London, at least, we saw the rainbow church take shape with many nationalities represented in the congregation. Jesus Army, London, with its kingdom aggression and Holy Spirit intoxication, was also a hit with many black churches.

The secret of Steve's success? He admired Noel's spirit, drank deep of the community vision and was a happy mix of prophetic spirituality and winning love. His team in London had a knack of attracting 'quality' people and were producing a new generation of community lovers.

Brokenness, soul freedom and yielding to God were vital ingredients. Steve had known frequent anointings since our general outpouring in 1988. They were a rocket boost into new ministry. Now, at the summer campaign in London, Steve was doing strange things again in the worship times (like running backwards with his eyes closed). During the mission his team was so 'intoxicated' that passers-by came in to the marquee looking for the bar!

We, like many Christians, were discovering a new closeness to God through what the media were calling the 'Toronto Blessing'. In May we'd heard the story of Eleanor Mumford's visit to Toronto and the subsequent 'bedlam' of laughter, shaking and 'swooning' in the highly-respectable London Anglican church, Holy Trinity Brompton. The power-wave, connected with Toronto's Airport Vineyard Fellowship, was nothing if not startling. Before long it had spread into hundreds of British churches and alerted the national press.

Some of the things they reported were pretty bizarre. Roaring like lions, jerking like chickens and pogoing about like pneumatic drills didn't easily fit into the British mindset! Inevitably evangelicals of a more rational bent questioned whether this was really the Holy Spirit at work. However research into genuine historic revivals showed that such manifestations were not entirely new.

We viewed the whole thing in a basically positive light. Our own leaders didn't make the pilgrimage to Toronto but we did receive fresh input and inspiration from all that was happening around the country. Renewed scenes of laughter and rolling in (and out of) the aisles were described in a *Jesus Life* supplement devoted to the worldwide 'refreshing'. Children and teenagers were especially touched. 'It was like eating lovely food!' Faolan told us at the July Festival.

Emotional experiences and physical manifestations had been fairly common amongst us; especially since 1988. This got a mention in Patrick Dixon's new book *Signs of Revival* in which Noel reminded us that pentecostal wine was not just to intoxicate us but to produce pentecostal results.[131] I guess our attitude now was similar to John Wesley's; we welcomed the signs, but got on with job.

Through our experiences of anointings in 1988 God had taught us to beware of selfishness and to pour the blessing out where the need was greatest – into a weeping world. The 'soft wind' of Toronto was bringing healing and refreshing to many of us. We welcomed that. But we looked forward to the stronger winds of repentance in the church and an awakening of the British people.

We were so grateful for the evident signs of a new breed now rising amongst us. These included many mature fathers like Rufus, Ian and Steve and inspired sons such as Jason, Phil and Nathan. The hymn 'Treasures of Zion' was apt as the Jesus Fellowship entered its second generation:

> Now pass the torch to precious sons,
>   Fathered from central Zion's ground.
> Trained in these costly truths, these ones
>   Like new Elishas flock around!
>
> Zion awake! Arise! Arise!
>   See now the depth that you have known;
> Transcend it far! Press for the prize.
>   Now bring the sons of Zion home!

So many of us, new, old or middle-aged were longing for all that 'Zion' stood for. As the year ended a new song expressed that strong undercurrent of hope.

> I see a golden age, a golden age
> And laugh at the days to come.

30

UK, We Love You!

1995

A figure emerged from the cold store outside the Goodness Foods building and stepped into the warm January sunshine. The scruffy young disciple sauntered through the warehouse and burst into the rest room singing cheerfully. Nathan paused to wipe the mist off his John Lennon glasses, stuck them back on his nose and strode over to Jason 'Tenderheart'. He gave him a boisterous bear-hug.

'Hallelujah! Praise God, bro!' he shouted. 'Your song was excellent last night.'

Jason had a reputation for being 'bananas about Jesus' and was a good songwriter. He was generally buoyant but this lunch time he looked down in the mouth.

'Hey, are you all right man?' asked Nathan stepping back.

'I suppose so,' muttered Jason. Then he straightened up and his eyes flashed.

'It does my head right in!' he blurted:

'What's that, bro?' asked Nathan.

'Babylon mate! Worldliness, negativity. It cabbages me. I see it leering at us, trying to get in. It does my head right in. Right in, I tell you. Ooow... You devil!'

'Calm down bro,' said Nathan soothingly.

'Calm down? – Grrr!' retorted Jason. 'I hate it! I hate it when the church isn't holy. She's supposed to be a praise in all the earth. She's the light, man, the light! And people whinge. I feel like smashing their Walkmans with a hammer!'

'Ah, I know bro,' smiled Nathan and picked up a guitar that was lying on one of the old beat-up armchairs.

'Don't let it bug you, Jase. There's some brilliant things cracking off. You know that. This is a new era, man!'

Nathan started to strum his guitar. Then he paused, and with a look of determination, he pointed a finger at Jason.

'It's going be better than its ever been – better than when I was a kid. They're hungry out there, bro. It's incredible. These new guys at the Farm – they're radical man!

'Yeah – they're buzzed right up,' chuckled Jason. 'You're right. You know I really love this church. I love Cornhill, and the warehouse, but I get frustrated sometimes.'

'It's gonna be all right bro!' grinned Nathan. 'You wait!' And he launched into a new song.

As the curtain fell on 1994 we didn't expect a huge applause – at least not from God. There were hard facts to face. We were well behind in our planting programme and had achieved less than two-thirds of our targeted membership increase. After several years of growth, numbers in community were showing a decrease, and finances were becoming stretched. Stunted growth and short supplies were signs of a diseased heart and clogged arteries.

A new apostolic spirit had certainly been released. There was 'a call to holy passion'. But it was meeting a backlash of dead institutionalism. This had been a repeated pattern amongst us when any new initiative dared disturb the slumberers. Though people nowadays were more free to be themselves, there was less 'holy fear' around – more of a casual attitude to God.

Community was a particular cause for concern. Through all the comings and goings, changes, phases and anointings, the number of core members had hardly grown. Had the vision dimmed? Did the high note of discipleship sound as sweet and acceptable as once it had? Some houses began to rattle as families moved out to their own place. The Bugbrooke estate began to fill up again. Only this time it wasn't the gold rush into the promised land. It was the quiet retreat out.

Not that anything was grossly wrong. There was no scandal, no rebellion – at least, none worthy of the name. Just the quiet ongoing work of discouragement and the drooping spirit of the settler. Some of us had been communified for twenty years. Maybe 'Mother Zion' was growing long in the tooth.

On the positive side a new spiritual generation was on the boil. But the question was, who was in it? Who was for the future? Some of us who'd been reckless idealists in the 70s were now hitting mid-life crisis. The challenge was to maintain our spiritual passion.

The renewed call to sacrifice was rocking the boat. For the apostolic challenged, by its very nature, all that was institutional and lukewarm. The mellow approach we had adopted for the 90s was now sharpened up and 'smoking guns' were again in evidence. As long as Noel was around sinners would definitely not be 'at ease in Zion'.

Reality had to be faced. When, at Vineyard, Cyril suggested repairing the crumbling path up to the brothers cottage, Mike 'Rockfast' sighed: 'The real need, bro, is for brothers to walk on it!' In his annual review Mike shared his longings to see community houses fully revitalised:

> What we have become in terms of counterculture fits exactly with Jesus Revolution and God's work of preparation in the nation. I believe that new creation community is the answer to the longings of many a seeking heart. But I am not so sure that the version of it practised in many of our houses is as attractive as we fondly imagine.

He likened our national movement to a bush fire: burning at the edges but smouldering at the centre. The map showed outlying areas as generally healthy and motivated but with a central base that was sluggish. The Farm was an exception but their scene majored on young singles.

Cornhill Manor was full and attracting new people. But established families were moving out. Did community, Jesus Army style, work in the real world of families, with so many children around? Some said a hearty yes but others struggled. For some it might be better to live in smaller houses with less pressure and yet remain in a common purse. We wanted to provide this as a positive option without the sense that they had 'failed'.

The vision of main community houses as radical discipleship centres was intensified. Struggling businesses too were receiving some emergency input both spiritually and practically from a team led by Mike 'Rockfast'. Zealous 'young Davids' like Jason, Phil and Nathan, responded wholeheartedly and with sights set on a new golden age of community, pushed things along, engaging any cynical Sauls, proud Goliaths or worldly Philistines they met on the way.

God's word to us was to 'cleanse the house of the Lord'. In spirit Noel saw an angel pouring out bowls of judgement and blessing on the church. The following months revealed the outworking of this as some scenes dwindled and others blossomed. As the Jesus Army steamed on into 1995 the growing cry was 'Lord, revive our church households' – from the roots up!

Towards the end of 1994 things had begun to hot up in London. The year had been OK, but not stunning, and they were a little weary with all the stress and pain of church building. Community families were struggling there too.

'There must be more' was a popular song and a common sentiment. Steve asked God for a new spirit of prophecy in the group. They had experienced a renewed soaking in the

Holy Spirit with ecstatic worship, laughter, people under the table and the like. But Steve was hungry for more. He wanted the complete Acts 2 power package: dreams, visions and prophecy – plus a startlingly new community.

As leaders we could motivate, push and preach the apostolic message. And we did. But the power of revival was personal encounters with the Lord Jesus and a prophetically awakened spirit. 'Your sons and daughters will prophesy, your young men will see visions, your old men will dream dreams' (Acts 2:17). That, in a nutshell, was our need.

Steve spoke about restoring God's house, quoting Ezra and Haggai. There was a marked prophetic anointing and a real sense that the Lord was coming through: 'You expected much, but it turned out to be little. What you brought home, I blew away. Why? Because of my house which remains a ruin, while each of you is busy with his own house' (Hag 1:9).

As Steve pressed the word home it sliced into self-motivation. Power was at the altar of sacrifice. Whilst in full flow he suddenly stopped: 'I've just seen an angel on his way with a golden bowl of oil and a scroll.' Then he began to prophesy. The response was dramatic. People were weeping and repenting all over the room. Some were freed from demonic oppression. Others just cried out for their first love. A hymn they often passionately sung was this:

> Jerusalem, ablaze with light;
> The gold, the glory in the night!
> Gaze on her till your spirit's flame
> Leaps upward, kindled at the name;
> Zion! Where Jesus reigns.

The message of Haggai was poignant: 'Who of you is left who saw this house in its former glory? How does it look to you now?' (Hag 2:3). Some tended to look back at 'the good old days'. There, in a hazy mist, before techno-colour, communications, Jesus Army, or even evangelism, lay the quiet green fields, the noble hymns and exquisite brotherhood we had known and loved. It was a rose-tinted memory. Now we had adapted to the culture and lowered the drawbridge it was inevitable that wordly influences should come. God's fire would purify them.

Two weeks later there was another outbreak. As Steve spoke about the bowl of oil it was if the angel had arrived and was pouring it all over them. People felt they were soaked in healing oil. Everyone was excited. They laughed, cried, prayed out or just shook and fell. Prophecy was unleashed; wherever this oil was allowed to flow there would be change. Eyes would be opened. Ears unblocked. Prison bars melted.

Around this time Steve attended a Toronto-style meeting and from then on kept waking up at exactly 5.55 in the morning. One Saturday night the Lord woke him up suddenly and urged him to go downstairs and look out of the window. Steve groaned. It was winter. But he dressed and went down.

'What do you see?' the Lord asked. Under the orange streetlights Steve watched someone unloading sacks of bread on the doorstep. (This was free bread for the homeless).

'Er, I see a white van — and lots of free bread.'

That was all. A puzzled Steve climbed gratefully back into bed. The next morning Steve intended to preach from Isaiah 55. He turned to the passage: 'You who have no money; come, buy and eat ... Why spend money on what is not bread?' Ah — free bread! That was why God woke him up! He was bringing living bread to the house.

In the morning meeting he spoke on the need to hear and eat God's word. Listen-eat-live-do: this was Isaiah. Remarkable things followed as others began to wake up at 5.55 and get words from Isaiah!

As the new year began Steve was inundated with words, dreams and pictures. He would be in his office and the phone would ring: 'Steve, I had a dream...'

One morning two sisters ran down excitedly from Spreading Flame. They'd just had a vision of lots of young men carrying batons and running up and down the stairs of Battlecentre and out onto the streets.

One scripture impressed itself on Steve – Isaiah 55.5: 'Nations that do not know you will hasten to you, because of the Lord your God, the Holy One of Israel.' Isaiah 55.5? 5.55am? He smiled at the coincidence. Now, when he awoke, Steve claimed the promise of 'nations coming to Zion'. He'd set his heart on a multiracial church. One prophecy said: 'When it rains, black umbrellas come out.' In the midst of blessing black people would come. That year three black churches in London joined the Multiply Network.

One day Steve suddenly declared; 'Zion's sons will arrive through the front door, the back door and even up through the floor!' Very unlikely! But when men came to work on the foundations, Steve bumped into a dusty workman climbing out of the cellar! Marian, a Romanian communist, stayed for dinner, found Jesus and moved in.

God told them to expect refugees. One black brother and his sister escaped from war-torn Africa both assuming the other was dead. Miraculously they met at Victoria Station. Both joined the Acton congregation.

Another word was about Spanish-speakers. That summer they found José, a Spaniard and heroin addict, in Leicester Square. He was powerfully saved. Mario, a flamboyant Spanish-speaker from Guadeloupe, also turned up and Miguel arrived from South America, soft-hearted and ready for discipleship.

Added to these, David 'Le Radical', romantic Frenchman and rasta, came via Amsterdam; Franceso arrived from Italy and Terry from the Emerald Isle. Terry, a near-invalid, found deliverance from alcohol addiction and stepped out of his wheelchair. Young men were now running up and down the stairs at Battlecentre. London, at least, was doing well.

Bowl and scroll; fresh oil for the lampstand and a new spirit of prophecy. This was the need of us all, especially Northampton which lacked the groundswell motivation of newer congregations. The newer units were small, urban and outward-looking. Risktakers needed God to survive. Not so settlers. Ensconced in rural comfort and routine, some could sit through the harrowing scenes shown in the latest multi-media event, 'Bleeding Life', and go home to sleep it off.

But God was anointing outward-lookers, those who, like Jesus, came 'not to be served but to serve'. If ever there was a day for harvest it was now. Our destiny depended on rejecting lukewarmness and being poured out for the nation.

Our vision focused down. We soft-pedalled our involvement overseas and planned an all-out offensive on the UK. The motto was: *UK People, We Love You!* – the plan: to evangelise all major cities in Britain. As Michael Green observed:

> Paul's strategy was urban. He made for the centres. The Acts of the Apostles records his visit to city after city of importance. This was part of a definite plan for planting the good news in key positions throughout the Empire.[132]

Mike 'Rockfast' saw a picture of arrows flying out from the centre of the church and hitting many targets in the nation. One thrust utilised the new coach which could house a whole team and had already 'done damage' in Yorkshire. Complete with stacks of literature, food, and the wild and inspired, it was to carry the UK Ignition Gospel Roadshow.

Ignition was to travel the land for three years sparking off spiritual fires. The pioneers' commission was to 'leaven with the gospel the strategic cities and towns of the UK, recognising groups and planting church households.' Their adventures would fill a book.

Mary and I had just been wed when we joined the Ignition team in the South West. We met the bus at Plymouth where it had been followed by the Mayor on a carnival procession! Our team (with an age range of 8 to 80) evangelised Torbay and Exeter. We had a warm reception. Anglicans lent us their church hall, an old Quaker invited us to tea, and policemen blessed us. God had gone before and there was an openness abroad.

Many were drawn by the colourful bus and the buzz of life around it. One travelling new-age artist joined our 'church on wheels' and later ripped up his occult paintings. A biker couple, who happened to stroll past the bus in Torquay, returned the next morning as new-born Christians, bright eyed and eager. Later Jim and Georgie wrote to *Jesus Life*:

> The presence of the bus sparked off a discussion about Jesus which went on into the night. We ended up reading a gospel booklet. Then the penny dropped. I couldn't believe the answer was staring me in the face. I'd got into New Age, Astrology, Spiritualism, Animal Medicine – you name it. I'd totally bypassed Christianity as a dead religion. Mind you, it wasn't religion I found but Jesus Christ. Our whole life changed and it greatly effected our friends. We were a bit upset when the Jesus Army bus moved on.[133]

But God looked after them. Jim continued:

> That weekend the church next door opened its doors for the first time in two years. People were dancing with joy, others were falling under the power of the Spirit. The room crackled with electricity.

This said it all: church in revival; people prepared; seekers searching; a generation turned off by institutions but attracted to the person of Christ. Here was Jesus Revolution, 90s-style. Ignition teams came home excited: 'They're wide open out there!'

Into this scene we flowed not as stingy Christians but as the generous-hearted. Marches with overtones of strength were transformed into relaxed, festive street-walks. Bearing bright crosses, butterflies, planet earths, and 'We Love Everybody' placards, we gave away stickers, flyers and even chocolate bars. People were beautiful – not only created by

God but precious to a Saviour who had 'died for all'.

One Bristol team attended a gay night-club carrying huge luminous butterflies and wearing the bright stage clothes from Bleeding Life. As the team listened to people, shared hearts and praised God to the dance beat, some of the clubbers were won over by their meekness and non-rejection.

Washing feet was a sign of the servant that we took amongst the people. 'Respect everybody' was apostle Peter's plea (1 Pet 2:17). Whether at London's Megatripolis nightclub or at Glastonbury Festival many were willing to have their feet washed, or receive prayer and anointing with oil.

Such trust! A pagan generation into symbols, vibes and mystery were ripe for a Christianity with its roots in experiential faith and sacraments. The cleansing blood, baptism or anointing with oil were commodities that non-rationals could grasp by faith. God stepped in through the open door. We saw 'unbelievers' fall under his touch.

The 90s youth culture was described by social observers as 'Generation X'. These youngsters were a product of a 'postmodern' society which was technologically advanced but morally rootless. Though turned off by 'religion' and wary of pre-packaged answers they were searching for something solid.

We had many friends like this who opened up to God once they'd seen his reality amongst us. 'Generation X' could become a generation for Jesus. God seemed to be targeting these spiritual 'orphans' and many were finding Christ.

Such 'modern believers', as we called them, were very non-religious. Open, warm and free, especially in worship, these young men and women were sensitive to atmosphere, hated self-righteousness and were hot on brotherhood. Many were keen to embrace a life of purity, often in stark contrast to the way they'd been. Members of 'Generation J' were as uninhibited in their Jesus life as they'd been in their sin. What's more they were daring.

Youth was not our only mission field. A typical Jesus Army meeting was a fair cross-section of humanity. However we still reached far too few people considering the current openness to God. 'Come to us' was the old mindset. This usually meant church on Sunday. The Jesus mindset was 'go to them'; sit where they sit, meet where they meet — whether in streets, shops, pubs or homes.

Evangelistic though we were, outreach-orientated though we'd become, our focus had always been on community houses. Get people along to the houses and they would find life. God corrected this. The way we were now growing, community folk were the minority. The focus swung out to the wider congregation. Congregation, not just community, was church. With an expectation of a spontaneous people movement, it was foolish to think otherwise. Could we even keep up with a revival movement, let alone hang it round community?

Our vision and structure adapted to maximise involvement with the people. Those in their own homes were well placed to network with locals. Revivals usually ran along the lines of family and friendship. Homes provided great opportunities to meet people and home-based cell groups could grow up into small congregations. We now baptised anyone, anywhere, who had faith in Jesus. Covenant membership was our strong heart, but anyone who loved us belonged. We were inclusive.

God was working fast in the UK. Was our gospel net ready? Were we geared for growth? We wanted passion and power but needed structures; wineskins that neither restricted nor wasted the wine. We believed in the dynamics of revival, with spiritual anointings being worked out in fruitful activity. God's goal was to reap the harvest.

Our profile to date was this: one national body, co-ordinated centrally and motivated by 18 senior men — one vision, one army, and one united church. This consisted of 75 church households scattered throughout the UK and led by

200 or so pastors and their trainees. In all 2,000 members and friends gathered regularly for our large Jesus Army celebrations.

Central Offices included Enquiries, Communications, Resources and a new Church Growth Department. We distributed 25,000 magazines and 100,000 streetpapers every quarter as well as *See You!*, a guide to the 14 Jesus Fellowship congregations and 8 other Multiply partners in the UK. We also had a colourful web site on the Internet.

Evangelism included regular household activity plus the centrally motivated Ignition, EDP, marquee and coach campaigns. Then there were multimedia productions like the recent 'Hot People'.

Strategies for training and nurturing people were firmly in place as mature brothers and sisters went about fathering and mothering a new generation. Community houses, with their raw, hands-on experience of living together gave extra opportunities for growth in grace – for us all!

Cell groups, 'Agape' love-feasts and household meetings were weekly features and there were slots in our programme for special nurture evenings, shepherding groups, covenant bands and leadership training sessions.

Very organised! I sometimes wondered if such tight structure was really spiritual. But when I considered John Wesley and General Booth I was reassured. Organisation was a servant to revival. Anointed men launch spiritual movements. Only when the anointing fails does the machinery take over and the movement become a monument. Our task was to keep the oil flowing.

It was twenty years now since we first saw the vision of a heavenly city shining through an earthly people. In real terms that city was more visible than ever before. Maybe we needed to recover the wild extremity of the pioneer. But we believed that the Jesus Fellowship was a structure God had prepared for the hour. We were on schedule.

31

Wild Spirit

1996–7

Nathan and some of the Farm brothers threw themselves into the jungle of housing that had mushroomed round the edge of Northampton. There they met with the drifting, searching youngsters and found acceptance in a whole new network of friends. Pubs, minibuses, staircases and squats were the venues of 'mid-week church'; Jesus Army boys sitting, sharing, singing; new friends passing round the spliffs (among themselves!).

Rob 'Rocket' went a step further. Young Rob had come to us 'a bit religious' but had found a whole new dimension in brotherly relationships at the Farm. His passion now was to meet ordinary people. Plain clothed, at first without badge, cross or 'religion', Rob spent his spare time in town amongst a new gang of friends, often returning home in the small hours.

Rob was a good guy to be with (plus he had a car) and got plenty of invites to parties, clubs and homes. His new mates soon found he was a Christian, and Jesus Army to boot. That, if anything, made him more popular. It was cool to have a Jesus Army guy as a friend. By the time Rob invited them to his own 'party' they were quite open to the idea. Up to twenty would trail back to the Farm for supper after 'Sunday Evening at Spinney'.

One scene sprang out of the Irish Centre in Northampton. There Rob, Nathan and crew met some lads who were into a deafening sound-barrage called 'thrash metal'. The musicians began to find God and three were baptised. On Sunday nights at Spinney the audience were treated to their contributions set to Christian lyrics. Noel called them the 'J Boys', an improvement on their former (unprintable) name.

One night Rob's mates got him to light a candle to remember a friend who'd died. As they prayed Rob sensed the presence of the Holy Spirit. Now these weren't born-again evangelicals. But something was happening. God was there.

Increasingly these 'modern believers' were reaching out to God. New age shops, with all their colour, fragrance and mystique, were catering to a trend. But the real search was deeper than any fad or philosophy. We were meeting people who really wanted to know, who opened their hearts and who prayed. God was responding too.

There was a move of the kingdom out there among the people.

THE JESUS EXPLOSION
The fervour that knows no bounds.

So ran the first *Independent Magazine* of 1996.[134] The front cover showed a light bulb. Glowing at its centre was a red cross. With a new millenium almost upon us, biblical Christianity was now being hailed by the media as a 'global revolutionary tide'. Its explosive power was the cross.

We often wore red crosses and gave them away at meetings. These bright, visual images symbolised a faith that had lain dormant in Britain but was rising again. A significant culture shift was underway with a deep desire for moral change. Polls indicated that large numbers believed in God and the Jesus of the gospels who was poor, selfless and spoke their language. It was church they couldn't cope with.

A major need was to break down the barriers with the people, to ditch religious language and to talk sense with the man in the street. We realised that effective outreach in these days wasn't blitzing the marketplace or standing on a soap box. It was being friendly and sensitive to where people were at.

This was a challenge to many of us who'd lived in a Christian sub-culture for so long. As Mike 'Rockfast' warned in his yearly report: 'For some of us old-stagers this will mean coming out from behind our walls of community tradition and Zion-speak assumptions and engaging in real heart contact with the rest of the human race!'

God told us to change our attitude towards our home town. The idea that Northampton was 'hard' stemmed from own pride. We now began to see the Northampton folk as our friends. We belonged to them and they to us. They were our people.

Noel was much impressed with a South American, Ed Silvoso, and his passion for city people. Ed Silvoso believed that 'If you want to reach your city for Christ, you must catch God's heartbeat. Listen carefully and you will hear two sounds: none...all. None to perish. All to come to repentance.'[135]

His book, *That None Should Perish*, described a strategy of 'prayer evangelism' that had impacted whole cities in Argentina. 'Prayer evangelism' was systematic spiritual warfare which engaged the enemy in aggressive prayer whilst mobilising cell groups to penetrate into the neighbourhood.

In comparison, our own activity was fairly laid back and unorganised. Wednesday night cell groups were flexible. This had its plus points, but there was wasted effort and laziness. Maybe these cell groups needed motivation and management.

Mobilising our 'troops' into Northampton would also challenge any complacency in the central church.

We were talking war here. It was useless trying to capture enemy territory if our own ground was vulnerable and insecure. As Ed Silvoso pointed out, Hezekiah first cleansed the temple before he was able to convert the city. Our community households needed cleansing and reviving.

The spirit of radical pioneering had been our genius over the years. This had to be recaptured. If residential community was to be a minority portion in the church, it must be the white hot centre, unadulterated and undiluted. Retaking the central ground was first priority.

We took a special pledge of sacrifice, inspired by the example of a dynamic Christian biker club. This was ours:

> We are the forgiven, the unstoppable. We are commissioned adventurers, self-deniers, cross-bearers. We pledge ourselves to the Kingdom cause. We have crossed the line. We will not give up, let up or slow up. We are pioneers. We cannot be bribed, compromised or side-tracked. We will not bargain with double-mindedness, but be pure. We are authorised to conquer Satan, move mountains, release captives. We will be compassionate. We will take healing to the lost. We will fulfil our destiny.

Stern stuff – the Pioneers Pledge. With this in mind, we commissioned our 32 local households to fulfil the vision of 'Pray Northampton'. The town map was marked off into six districts, sub-divided into sections of about 2,000 people. With a population of 200,000, the 80 or so cell groups would just be able to cover each neighbourhood.

Preparation then began in earnest. In some sections we had homes of friends and members. The beauty of non-residents was their position among the people. But with or without a home, each cell took one little neighbourhood to heart, and owned it. This was their parish. Many prayer-walked their area, feeling the atmosphere, sensing the needs and praying accordingly. It was time to listen and be led by the Spirit.

Even with this first step some felt a change:

> We walked around seven times praying for the breaking down of strongholds. With each round we understood more of the needs, found increasing love for the people and longed to meet them. We felt God moving supernaturally for them and dealing with our own fears and negativities too.[136]

The next move was to post 'friendship cards' introducing us as their friends and offering help and prayer (plus a video and a New Testament). Many people had deeply felt needs and were much more open to prayer than we had imagined, as one sister found when she followed up with doorknocking:

> A junkie woman invited us in and poured her heart out. Another lady burst into tears on the doorstep. God is widening our hearts and it's painful yet beautiful as these ones become dear to us. When we got home we just wept.[137]

The vision was to build up six distinct congregations in the town, one for each of the Pray Northampton districts. We began this transition slowly. On just one Sunday a month the large Northampton congregation divided up into six 'neighbourhood' gatherings of around 100 people.

At first the Sunday morning meetings held in various halls and community centres were not well attended by new friends. Young people, after a long Saturday night in pubs and clubs, were hardly geared up to morning meetings however informal we might make them. Sunday mornings didn't register with a comatose youth culture!

However I thought the smaller groups were an excellent challenge for those of us in the central church who'd grown used to a platform-directed programme on Sunday morning. Neighbourhood meetings provided another fresh experience of being church.

The evening celebrations were held as usual in the Spinney Hill school theatre in Northampton. The atmospheric meetings were becoming very popular. New friends (now wide awake) that our cell groups brought along with them were attracted by the music, the visuals and the creative exuberance.

Many found the life of the Spirit at these events. This was church and it was exciting! I was reminded of the early days at Bugbrooke chapel, when the Northampton hippies, who were nowhere to be seen before lunch, all turned up for the vibrant (and sometimes dramatic) evening meetings.

Now, apart from Sunday evenings, it was the team spirit of mid-week cell groups, meeting in homes and evenings spent in community houses that gave new friends their bread and butter experience of church. That spoke of the future.

Nathan and Rob noted the friendly buzz at a popular nightclub. Amidst the lights, mobiles and music, people shared, flowed, and danced freely with hands raised as if in worship. Seeing their tremendous potential for God, Rob and Nathan just wished they could bring them to Jesus, set up a pool on the dance-floor and baptise them there and then!

These brothers spotlighted the need to get in amongst people – not with dogma or a slick answer – but with sensitivity. We too were searchers, as one song made plain:

> I'm still seaching, Lord, on a journey,
> Learning, yearning – and yes, I do believe in You.

We hadn't arrived, had we? Christians were so keen for people to come to their party. Maybe God was saying, 'I'm out there amongst the people. Come and join Me.'

Steve 'Capable' and his London team were putting this into practice at 'Heaven', a famous West-End club. The manager liked the 'footwashers', as he called them, and often led them out of the queue and escorted them in like kings. Once on the dance-floor the Jesus team generated a lot of energy, loving people, handing out red crosses or grapes and praising God 'in the midst of Babylon'.

One night Tony, a Jamaican from Battlecentre, was

dancing up front when there was a sudden hush. Tony took the moment. 'Who's in the house?' he shouted.

'God!' they all cheered. 'God is in the house!'

The DJ smiled.

That Spring the BBC showed a documentary about the Jesus Army. *Brothers in Arms* focused mainly on the Farm and their evangelistic exploits with the homeless in London. Despite our initial misgivings, it gave a pretty fair, though selective, portrait of our church and its work. Some came to join us in community as a result of seeing the film. Many others expressed their appreciation of what we were doing.

Positive media coverage was helpful but we found God reaching many people through more supernatural means.

Sonja worked as a medical officer in London. She told us how she was attending a patient after an operation when he had a sudden heart attack. As the nurses rushed out for the resuscitation trolley Sonja felt the Spirit's nudge to look at his arm. He wore an African wristband. She removed it and prayed against a spirit of witchcraft. Immediately the blood pressure normalised and he recovered. Later the man told Sonja he was out of his body when she prayed, but the evil power was broken and he came back. Sonja led him to Jesus.

Dreams and visions played a part in the Spirit's activity amongst us. This account of a supernatural 'link-up' was reported in *Jesus Life*:

> While praying, Aase saw a deer coming down to a stream to drink. The setting was a Bavarian forest. The Spirit interpreted the picture in this way: 'A man is coming from Germany who is thirsty for more of God. He wants to speak to someone who speaks fluent German.' Aase passed the wisdom on to Trevor, one of our German-speaking leaders. A few weeks later in Nuremburg, Bavaria, Mathias had a dream. 'I was somewhere in England talking with a man in his 40s who spoke fluent German. He really understood my heart.' Mathias felt that the man belonged to Pioneer Ministries or the Jesus Army. When he awoke, the Spirit said, 'This man is Trevor. He will strengthen your faith.' Mathias mentioned the dream to a

friend just back from the UK; she'd already met Trevor from the Jesus Army. Mathias wrote a letter and they met up in the UK, both awed that God had arranged the meeting.[138]

Another remarkable event was the 'miracle oil'. One evening, as a few London sisters worshipped together in their covenant band, a mysterious oil began to appear on their hands. One sister didn't receive this, so the rest prayed with her. Soon oil began to appear all over her hands and forehead. They then layed hands on someone who was on her back with chronic neck pain. Her face first turned a healthy pink, then she got up and danced around.

One woman, partly deaf through an infection, was healed after she felt oil dripping into her ear. The healing was impressive but they found the most powerful effect of the 'miracle oil' was new breakthroughs with the locals.

'Pray Northampton' was now well underway, its progress monitored by a team who turned out bulletins of inspiration, stories and statistics. As the number of friends slowly increased we considered new ways of nurturing them.

The Alpha Course that had originated from Holy Trinity Brompton was being well received in Britain. Alpha was a mid-week introduction to the Christian faith for those interested but not ready for 'church'. It centred round a meal, an informal talk and discussion round the table.

We took our cue from Alpha and held a New Friends Course for our own 'rough and readies' in a modern sports centre. We used a tailor-made *New Friends* booklet we'd written in addition to *Why Jesus?*[139] from Alpha and a colourful booklet, *The Church – Relic of a Bygone Age?*[140]

The question mark was a symbol of the times. But people were now finding answers in the church. As they were touched by God, relatives and friends of friends were drawn in. As the network widened, so the gap between church and people narrowed. We began to see the reality of the multitudes.

The multitudes in New Testament days were the huge

numbers who were attracted to Jesus, if not yet disciples. The curious, like Zaccheus who shinned up a tree to get a closer look, often got more than they bargained for! We wanted to belong to these 'multitudes' and felt that Jesus ought to be the national folk hero. At one Festival the band blew a horn and launched into the theme tune of 'Robin Hood', with new lyrics:

Jesus Army, Jesus Army, moving through the land.

During the song a troop of brothers marched through the tent in their rainbow jackets and red sweatshirts. My mind conjured up images of Robin as a type of Christ and Sherwood Forest as Christian community (Style 3). I guess we were the merry men! I smiled. We weren't very adept at robbing the rich, but the poor seemed to like us anyway!

The red sweatshirts were significant. Noel launched 'Jesus Army Reds' as a new dynamic for our church, but by the end of the year a 'Jesus Red' described any red-hot, red-alerted, blood-and-fire Christian. This red thrust put some guts into being out and out, dare-devils for God. A new dance song 'We're wild and we're Christians!' captured the exuberance of this 'total consecration' and enthusiasts wore something red as a declaration of intent.

As some gripped hold of this vision we began to see definite Jesus Red teams taking shape. Rob, Nathan and Hannah, all Farm members, were but three examples of people who naturally gathered friends around them. These warm, charismatic youngsters were getting quite a following, especially amongst the clubbers of Northampton.

'I'm a leader, I'm a leader of Generation J!' was a techno song, belted out mercilessly at Spinney, which praised this type of leadership dynamic. These informal friendship circles were magnetic. People wanted to be part of the team. In the process they got to know Jesus, the motivator.

Young leaders began to baptise their converts from the club

scene, sometimes at the break of dawn in a river. Friends from the club and a few cows looked on in wonder.

The inspiration of the early Celtic Church was now coming through and encouraged the wild spirit of the Jesus Reds. At the outset of Christianity in Britain there was a powerful movement of God amongst the Celts. This simple, charismatic brotherhood, led by the Holy Spirit (whom they called the 'Wild Goose') gained a vast influence over the people – so much so that their searching, pagan culture was turned towards God.

These believers were intuitive creation-lovers who devoted themselves to a life of hard work and prayer. Marrieds and celibates often joined together in communal settlements in wild places like Iona and Lindisfarne. And from these spiritual power-houses they ventured out amongst the people, identifying with them and leading them to Jesus.

Now, many centuries later, God was reminding his people of these lovable Celts. Roger Ellis was very enthusiastic about them when we interviewed him:

> When I read and prayed about the Celtic Christians, the impact of God speaking to me was stronger than anything I'd known – stronger even than 'Toronto'. I believe God is saying something prophetically through them. They are a symbol communicating something to us with regards to mission, community, creation and creativity.[141]

When Channel 4 was doing a series on alternative youth services, one of the team, who was not a Christian, told Roger, 'We've been to 70 of these and the most interesting message is this one on the Christian Celts. This is the first thing we've heard that really engages and gives a Christian alternative as relevant culturally as the New Age movement.'

Primitive, spiritual, colourful; something in these days was coming through about pre-institutional Christianity. This was as much for the hungry believer as for 'pagan' seekers. At one level the appeal was to the mystical, the symbolic. A post-modern culture was responding to images, music and drama. They were looking for humble bards not preachers. At another level they were seeking an alternative.

The example of the Celtic Christians helped to clarify the future role of our community houses. The key to Celtic evangelism was the network of communities which were both mission centres and spiritual oases. The numbers who embraced their rigorous lifestyle were small in comparison with the multitudes caught up in the wider movement. But the communities stood like priests, blessing and serving people.

The Celtic spirit resonated with so much we held dear. It crystallised our whole apostolic call; combining radical discipleship with a passionate sense of mission. Like them we were to move with sensitivity amongst the people, showing Jesus as the answer to their search. Maybe we too, together with other Christian streams, would see the 'post-modern' culture of our day powerfully influenced by the gospel.

In the late sixties God moved in a remarkable way upon the churches of this land. We were one of many little groups at that time who sprang to life through the Holy Spirit. God took hold of us and opened our eyes. He showed us a people who had been scattered coming together to live for Jesus and his kingdom. And we said goodbye to lesser things.

We have seen that vision fulfilled. Now, it seems, we stand at the threshold of something bigger. God's movement is among the people and it is spreading daily. We want to be in the thick of it, where Jesus is.

But that will depend, as ever, on the fire in our hearts.

Roger Forster interviews Noel Stanton

We decided to give the last words in this book to Roger Forster, the leader of Ichthus Christian Fellowship and Vice-President of TEAR Fund. Roger, who has known us for many years, agreed to interview Noel and to write an Afterword. In the interview Roger included questions from his various contacts.

Roger: Noel, why do you think the Fellowship has travelled such a distinctive road?

Noel: The important factor has been our obedience to the prophetic directional word. We've received the Spirit's word as a step-by-step process causing the church to be built. We haven't 'flirted' with the word by receiving some 'new' direction and then giving it up and going on to something else. We've obeyed the word and allowed it to become creative amongst us. That's taken us into a radical kingdom of God lifestyle as barriers of class and race have come down. It's included community, discipleship, covenant and all the other things that have made us controversial!

Roger: Do you think you could have avoided some of the suspicion you encountered in Christian circles?

Noel: Yes, we could have been more open and trusting of other Christians. We felt unjustly persecuted, and felt that accepting isolation was really the only answer. I think we were wrong in the way it got hold of us.

On the other hand, we have been faced with somewhat hysterical opposition, especially from 'anti-cult' groups. Sadly, many Christians seemed unable to differentiate between groups opposing heretical movements such as the Jehovah's Witnesses or the Mormons for reasons of basic truth, and those 'anti-cult' groups opposing on sociological grounds, who have a problem with any church moving in strong kingdom-of-God covenant commitment and zeal.

Now that we have put away the defensiveness that characterised us for a number of years in the heat of the battle we are flowing much more freely with Christian leadership in the nation.

Roger: You've received a good deal of personal criticism in the past. What effect has that had on you?

Noel: At first I found it very difficult, very unjust and very painful. However I had to come to terms with the fact that any ongoing work of God will receive the persecutions and false accusations of which Jesus spoke. In that light I've learned to accept it as a commendation and a blessing and have come to a point where I'm just about able to pray for my accusers! Personal criticism has drawn me closer to God, helped me get rid of prides and caused me to need the brethren.

All of us in prophetic leadership must expect strong criticism. Some of it will be worth listening to. Some of it will spring out of jealousy. Much of it will come from those carrying particular doctrinal standpoints. In my case, much of it has been originated by Christians. I find that sad. All in all, of course, one must see it as belonging to the realm of spiritual warfare.

Roger: You've put a lot of effort into bridge-building in recent years, Noel. Has it achieved all you hoped it would?

Noel: Generally yes, though it appears some still find us difficult! Like many others we responded to God's call to affirm our brethren and to stand together. It hasn't been a matter of sacrificing God-given distinctives, but of dismantling the barriers of mistrust and suspicion.

Roger: How do you see your links with other evangelicals and charismatics developing?

Noel: We realise that if we are going to make maximum impact with the gospel then we all have to learn to recognise other churches and networks and not to compete; to give them space, refuse to duplicate and so on. The world has to see that we do love and trust each other. I'm happy about bringing into being more leadership links in those ways.

But distinctives need to be safeguarded. For example, there's a tendency for people to support a gospel that's far from full, with no proclamation of water baptism, let alone of Holy Spirit baptism, discipleship or the use of spiritual gifts. We must not compromise! We've all got to bridge the barriers, but also allow one another to develop our own distinctives under the calling of God. We mustn't feel threatened by one another.

Roger: Why does your leadership appear reluctant to establish local links rather than just nationally?

Noel: Well I don't think we are reluctant! Sometimes it's other local leaders who are the reluctant ones! Of course we are now very widely spread from the south coast up to Liverpool and even Glasgow. That all means we've become a national movement with a need for relationships with national leaders.

Having said that, we encourage our local leaders, especially in areas which are new to us, to make contact with other leaders. There may be liaison over pastoral matters, church planting, and events like March for Jesus.

Roger: How can we help you overcome the prejudices

which some people hold against you in some of the cities where you are working?

Noel: First to support our integrity and faith! We're very keen for Christian leaders to visit us, ask questions, see things and make whatever enquiries they want. It helps greatly, Roger, if national leaders speak well of us. I'm always willing to meet leaders if that would help.

Secondly, we need to be forgiven for situations which have arisen over the years which we've not handled too well. It's the way of pioneers to hold to the vision and press into it and not deal too well with the 'spin-offs'. We've made many mistakes in the course of our journey.

Then we all need to be very careful of hearsay and gossip. People who have specific criticisms should be encouraged to speak direct to us. People should also feel free to join us on the streets, or to attend our events so that they will know what we're about!

Roger: I notice, Noel, that you sense there are things where you do need the forgiveness of your brothers.

Noel: There are bound to be cases where hurts have resulted from our handling of situations and we are sorry about that. We have moved quite fast and not everyone has been able to keep up with us! So, yes, where we haven't been sensitive to others, we ask forgiveness.

But we are determined to respond to God's word to build. In the earlier days I was involved in denominational matters and God said there should be a full concentration on building the church. That has meant radical commitment on our part. Working it through has at times been somewhat traumatic but it has led on into fruitfulness.

Roger: Turning now to some of the questions that people have asked about the Jesus Fellowship, how do you prevent over-dependency on the leadership?

Noel: We see it as important that people develop their own individual identity, ministries and gifts. We emphasise personal devotions, Bible reading and so on. A personal walk with God is vital. Speaking generally, while we do believe in shepherding, I don't think we produce an over-dependence on the leadership. People soon realise that all leadership is fallible! But we do believe in discipleship. Our aim is to produce strong characters – strong men and women of God.

Roger: Some people have criticised 'authoritarian structures' that folk picked up off the street have been subjected to. Do you think there is a value in having a strong authority to begin with?

Noel: We are, of course, a church and not just a set of community houses. We have a wide spectrum of commitment. The majority of our people nowadays are what you might call ordinary church members living in their own places. But it's the more accountable lifestyle of community that gets criticised. In community houses we must have holiness, standards, discipline. Most people coming off the streets come to appreciate the need for that. A right authority gives security. Some, of course, can't cope with the disciplines and move elsewhere.

Roger: What about suggestions that the Jesus Army takes advantage of the weak and vulnerable members of society?

Noel: Those suggestions are untrue. Obviously we are keen to help the poor and needy – that's biblical, after all. Many are helped on their way in life, often breaking with various addictions and gaining confidence while they are with us. Society benefits from this kind of help. A number have real conversion experiences but relatively few will actually join us. If anything, Roger, we are the ones that lose out – certainly financially and in terms of stress! But that's part of our ministry.

Roger: And the charge of recruiting people?

Noel: I think Jesus could have been open to that accusation! We think the Christian faith is good for people. We gladly say 'Come and join us!' But we wouldn't pressurise a person into commitment. If people who've found Jesus want to be fully involved, they will normally enquire into everything. We encourage them to be sure of what we are; our faith and lifestyle, our various styles of membership and all that sort of thing, so that they can make an intelligent decision. And we have particular safeguards for those under twenty-one who want to move into community. There's no question of just grabbing people and pulling them into what we are, without them fully understanding what is involved!

Roger: How do you answer the accusations that in community there is a potential for breaking up families and separating those who have joined from families who are outside?

Noel: We've no desire to break up families! Often it works the other way round, and families are reconciled, especially young people with parents. Our members generally maintain good loving contact with their families and visit them regularly, but, as Jesus taught, the gospel does bring tensions. He made it clear that there would be 'division' in natural families, some choosing for him, and some against him.

As for families in our community houses, there is little evidence of serious family break-up. Of course some teenagers leave when they start work, but they keep in touch.

Roger: Are people encouraged to make friendships outside the Fellowship?

Noel: Very much so. A lot of new friends are made through evangelism and work. Friendships with other Christians are often retained and new ones may develop. And maintaining contact with non-Christians may lead to their finding Jesus too. However, it would be difficult if old friends were going to draw someone back into his old ways and habits, and we would caution against that kind of bad influence. We would also caution against the 'jungle' of Christianity where people have no definite commitment to a church.

Roger: What happens when committed members 'break covenant'? Are there really no bad vibes?

Noel: Of course people are always free to leave us and

many who do so remain on good terms. We have many in our congregations who truly belong to us but have not made covenant. Those that do, accept a covenant of membership with pledges concerning faith and lifestyle. Covenant does bring a spiritual obligation. But we never say, Roger, as we've been accused of saying, that covenant members who leave us are damned. We do warn them of the dangers of backsliding. But those who leave us are loved and prayed for.

Roger: Some people think that once you get into a community house it's very hard to get out again and that there's some kind of sinister hold over people.

Noel: That's rather silly! Up to two years is a trial period in which people can assess their call to community. There's no problem in their withdrawing during that stage. The trustees will not accept capital or goods until after at least a year has passed and then they have the authority to return any wealth that's been handed in, or to make payments in certain circumstances.

If established people want to leave community there will naturally be pastoral activity to understand the problem. In many cases a move to non-community membership proves helpful. Others do leave us altogether and, of course, that's painful.

Roger: Now I've a few questions about money, and it always raises people's hackles once we start to touch on the alternative god of mammon! Who makes the decisions about the use of money?

Noel: As far as our businesses are concerned, the directors or partners. As far as church and community funds are concerned, there are trustees. These are accountable to the members and give reports at the annual general meeting.

Roger: Presumably you're on the executives that make those decisions?

Noel: I'm on a number of the executives, but not all.

Roger: Obviously people are always concerned about the power that money brings.

Noel: We fully understand the danger of money power. We've seen how Jesus said, 'Sell your possessions.' We've sought to move away from the power of personal possessions. Like all our elders and full community members, I have no personal possessions or wealth.

Roger: How do the funds get used?

Noel: We accept that all the funds of the church and community belong to the Lord, and we seek to use them with wisdom in the Spirit within proper, constitutional, legal and accounting structures. We don't want to be rich, just to be able to share the gospel and build the church, including community. We do not ask the general public for funds and rarely take collections in our meetings. We spend a fair amount of money on our evangelistic campaigns and literature. We don't use money to wield wrong 'influence' over people and society, but we do want to spread the gospel and engage in social action as God directs.

Roger: Do you use your money to support any missionary or aid organisations which don't actually belong to you?

Noel: We have a charity budget and support financially a few evangelical organisations. We still find the main call of God on available funds is for direct charity or direct help. We give 'relief of need' gifts to members and non-members in cash or kind. There's also a lot of board and lodging that for one reason or another we never get paid. On top of that, paying off the debts of people joining us amounts to many thousands of pounds a year. We also have a bursary fund which pays the costs of several overseas members who are staying with us. Altogether our outlay must be approaching £100,000 a year.

Roger: Have you given to third world charities or third world relief over recent years?

Noel: Not directly. We are involved with a number of churches in Africa and elsewhere in the third world, but we feel God's main call to the Jesus Army is to reach the poor and marginalised of Britain.

Roger: How has the Fellowship developed over recent years?

Noel: We now feel we're an accepted part of the Christian scene and can concentrate on our particular mission. God has been refining our community houses. The call to sacrificial living has been re-emphasised and we're seeing a new generation keen to take us further.

Most of our recent numerical increase has been outside community. Learning to flow with people in their pain and searching has been the main emphasis. We've been tapping into the modern youth culture. That's meant a culture shock for some of us, but has borne remarkable fruit.

People are more open now, Roger, than we've ever seen them. There's a whole movement of people seeking God. We want to flow in with this, to be their friends – like Jesus.

Roger: So, you're forward-looking?

Noel: Yes. Definitely!

Roger: What steps are you taking to ensure the continuation of the vision when you are no longer here?

Noel: Our governing body these days is a Senior Leadership of around seventeen men of whom I'm the eldest. Most of them are in their forties, so I don't think there's much difficulty in the vision continuing. We've grown together, lived together and worked out many things together over many years and the vision is well established in our hearts. At the same time, we are continually training new leaders. We have over 200 men in pastoral leadership and as many again in some stage of leadership training.

Of course in the end one realises that God has got it all in hand anyway. I'm not a General Booth! I've not written down my successor's name. It will all be dealt with in the Spirit.

Roger: What in particular do you think God is now saying to the wider church through the Jesus Fellowship?

Noel: I would suggest that God is pointing to the need for a church that is welcoming to today's 'modern believers' and seekers that includes people of all sorts of levels of commitment. It must have a clear identifiable core of truly regenerated disciples of Christ Jesus, demonstrating the kingdom of God in a 'new creation' culture. We've found that Christian community, in spite of its pressures and problems, is a foundation for this.

I would also hope that we might show the way of the cross, of sharing Christ's sufferings.

I think God may challenge other churches through our Jesus Army work amongst the neediest in society, especially those trapped in various forms of evil. We're called to storm the strongholds of Satan and release the captives. This means receiving those who are unstable and sticking with them as they find healing, security and strength.

Roger: Finally, Noel, if you had the choice, would you do it all again?

Noel: Yes and gladly! But hopefully much better! There are still unfulfilled visions and dreams that we're working on. Oh for more holy, radical, Spirit-filled men and women ready to take up the torch!

Afterword
by Roger Forster

'Tax collectors can love tax collectors, sinners can love sinners' says Jesus, and adds in Luke 6:32–34 'what grace (*charis*) is that?' The test of grace and of true discipleship is, Jesus goes on to explain, to love those who are different from us. Sadly, many who would claim Christ's name as theirs have abandoned the place of grace to criticise those who are different from themselves. The Jesus Fellowship has often been the victim of such brotherly intolerance and gracelessness.

This volume shows, and their leader has acknowledged, that they have made mistakes. They have deserved censure and also at times may have returned it. Which movement or denomination escapes this charge? Christian history is an appalling story of hatred, persecution and intolerance. Conquistadors, inquisitions, burning of dissidents, drowning preachers, vilifications in the twentieth-century press, litter the history of the people who are called to love God, their neighbours, and their enemies as a mark of their loyalty to Christ. May God forgive us all.

Our God is a triune God, a unity in diversity, a God existing in varieties, joining our different and various expressions of obedience, which we give to our triune God, and enabling us to respect each other's contribution to the oneness Christ prayed for and won by his crucifixion.

I have known Noel Stanton for over forty years. He has grown more like his master over this time. I hope I have too. He has tried hard to build and rebuild lost relationships over the more recent years, abandoning the movement's earlier isolation. The Jesus Fellowship, which salvages many damaged people from broken society, has matured. Mistakes have been admitted, forgiveness asked for: what a grand opportunity to embrace the radical discipleship contribution they have made to the church, and to be enriched by them.

True Trinitarian believers should not be marginalised. Without fellowship, maturity is impossible. Reconciliation is at last on the agenda, not only in the context of this book and its history, but throughout the body of Christ. Truly this is a move of God's Holy Spirit. Accepting the oneness of the body is essential if the world is to be evangelised and Christ's mission completed. For Christ's sake let us be radical enough to love one another! May the Jesus Fellowship story be an incentive to this end-time obedience.

Roger Forster
Leader of Ichthus Christian Fellowship,
London, UK

Keep up to date

If you would like to keep abreast of the Jesus Fellowship story, write for our free *Jesus Life* magazine. We'll be glad to offer any other help of information we can.

> Jesus Fellowship Central Offices
> FREEPOST
> Nether Heyford
> Northampton NN7 3BR
> United Kingdom

> Phone: (01327) 349991
> Fax: (01327) 349997
> E-mail: info@jesus.org.uk
> Web: http://www.jesus.org.uk

Also available is a variety of Christian resources:

Live worship tapes
Worship cassettes of new and old songs convey the anointed atmosphere of the Celebrate Jesus events and other gatherings

where they were recorded. The tapes feature Jesus Fellowship songs, as well as other current material and rediscovered hymns.

Videos
Jesus Fellowship videos show the Jesus Army in action and cover the worship, ministry and other highlights of various powerful meetings.

Books and Booklets
Multiply Publications produce a range of books and booklets containing teaching and information.

Other Resources
Tee-shirts, sweatshirts, crosses, stickers and badges form part of the Jesus Army's campaign to let the name of Jesus be heard on the streets.

Notes

1. *Such Is Our Story: A Brief History of Bugbrooke Baptist Church 1805–1955*, Payne, E and Perkin, James (Carey Kingsgate Press, 1955).
2. ibid
3. *In The Day Of Thy Power* Wallis, Arthur (CLC, 1956).
4. *Evangelism Today* August 1974.
5. *The Cross and the Switchblade* Wilkerson, Dave (Spire Books, 1964).
6. *Evangelism Today* August 1974.
7. ibid
8. *Buzz* April 1986 'Bugbrooke – Cultic or Christlike?'
9. *Face Up With A Miracle* Basham, Don (Voice Christian Publications, 1967).
10. *Northampton Chronicle and Echo* June 19 1972.
11. ibid
12. ibid
13. *The Normal Christian Life* Nee, Watchman (Victory Press, 1961).
14. *Jesus Power* Wirt, Sherwood (Coverdale House, 1972).
15. *Run Baby Run* Cruz, Nicky with Sherrill, John (Logos, 1968).
16. Letter from a communist student to his girlfriend.
17. Pastor J Sands.
18. *The Cost Of Discipleship* Bonhoeffer, Dietrich (SCM, 1959).
19. *Love Not The World* Nee, Watchman (Victory Press, 1968).
20. *The Set of the Sail* Tozer A W (Christian Publications [CP], 1986).
21. *A New Way of Living* Harper, Michael (Hodder and Stoughton, 1973).
22. ibid
23. ibid
24. ibid
25. *The Daily Mail* 16 Sept 1973.
26. *New Society* 20 Sept 1973.
27. *The Daily Telegraph* 26 June 1974.
28. *The Root of the Righteous* Tozer, A W (CP, 1955).

29 *Worship – The Missing Jewel* Tozer, A W (CP).
30 *That Incredible Christian* Tozer, A W (CP, 1964).
31 *Pray in the Spirit* Wallis, Arthur (Victory Press, 1970).
32 *Nine O'Clock in the Morning* Bennet, Dennis (Logos Int, 1970).
33 Pat Bilbrough, Thankyou Music.
34 *Dust of Death* Guinness, Os (IVP, 1975).
35 *ibid*
36 *ibid*
37 *ibid*
38 *Enough is Enough* Taylor, John (SCM, 1975).
39 *ibid*
40 *ibid*
41 *Disciple* Ortiz, Juan-Carlos (Lakeland, 1976).
42 *The Radical Christian* Wallis, Arthur (Kingsway, 1981).
43 *Disciple* Ortiz, Juan-Carlos (Lakeland, 1976).
44 'Charismatic Crisis' article by Harper, Michael.
45 *Restoration in the Church* Virgo, Terry (Kingsway, 1985).
46 *House Churches Will They Survive?* Noble, John, Introduction by Forster, Roger (Kingsway, 1988).
47 *Rain From Heaven* Wallis, Arthur (Hodder and Stoughton, 1979).
48 *Pilgrims of a Common Life* Saxby, Trevor (Herald Press, 1987).
49 *ibid*
50 *ibid*
51 *ibid* (modern paraphrase).
52 *The Life of David Brainerd* (Baker Book House).
53 *Against the Tide* Kinnear, Angus (Kingsway, 1973).
54 *The Radical Christian* Wallis, Arthur (Kingsway, 1981).
55 *Renewal* magazine No 87, June/July 1980.
56 *New Wine* magazine, Baxter, Ern, Jan 1980.
57 *New Wine* Basham, Don, Feb 1980.
58 *Oxford Journal* March 14 1980.
59 *Baptist Times* April 10 1980.
60 *Baptist Times* April 24 1980.
61 *Pilgrims of a Common Life* Saxby, Trevor (Herald Press, 1987).
62 *Thy Kingdom Come* Baxter, Ern (CGM Publications, 1977).
63 'The New Creation At Bugbrooke' Jebb, Stanley in *Renewal* Sept 1982.
64 *Evangelism Today* Oct 1980.
65 *Buzz* Aug 1980.
66 *Buzz* Oct 1980.
67 *Buzz* Aug 1980.
68 'Fair Official Information Document' Sept 5 1978.
69 *ibid*
70 *News Of World* April 12 1981.
71 *Azusa St* Bartleman, Frank (Logos Int., 1980).

NOTES

72 *You Are My God* Watson, David (Hodder and Stoughton, 1983).
73 *Restoration* magazine March/April 1981.
74 *Restoration* magazine May/Jun 1982.
75 *Jesus People Lifenews* 1 1984.
76 *Mercury and Herald* 17 March 1984.
77 *Restoring the Kingdom* Walker, Andrew (Hodder and Stoughton, 1985).
78 *Jesus People Lifenews* 2 1984.
79 *ibid*
80 *Holy Fire* Urquhart, Colin (Hodder and Stoughton, 1985) also *Faith For The Future* (Hodder and Stoughton, 1982).
81 *Buzz* June 1985.
82 *Buzz* April 1986.
83 *ibid*
84 *The Fight Of Your Life* Calver, Clive and Copley, Derek (Kingsway, 1986).
85 *Leaning Into The Wind* Christian Life 1983 (Kingsway, 1985) foreword by Calver, Clive.
86 *Church Adrift* Matthew, David (Marshalls, 1985).
87 Sabbatical Report 1986 Perris, Roger Swallownest Baptist Church.
88 *Power Evangelism* Wimber, John and Springer, Kevin (Hodder and Stoughton, 1985).
89 *Jesus Army* magazine No 1 Sept/Oct 1986.
90 *Nottingham Trader* May 28 1986.
91 *Sunday Mirror* September 14 and 21 1986.
92 *ibid*
93 *Jesus Army* magazine No 1 Sep/Oct 1986.
94 *C. T. Studd* Grubb, Norman (Lutterworth Press).
95 *Buzz* April 1986.
96 *Jesus Lifestyle* No 8 2nd Quarter 1989.
97 *ibid*
98 John 18:6 Acts 9:4, 10:10, 11:5, 22:17 2 Corinthians 12:2 Revelation 1:17, 4:2.
99 *Jesus Lifestyle* No 6 Autumn 1988.
100 See 2 Chronicles 5:14.
101 *21st Century Christian* July 1989.
102 For prophetic drama, see Acts 21:11 Ezekiel 4:1 Jeremiah 13:1, 19:1, 27:2.
103 Paris, Twila Ariose Music 1988.
104 See Acts 10:9 ff.
105 *Jesus Lifestyle* 4th Quarter 1989, reprinted from *Equipping The Saints* Summer 1989.
106 *Jesus Lifestyle* 3rd Quarter 1990.
107 *The Gravedigger File* Guinness, Os (Hodder and Stoughton, 1983).
108 *Daily Mirror* 5 March 1991.

109 *'Christian' England* Brierley, Peter (Marc Europe, 1991).
110 *Daily Mirror* 5 March 1991
111 *ibid*
112 *The Independent on Sunday* 13 Jan 1991.
113 *Daily Mirror* 5 March 1991
114 *ibid*
115 *Fire in our Hearts* Cooper & Farrant (1st edition Kingsway Publications, 1991), Foreword.
116 *'Christian' England* Brierley, Peter (Marc Europe 1991).
117 *Alpha* Oct 1991.
118 *Elle* Nov 1991.
119 *Spiritual Power and Church Growth* Wagner, Peter (Hodder and Stoughton, 1987).
120 *Jesus Lifestyle* 3rd Quarter 1989.
121 *DAWN 2000* Montgomery, Jim (Highland, 1989).
122 *Jesus Lifestyle* 2nd Quarter 1991.
123 *The Radical Kingdom* Wright, Nigel (Kingsway Publications, 1986).
124 *Renewal* June 1992.
125 *Jesus Lifestyle* 1st Quarter 1992.
126 *Jesus Revolution Streetpaper* 3rd Quarter 1992
127 *The Magician's Nephew* Lewis, C.S. (The Bodley Head, 1955).
128 *Jesus Revolution Streetpaper* 4th Quarter 1993.
129 *Jesus Life* 3rd Quarter 1994.
130 *Jesus Life* 2nd Quarter 1994.
131 *Signs of Revival* Dixon, Patrick (Kingsway Publications, 1994).
132 *Evangelism in the Early Church* Green, Michael (Hodder and Stoughton, 1970).
133 *Jesus Life* 2nd Quarter 1996.
134 *The Independent Magazine* 6 Jan 1996.
135 *That None Should Perish* Silvoso, Ed (Regal Books, 1994).
136 *Wind & Wine 3* Pray Northampton bulletin, March 1996.
137 *Wind & Wine 9* Pray Northampton bulletin, Sept 1996.
138 *Jesus Life* 2nd Quarter 1996.
139 *Why Jesus?* Gumbel, Nicky (Kingsway Publications, 1991).
140 *The Church – Relic of a Bygone Age?* Halloway, Andrew (CPO, 1995).
141 *Jesus Life* 1st Quarter 1997.

Index

Acts 28, 41, 48, 51, 53, 62, 77, 80, 92, 109, 135, 167, 269, 338
Accountability 90, 124, 300, 361
Africa 264, 265, 290, 296, 300, 303, 317, 340, 364
Agape meal 167, 182, 197, 210, 256, 281, 346
Alberts, Larry 283
Alpha 295
Alpha course 353
Alternative culture *see* Counterculture
Anointings 32, 35, 54, 63, 67, 217, 246, 248, 252, 263, 273, 281, 283, 291, 309, 331–2, 339, 345
Anabaptists 137, 178, 301
Angels 114, 213, 255, 266, 291–2, 304, 337, 338
Anti-cult groups 178, 358
Apostolic spirit 325, 329, 335, 356
Authority 47–8, 58, 72, 84, 90–1, 120, 122–3, 127, 130, 159, 168, 175, 177, 191, 226, 229, 360–1
Ashburnham Place 93, 95, 106, 123, 137, 146, 331
Awakening 268, 273, 286, 288, 295, 297, 332

'Babylon' 147, 159, 167, 323, 335, 351
Backsliding 158, 162, 208, 216, 238, 275, 279
Banbury 201–2, 210, 225
Baptism 22–3, 25, 27, 35, 39, 41–2, 50, 54, 64, 72, 103, 137, 173, 178, 209–10, 238, 267, 268, 290, 310, 319, 344, 351, 354
  rebaptism 171
Baptism in the Spirit 12, 28–30, 32, 36, 39, 42, 77, 103, 155, 224, 257, 258, 294
Baptist Union 22, 25, 48, 132, 170, 230–1, 277
Basham, Don 35, 167
Baxter, Ern 110, 167, 174
Bedford 22, 25, 50
Bible 23, 26, 28–9, 37, 41, 46–7, 62, 66, 69, 70, 72, 79, 92, 100, 105, 119, 122, 124, 131, 135, 138, 169, 175, 182, 186, 192, 196, 202, 223, 244, 256, 257, 281, 283, 315, 324, 350, 360
Bikers 43, 52, 70, 78, 95, 98, 111, 162, 201, 222, 224, 342, 349
Bilbrough, Dave 264
Birmingham 181, 190, 201, 213, 234, 238, 255, 262

Bonnke, Reinhard 252–3, 264, 265
Booth, William 204, 213, 230, 232, 241, 264, 301, 345
Brainwashing 130, 179
Bridge-building 171, 174, 253, 261ff, 265, 275, 298, 301, 359
Bristol 324ff, 343
Britain *see* UK
British Youth for Christ 268, 297
Brokenness 23, 87, 110, 126, 140, 143, 218, 263, 278, 280, 331
Brotherhood 43, 46, 48, 54, 58, 64, 68, 72–3, 81, 89, 91, 95, 99, 101, 104, 110, 117, 119, 125, 127, 132, 137, 139–40, 143, 159, 182, 191, 210, 225, 244–5, 247, 250, 253, 257, 282, 283, 311, 319, 326, 338, 343
Bugbrooke 21, 25, 29, 37, 47, 85, 91, 102, 122, 126, 248, 250, 253, 257, 293, 300, 329, 330, 336, 351
  Baptist Chapel 22, 37, 40, 44–8
Buzz 177, 222, 229, 245
Businesses 101, 118, 128, 134, 138–9, 142, 168, 190, 198–200, 233, 240, 252, 337, 363
Cain, Paul 276, 279
Calver, Clive 228, 231
Celebration 10, 30, 36, 37, 40, 63, 67, 95, 114, 210, 244, 249, 257, 262–3, 269, 274, 350
Celibacy 97, 149, 161, 171, 203, 230, 233, 263, 278, 281, 282, 290, 304, 305
Cell groups 190, 201, 328, 345, 348–50
Celtic Church 355–6
Central Office 253, 298, 330, 345
Chadwick, Samuel 12, 14
Chard Fellowship 35
Charismatic movement 28–9, 33, 40, 46–7, 50, 83, 105, 133, 135–6, 178, 257, 263, 285, 287, 315, 356
Charities 364
Children 44–5, 91, 105, 108, 120, 134, 172, 179, 187–8, 219, 226–7, 305–7, 325, 332
Cho, Yonggi 200, 204
Christian individualism 82–4, 90, 101, 115, 119, 127, 138
Christian 'jungle' 362
Christian meditation 93, 95, 101, 104, 117, 124, 249
Christian mystics 94, 97, 120, 124, 255, 257, 310
Christmas, etc 51, 73, 91, 169, 227
Chronicles of Narnia 307–10
Church 47, 61, 108, 115, 319
  as army 73, 167, 204, 213–4, 225, 232–3, 236, 241, 243, 261, 269
  as body 40, 48, 82, 171, 327, 330
  as bride 115, 237–9, 288, 323–4, 327
  as city 108, 200, 204, 252, 261, 277, 281, 303, 323, 324, 338, 345
  building 83, 167, 171, 208, 280, 302, 329
  growth 61, 71, 85, 89, 182, 200, 209–10, 214, 233, 238, 248, 252, 278, 285, 296, 298, 324, 335, 345, 365
  history 131, 135–6, 197, 301
  households 134, 144, 202,

225, 227, 234, 240, 251
- planting 22, 47, 152, 171, 200, 227, 230, 234, 251, 262, 267, 278, 297–8, 300, 302, 329–31, 335, 341
- streams 263, 283

Cities 181, 201, 213, 225, 243, 261, 310, 324, 329, 341

Coates, Gerald 9, 10, 33, 46–7, 50, 170, 175, 253, 262, 263, 289, 292

Colour 261, 266, 277, 288, 311, 324

Commitment 61, 71–2, 78, 83, 90–1, 133, 167, 171, 194, 224, 229, 241, 275, 325, 358, 360, 362–3; *see also Membership styles*

Common purse 104, 121, 128, 134–6, 178, 194, 269, 300, 337, 364

Communication 170–1, 174, 180, 261ff, 298, 325, 338, 345

Communion *see Sacraments*

Communism 32, 67, 68, 78, 111, 297

Community 49, 51, 53, 60–4, 77, 86, 95, 105, 113, 137, 172, 194, 210, 227, 243, 261, 263, 275, 289, 300, 336, 344, 349, 355–6, 361

Community houses 64, 70, 80, 88, 91, 96, 128, 134, 138–9, 144, 146, 157, 168, 175, 190, 198, 201, 210, 213, 233–4, 242, 251, 265, 267, 278, 289, 330, 336–7, 344, 355–6
- Battlecentre 276, 280–2, 298–300, 313, 331, 337–40, 353
- Cornhill 157, 188, 202, 214, 235, 251, 256, 260, 267, 273, 275, 280, 295, 301, 303, 323ff, 335, 337
- Farm 114–6, 134, 141–2, 146, 162, 174, 191, 196, 202, 272, 286, 289, 301, 306–7, 313, 325, 346
- Living Stones 144ff, 291
- New Creation Hall 21, 91, 98, 114, 128, 196, 202, 225, 260, 276

Community foodstore FDC, 101, 197, 211

Community Trust 173, 363

Congregations 330, 344, 350

Constitution 41, 168

Conversion 23, 25, 27, 32, 39, 50, 59, 62, 66, 99, 161, 164, 211, 222, 224, 233–4

Conviction of sin 23, 27, 36, 39, 50, 59, 66, 112, 186, 217–8

Counterculture 49, 70, 72, 74, 103, 109–13, 119–23, 132, 136–7, 167, 170, 174, 176, 191, 200, 244, 250, 274, 281, 287, 293, 301, 302, 326, 336, 355, 365

Covenant 15, 22, 34, 78, 138, 167, 171, 173, 175, 182, 192, 194, 210, 239, 241, 243, 251, 254–5, 263, 275, 280, 282, 304, 353, 358

Coventry 102, 157, 175, 203, 249

Covering 48, 84, 120, 240

Creation 308–10, 315

Creativity 103, 104, 110, 114, 119, 145, 184, 264, 311, 324

Criticism 9, 10, 59, 61, 74, 83, 91, 122, 130, 132, 137, 174–5, 179, 191, 225–6, 247, 264, 269, 271, 277, 279, 358, 360, 367

Cross 27, 34, 39, 71, 83, 90, 95, 97, 105, 160, 188, 210, 223,

237–8, 241, 277, 347
red 318, 347, 351
Cults 55, 65, 89, 110, 112, 125, 129, 145, 148, 159, 178, 224, 226, 231, 358
Cultural relevance 266, 287, 288–9, 293, 314, 319, 326, 342, 350, 355–6; *see also* Sensitivity to people
Dance 107, 253, 262, 269, 311
DAWN 298
Deacons 36–7, 41, 44, 46, 95, 198
Deaths 38, 65, 130, 142, 179, 189
Demons 41, 49, 57, 83, 85, 89, 93, 99, 162, 191, 201, 213, 222, 233, 238, 254, 256, 265–6, 281, 282, 285, 312
Denominations 47, 77, 183, 229, 264, 298
Discipleship 47, 49, 51, 61, 72, 90, 95, 98, 106, 119, 121, 123, 128–9, 134, 144–5, 148, 174, 200, 208, 249, 325, 328, 345, 356, 361
Disciple bands 124, 190, 211, 345
Distinctives 263, 275, 282, 359
Drama 265, 268, 270, 294–5, 308–9, 311
Drugs 29, 69, 49, 52, 65, 72, 162, 189, 221, 234, 282, 290, 294, 306, 316, 346
Early church 28, 41, 51, 53, 62, 80, 112, 135, 167, 171, 180, 208, 231, 303, 305, 329
Earth 106, 110, 288, 308–10, 315, 342
Eat, Drink and Pray (EDP) 268, 345
Ecstasy (spiritual!) 254–7, 291, 310, 332
Education 138, 172, 197

Elders 41, 78, 95, 123, 142, 179, 192, 219, 251, 344, 365
Elderly 45, 249
Ellis, Roger 287, 355
Entertainment 73, 90, 103, 121, 177, 187, 311
Equality 112, 168, 172, 181, 232
Europe 181, 296–7, 301, 328, 340
Evangelism 23, 25, 26, 48, 52, 83, 88, 95, 137, 139, 152, 157, 160, 171, 187, 197, 202, 207, 220, 224, 234, 254, 261, 268, 270–1, 292, 313
Evangelical Alliance 175, 227, 277
Faith 35–6, 60, 92, 135, 138, 200, 220
Faith targets 210, 214, 233, 238, 298, 335
Faith and Practice 168
Falling in the Spirit 63, 67, 88, 217, 246, 252–3, 263, 267, 273, 315, 331–2; *see also* Anointings
Families 36, 88, 91, 102, 105, 118, 137–8, 157, 168, 172, 217, 229, 275, 336–7, 362
Farmwork 114, 117, 134, 141, 190–1, 196–7, 214, 226
Fathering 156, 288, 289, 305, 306, 313, 328
Fear of God 34, 94, 187, 216, 335
Fellingham, Dave 283
Festivals
Bank Holiday 267, 268, 278, 279, 281, 316, 354
Festival of Light 50
Glastonbury 212, 247, 267, 282, 286, 314, 343
Greenbelt 178

INDEX

Knebworth 161
Finney, Charles 28, 30, 187
Fire of God 55, 61, 215, 217–8, 241, 252, 256–7, 260, 262, 273, 279, 299, 304
Flesh 141, 145, 182, 302
Footwashing 104, 117, 167, 343, 351
Forgiveness 263, 277, 360
Forster, Roger 26, 135, 170, 253, 263, 264, 279, 357ff
Fountain Trust 33, 37
Francis, St 64, 97, 124, 150, 328
Friendship 100, 103, 108, 110, 141, 146, 148, 151, 202, 208, 212, 214, 224, 243, 265, 289, 350, 362
Generation J 14, 343, 354
Generation X 14, 343
Glasgow 267, 301
Gordon, Bob 281
Gospel 22, 131, 188, 197, 201, 242, 250
Grace 46, 72, 84, 121, 135, 174, 192
Graham, Billy 24, 223
Green, Lyn 278, 297
Greenwood, Harry 35
Guinness, Os 111, 281
Gumbel, Nicky 353
Harper, Michael 14, 33, 79, 83, 133, 175
Healing 32–4, 36, 46, 54, 72, 89, 112, 135, 162, 209, 212, 233, 238, 340, 352–3
Hippies 29, 49–57, 64, 87, 247, 257, 267, 287, 317, 327
Holiness 58, 61, 69, 90, 94, 111, 118, 122–3, 135, 145, 147, 175, 201, 204, 216, 219, 229, 240, 247, 258, 276, 278, 279
Holy Trinity, Brompton 331, 353

Homeless 226, 232, 238, 260, 268–70, 286, 289, 294, 300, 313, 319, 339, 352
'Hope Now' 268
House churches 33, 35, 46–8, 133, 167, 194, 229, 243, 264, 285; see also New churches
Hutterites 137, 172, 178, 195, 214, 301
Hymns 147, 159, 180, 188, 190, 192, 193, 196, 250, 280, 288, 304, 332, 333, 338
Ichthus 263
Ignition Gospel Roadshow 341–2, 345
Institutionalism 274, 335–6, 341, 348
Isolation 159, 173, 262, 264
Israel 109, 169, 194, 303
Jebb, Stanley 175, 226
Jerusalem church 28, 33, 51, 53, 80, 92, 134–5, 137, 160, 231, 269, 329
Jesus
 blood of 33, 57, 181, 188–9, 201, 216, 218, 227, 241, 261, 343
 name of 36, 156, 189, 208, 241
 person of 267, 288, 310, 318, 342
 teaching of 40, 72, 121, 132–3, 149, 263, 325
 practice of 49, 71, 104, 111, 117, 121, 133, 294, 297, 325
Jesus Army 225, 232, 234, 236, 239, 242–7, 250, 261–2, 266, 275, 298, 325, 338
 jackets 265, 266; see also Uniform
 Modern 310
Jesus Fellowship 91, 138, 156, 227, 233, 285, 326, 332, 345

379

literature 60, 63, 71, 175, 208, 212, 214, 225, 230, 232–3, 236, 246, 261, 263–6, 345
resources 265, 314, 345
tapes 265, 291, 329
videos 264, 265, 267, 310, 317, 319, 350
Jesus Live 311ff, 324, 325
Jesus People 48–9, 53, 58, 60, 64, 116, 208, 213, 223, 229, 250
Jesus Rebellion 223, 232, 234, 242
Jesus Reds 354
Jesus Revolution 49, 51, 64, 71, 111, 236, 266, 280, 285, 295, 306, 328, 336, 342
Joining 164, 173, 254, 325, 361
Jones, Bryn 292
Judgement 182, 188, 279, 283, 337
Kansas City Prophets 279
Kendrick, Graham 262
Kingdom of God 28, 61, 72, 90, 97, 101–6, 109, 114, 121, 133, 160, 168, 170, 194, 200, 208, 210, 214, 225, 250–1, 264, 293, 304, 324, 347, 356
Kirby, Gilbert 175, 227
Laying on hands 33, 61–2
Leadership 28, 36–7, 41–2, 43, 70, 91, 95, 118, 124, 138, 151, 174–5, 188, 190–1, 204, 218, 240, 251, 273, 278, 280, 298, 305, 344, 361, 365
Leaving 81, 95, 114, 130, 173, 183, 189, 193, 211, 214, 226, 230, 260, 280, 361–2
Legalism 91, 121–2, 170, 174, 183, 192, 226, 283, 313
Leicester 139, 162, 175, 190, 232
Lewis, C.S. 307–9
Liberty 33, 35, 40, 43, 48, 68, 84, 88, 91, 113, 124, 188, 192, 253, 262
Lifestyle 64, 70, 72, 91, 103, 111, 121–2, 130, 151, 159, 244, 275, 326, 361–2
Liverpool 234, 261
London 67, 70, 234, 242, 246, 263, 280–2, 331, 338–40
London Bible College 301
Lyne, Pete 33
Maclaughlin, John 33
Mainstream churches 262ff, 281, 319, 361–2
Manifestations FWD, 254–7, 273, 275, 292, 332, 338; *see also* Anointings
Maps 242, 298, 349
March for Jesus 246, 252, 285, 286, 297, 359
Marches 63, 221–2, 235, 242–3, 245, 297–8, 342
Marquee, Golden 221, 225, 234, 238, 256, 268, 291, 299, 325
Marriage 47, 57, 77, 99, 149, 171, 216, 324, 355
Materialism 277, 283, 284
Maturity 94, 125, 127
Media 49, 56, 60–1, 85, 86–7, 131, 136, 169, 175, 176, 179, 189, 209, 227, 235, 245, 247, 264, 284ff, 295, 301, 329, 331–2, 347, 351
Membership styles 300, 361
Men 91, 95, 96, 104, 119, 149, 169, 225, 238, 305
Men's Day 277, 326
Mentoring *see* Fathering
Methodists 22, 131, 135, 160, 167, 208, 230–1, 257, 260, 276

Middle classes 48, 59, 71, 80, 91, 231, 287, 302, 326
Midlands 21, 190, 197, 202, 225
Milton Keynes 175, 208, 212, 223
Ministry 25, 37, 41, 46–7, 61, 82, 119–20, 124, 157, 202
Miracles 35, 55, 77, 129, 135, 209, 222, 257, 292, 352–3
Mission England 210, 223
Misselbrook, Lewis 170
Modern believers 305, 343, 347, 365
Modern worship 274, 293, 310, 311, 314, 317, 326; see also Multimedia
Modesty 120, 122
Mohabir, Philip 277
Money 25, 27, 60, 68, 80, 83, 92, 104, 121, 138, 173, 199–200, 252, 265, 364
Moravians 204
Morton, Tony 301
Multimedia 311, 317–9, 341, 345
Multiply network 301, 345
Multiracialism 201, 207, 224, 235, 300, 331
Music 26, 40, 45, 48, 50, 65, 86, 90, 107, 114, 126, 210, 253, 262, 267, 288, 290, 307, 314, 317, 350, 355
'Natural' life 190, 238
Nee, Watchman 41, 62, 73, 151
New Age 247, 260, 262, 286, 288, 290, 303, 310, 314–6, 328, 342, 343, 347, 355
New churches 9–10, 292–3, 295, 301
New creation 73, 103, 114, 116, 140
New generation 324ff, 332, 337, 365
New Testament Christianity 46, 51, 60, 62, 65, 73, 132, 135, 150, 159, 169, 171, 178, 225, 240, 257, 283, 338
New society see Counterculture
Noble, John 261, 277, 289
Nonconformity 21, 48, 135, 231
Non-residents 134, 173, 201–2, 210, 329, 330, 344, 349, 363
North, the 300, 329–30
Northampton 21, 34, 50–1, 63, 78, 88, 117, 146, 189, 221, 234, 242, 252, 269, 308, 314, 329, 346ff
Nottingham 212, 235
Nurture 189, 208, 210, 238, 240, 247, 345, 353, 360–1
Obedience 72, 124, 232, 357, 368
Occult 49, 56, 57, 70, 129, 162, 213, 234, 352
Openness 33, 40, 64–5, 82, 87, 101, 110, 119, 124, 158, 263, 350
Opposition 22, 45, 46, 54, 59, 61, 73, 91, 111, 160–1, 166, 176–7, 181–2, 189, 214, 227, 267, 358
Organisation 344–5, 361
Ortiz, Juan-Carlos 124, 133
Overseas links 94, 117, 128, 195, 234, 265
Oxford 62, 88, 99, 102, 122, 129, 168–9, 209–10, 302
Parents 23, 34, 38, 64, 102, 121, 141, 225, 306–7, 362
Pastoring see Shepherds, Leaders, Elders
Pentecostalism 25, 28, 33, 35, 42–3, 59, 74, 131, 135, 146, 179, 212, 220, 230, 255, 257, 332
People movement 288, 296, 297, 344, 347–8, 361

Perrins, Graham 33
Persecution 22, 46, 73, 109, 131, 134, 137, 169, 179–80, 193, 204, 227, 358, 367
Pioneer Ministries 263, 352
Pioneering 132, 135, 137, 157, 166, 170, 191, 201, 220, 227, 231, 267, 345, 349
Pioneers Pledge 349
Poor 9, 181, 200, 213, 232, 238, 242, 247, 270, 296; see also *Homeless*
Possessions 80, 90, 100, 103, 121, 135, 137, 325, 364
Post-modern culture 355–6
Praise 30, 36, 37, 40, 67, 95, 210, 244, 249; see also *Celebration*
Pray Northampton 346ff
Prayer 22, 24, 28–9, 32, 94, 101, 124, 141, 168, 182, 188, 201, 203–4, 211–2, 214, 216–7, 233, 244; see also *Spiritual warfare*
Presence of God 36, 38, 56, 67, 69, 79, 81, 94, 95, 104, 107, 183, 186–202, 216, 218–9, 256, 273, 303, 331
Privacy 84, 99, 100, 130
Professionals 64, 74, 77, 89, 92, 102, 163, 168, 170, 182, 224, 314
Prophecy 24, 33, 41, 45, 54, 61, 68, 78, 91, 101–3, 110, 124, 127, 133, 157, 191, 225, 260, 264, 273, 282, 283, 289, 337, 340
Prophetic church 91, 112, 127, 132, 134, 169, 174–5, 181, 194, 220, 223, 230, 232, 248, 357
Prophetic drama 268, 308–9, 311–2
Prophetic ministry 61, 91, 112, 132–3, 188, 217, 219, 243, 250, 257
Prophetic vision 91, 114, 133, 135, 276, 281, 326
Prophetic wisdom 33, 37, 61, 72, 98, 101, 103, 125–7, 110, 161, 182, 184, 211, 237, 252, 261, 282
Prophets 47, 95, 133, 276, 279
'Psalming' 86, 94, 107, 124, 126
Purity 47, 55, 122, 138, 241, 252, 260
Quakers 21, 131, 231, 257
Radicalism 41, 51, 61, 111, 120, 123, 129, 132, 134, 137, 165, 175, 230–2, 243, 282, 283, 294, 301, 303, 305, 316, 318, 326, 349
Raj, Paul 289
Redeemer Church 81, 83, 86, 102
Reformation 111–2, 135, 138
Regions 298, 304
Renewal 33, 37, 41, 46–8, 74, 132, 166, 171, 175, 226, 264
Renunciation 138, 169, 172, 325
Repentance 186, 188, 214, 216, 218, 222
Restoration 46–8, 83, 106, 109, 132, 135, 160, 167, 194, 210, 223, 243, 264
Revival 24, 26, 28–9, 34, 36, 38, 43, 49, 60–1, 71, 90, 147, 167, 181, 183, 186ff, 200, 216ff, 246, 255, 261, 268, 280, 285, 288, 289, 297
Roberts, Evan 38, 187, 190, 216
Roles of men and women 119, 164, 169, 177, 203
Rugby 156, 188, 190
Sacraments 311, 343
  bread and wine 44, 79, 167, 197, 240, 343; see also

INDEX

Agape meal oil 343, 353
Sacrifice 71, 90, 95, 97, 114, 138, 147, 190, 214, 236, 238, 241, 243, 250, 281, 288, 301, 305, 319, 326, 338, 349
Salvation 66, 69, 73, 110, 134, 139
Salvation Army 9, 131, 204, 213–4, 225, 240, 244, 260, 276
Sanctification 94, 135, 147–8, 252, 260, 264, 276, 278
Satan 57, 60, 112, 129, 139, 180–1, 223, 225
Scriptures *see Bible*
Searchers 268, 281, 287, 310ff
Self-love 90, 121, 148, 160, 187, 238
Sensitivity to people 266, 310, 314, 324, 346ff
Separation 22, 51, 61, 71, 73, 91, 109, 111, 121, 137, 160, 194, 225
Servant groups 190, 197, 200–1, 211–2, 233
Servanthood 58, 96, 100, 145, 148, 190, 277
'Sheep' 23, 95, 96, 127, 158, 174
'Sheep-stealing' 158, 178
Sheffield 234, 267, 292, 329–30
Shepherding groups 96, 280, 345
Shepherding movement 105
Shepherds 23, 28, 95, 96, 101, 144, 174–5, 179, 182, 211, 226
Simplicity 46, 103, 110, 113, 121, 167, 194, 246, 263, 265
Single parents 134, 302
Singles 105, 120, 134
Sisters 23, 37, 42, 60, 63, 99, 102, 104, 119–20, 123, 125, 138, 144–6, 149, 159, 164, 169, 177, 188, 203, 218
Soul-healing 262, 268, 303, 313
Spiritual family 34, 42, 46, 84, 143, 211, 225, 303, 313, 319, 328
Spiritual fathers, sons *see Fathering*
Spiritual gifts 33, 39, 41, 45, 47, 54, 82, 89, 101, 103, 124, 240, 260
Spiritual warfare 73, 81, 92, 127–8, 139, 160, 166, 182, 191–3, 213, 222–5, 232, 236, 238, 243, 250, 254, 349, 358
Spirituality 94, 108, 124, 142, 145, 182, 257, 279, 331
Sport 73, 121, 305
Spurgeon's College 301
Stoke 209, 211
Street people 29, 51, 162, 168, 201, 222, 232, 242–3, 246–7, 263, 268, 269, 270, 286, 294, 361; *see also Homeless; Jesus revolution; Youth*
Studd, C.T. 26, 236, 241
Students 31, 35, 36, 45, 61, 71, 89, 99, 102, 128–9, 155
Submission 84, 119, 137, 147, 168
Subritzky, Bill 258
Suffering 22, 137, 143, 181, 193, 229, 239, 243, 263, 280, 358, 366
Surrender 29, 61, 68, 70, 72, 80, 84, 95, 278
Symbols *see Visuals*
Taylor, John 113
Television 71, 86, 89–90, 103, 122, 132, 176–7, 193, 245, 247, 261, 351, 355

Theology 35, 168, 171, 175, 197, 227, 229

Third world 278, 296–7, 364

Thompson, Hugh 33

Tongues 28–30, 32–40, 36–7, 39, 42, 45, 77, 93, 124, 191, 214, 217, 246

Toronto Blessing 9, 11, 331–2, 355; see also Anointings

Tozer, A.W. 73, 74, 91, 94, 97, 310

Tradition 33, 37, 40, 44, 47–8, 51, 71, 73

Trafalgar Square 268, 288

Training 25, 47, 83, 124, 128

Uniforms 9, 240–2, 247; see also Jesus Army jackets

United Kingdom 24, 46, 48, 83, 166, 181, 191, 204, 214, 222, 236, 242–3, 263

Unity 26, 27, 36, 39–40, 43, 61, 65, 83, 84, 101, 112, 119, 122, 125, 128, 138, 144, 148, 167, 177, 191, 223

Videos 260, 263–4, 267

Vineyard Fellowship 262, 276

'Virtue' names 18, 117, 215

Vision 25, 83, 91, 97, 110, 114, 120, 124, 133, 139, 152, 160, 166, 170, 173–5, 190, 192, 200, 204, 230, 232, 243, 247, 250, 289, 365

Visions 27, 32, 34, 45, 255–7

Visitors 33, 61, 64, 100, 102, 104, 108, 119, 132, 164, 174–5, 195, 259

Visuals 264, 311, 347, 355

Vows 276, 278, 280

Wallis, Arthur 26, 46, 102, 127, 132, 136, 166, 170, 175

Warwickshire 157, 190

Watts, Isaac 115, 122, 144

Wembley Praise-Day 277–8, 283, 285, 293–5, 296, 317–9

Wesley, Charles 26, 35, 115, 119, 122, 160

Wesley, John 26, 86, 159, 230, 332, 345

Westminster Central Hall 264, 311

White, Rob 259

Wilkerson, David 29, 268

Wimber, John 233, 251–2, 265, 276–7

Wisdom pictures see Prophetic wisdom

Word of God 86, 136, 223, 232, 243, 250, 257

Word of knowledge 33, 68, 158, 164, 165, 260, 282, 327, 340, 352

Worldliness 22, 51, 61, 64, 71, 73, 84, 90, 112, 121, 129, 138, 145, 158, 172, 174, 177, 200, 214, 222, 225, 275, 281

Women see Sisters

Worship 63, 94, 97, 101, 107, 132, 252, 309, 311

Wright, Nigel 301

Yarmouth 212, 223, 234

Youth 23, 24, 26–7, 32, 45, 49–50, 54, 156, 212, 214, 216, 220, 223, 238, 246, 268, 284, 287, 288
  culture 284ff, 289, 305, 343, 347, 351

YWAM 268, 278, 282, 297

Zion 22, 25, 75, 107ff, 119, 121–3, 126, 128, 131–2, 135, 146, 148, 152, 156, 160, 169, 174, 176, 180, 189, 195, 210, 216, 223, 225, 232, 219–20, 247, 250, 252, 273, 274, 275, 279, 280, 281, 282, 293, 303, 307, 323, 326, 332–3, 336, 338